GLASS

'Brightness and sunshine pour from every page of this book. The brightness of the spirit, informed by love and nourished by the enchantment of everyday life ... it is a mad, beautiful book full of dreams and fancies and homely realities and idealism ... when you have finished reading it, you will be a happier person than you were before you began' *Canberra Times*

'*Glass after Glass* introduces us to the secret and fascinating world of Barbara Blackman; a very unique soul, with an ability to see further than most ... she has used her blindness as a shortcut to a world of wonder that many of us fail to see.' *Betty Churcher*

'[Blackman] makes us see what she cannot see; and she turns our seeing eyes to the barriers we live behind, the luminosity we so rarely achieve.' *Sydney Morning Herald*

'Barbara Blackman sees the world in ways that elude most people. She has many riches to share.' *Courier-Mail*

'A marvel of understatement and stoicism ... a welcome relief from the tenor of our time.' *Weekend Australian*

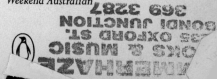

BARBARA BLACKMAN, essayist, librettist, letter writer, was an only child, born and bred in Brisbane, caught up into the Barjai art/literary group of the Forties, the Melbourne Contemporary Art Society of the Fifties and the Australian wave in London of the Sixties. She was married to painter Charles Blackman for thirty years. She has worked as a child psychologist, an artists' model, a magazine columnist, a radio producer for Radio for the Print Handicapped, and an oral historian for the National Library. She was a co-founder of the Little Lookout Theatre in Sydney and is a member of the C.G. Jung Society and the National Federation of Blind Citizens. Her pleasures are contemporary music, coffee drinking, visiting Perth, solitude, and her three offspring and six grandchildren.

glass AFTER glass

Autobiographical Reflections

BARBARA BLACKMAN

Penguin Books

Penguin Books Australia Ltd
487 Maroondah Highway, PO Box 257
Ringwood, Victoria 3134, Australia
Penguin Books Ltd
Harmondsworth, Middlesex, England
Viking Penguin, A Division of Penguin Books USA Inc.
375 Hudson Street, New York, New York 10014, USA
Penguin Books Canada Limited
10 Alcorn Avenue, Toronto, Ontario, Canada M4V 3B2
Penguin Books (NZ) Ltd
Cnr Rosedale and Airborne Roads, Albany, Auckland, New Zealand

First published by Penguin Books Australia Ltd 1997
This paperback edition published by Penguin Books Australia Ltd 1997

1 3 5 7 9 10 8 6 4 2

Cover design by Beth McKinlay
Text design by Stacey McEvoy, Penguin Design Studio
Typeset in Perpetua by Post Pre-Press Group
Made and printed in Australia by Australian Print Group

National Library of Australia
Cataloguing-in-Publication data:

Blackman, Barbara, 1928– .
Glass after glass: autobiographical reflections.

ISBN 0 14 026033 1.

1. Blackman, Barbara, 1928– – Biography. 2. Blind women – Australia – Biography.
3. Women poets, Australian – 20th century – Biography. I. Title.

A821.3

Australia Council
for the Arts

$\mathcal{C}$ONTENTS

ACKNOWLEDGEMENTS   vii

PROLOGUE   1
The Autobiographical Archaeological Dig   3

PART ONE   21
My Life with Joey   23
Grandmothers   35
15 Edmondstone Street   53
Four Oaks in the Forties   71
In 1945: 'How to Be Happy'   87
Barjai Days   103

PART TWO   125
Daise of Our Lives   127
The Fish Bowl   139
Life Class Life   155
The Good Ship Mora   169
Portrait of a Friendship   191

PART THREE   225
Poetics of Family Life   227
Our Life with the Bears   251
Days of Wine and Roses   257
A Year in Paris   271
Pleasures of Solitude   291
The Cat That Got Away   301
Tell Your Mother Lovely   307
On First Looking into Blackmans' Home Life   313

PART FOUR   329
Nature's Poems   331
Into My Looking-glass Land   339
Unlikely Gifts   353
Whitefellers Walk All Around   359
Transparencies   373

CREDITS   402

$\mathcal{A}$CKNOWLEDGEMENTS

I wish to thank my family and so many friends for their help with this work, among them, as readers, John Yule, the late Barrie Reid, Karen Lamb and Chris Mansell, Ross Mellick and Susan Alexander; with the visuals, Meegan Bussey, Peter Daltoe, Lorraine Forden, Thelma Furlong, Adrian Keenan, Jonathan Ladd, Felicity Moore, Yaffa Adari Moore, Tim Murray, Mary Perceval (Lady Nolan), Evva Sek-Sekalski, and particularly Marcel Veldhoven – and all those patient friends who have read my scripts back to me in human voice. I thank Charles Blackman for permission to use his painting on the jacket. I thank the Literature Board of the Australia Council for a grant for a 'seeing eye' assistant and Martin Thomas for his fulfilment of this role, and Shirley Fenton Huie for proofreading. I want to thank Bryony Cosgrove, Clare Coney and Alex Watts at Penguin and my agent Barbara Mobbs for editorial help beyond measure, and Stacey McEvoy for her sensitive design.

This book, dedicated to
My Mother,
Gertrude Olson Patterson
1891–1987,
is my humble offering to
St Peter at the Pearly Gate who,
I have it on good authority,
has only one question:
Did you have fun?

'I drink glass after glass of love.
Neither does that wine finish nor my thirst'

– Bayazid Bestami

PROLOGUE

THE AUTOBIOGRAPHICAL ARCHAEOLOGICAL DIG

September 9th 1994. It is a beautiful day; wattle, blossom, bush daphne all out, possibly also brown snake. Our letter box is a good kilometre away from the house, marking the spot of the postal address. I take my hat and stick, swing out along the gravel path, turn south down the dirt road, across the little creek, steeply up the other side. This walk with white cane in my invisible world is all air and odour, familiarity and fancy. My long white cane guides – 'good dog' – sniffing, tapping on stone, leaf, puddle, wood. My feet sculpt the path. The stick, a conducting baton, makes landscape percussive. This walk, so familiar, is endeared to me like a lover's face, known though unseen, felt and caressed, a beloved portrait, an intimate topography.

Today's mail: Rural Co-op bill, just as expected; notice of Fire Brigade next meeting, pin on board; Jung Society newsletter, regular; yes, thick and hand-written, one personal letter. Thank you, Dorothy Cameron, a smell of the sea and of your advances in the pre-history research, photocopy of your latest piece on women's symbols in the Minoan murals, sourced from your archaeological dig – well worth keeping, a little bit of happening history that laps my shore. Like this since my teens I have sifted the daily mail debris for human content, saved the good letters, just as I have saved snatches of my days in diaries, netted the press cuttings, culled the photographs – documentary evidence of my path through life.

'Nature, the House of the Soul' is the title of an essay by Kathleen Raine. Walking my familiar bush path is a meditation, the chance to join one's own minute and sensitive being to the great eternal, a redemptive moment. A questioning of soul. How is it that I, whoever I am that has inhabited this body for three score years and more, comes to be here, now, today, in this place on earth and no other, an atom of the mystery of the whole, a free spirit and a happy creature, picking up kindling to light the evening fire?

Tradition allocates three score years and ten for a human life. Understood, not literally but esoterically, interior rather than exterior measurement, this seventy means 7 for becoming, 0 for a long time in the process. Three, on the other hand, is for being. At three the child begins to know himself. That is to say, the creature begins to ask the question of the soul and has the lifespan to pursue or be pursued by the answer; to flee until the final flash of recognition, or seek a slow illumination.

> God bless this tiny little boat
> And me that travels in it.
> It stays afloat for years and years
> And sinks within a minute.
> And so the soul in which we sail,

Unknown by years of thinking,
Is deeply felt and understood
The minute that it's sinking.
(Michael Leunig)

Last November a young friend came to live here as seeing-eye secretary–archivist – a researcher, a white cane of patience tapping into my past landscape, stratum by stratum. Persistently, sensitively, ruthlessly, together we have sorted through all the fifty years of kept papers. Victoria, dear Queen, I have sighed your daily sigh: 'O the boxes, the boxes!' Now a filing cabinet is filled with diary remnants rendered chronological, photographs captioned, documents dated, kept letters in order dramatis personae; some letters returned to source, some documents to museums; much paper shredded for garden mulch, pieces of poetry and snatches of tax figures nourishing the tender roots of vine and vegetable.

Today the last box is emptied, storehouse swept. That day, mythical for so long among all my friends, 'Barbara Blackman getting her life in order', has actually happened! This is the archive. These papers are the artefacts. Here is evidence of a life lived. Here are the leaves of this particular Tree of Life, leaves fallen in their season, swept up and kept, unearthed now from their boxes and camphor to be sifted and savoured. These are the shards, bones, parts of tools, dug up and looked at in themselves, documents recording material facts – the flesh, the people, the passions, the enterprises, the conflicts, the dialogues are all secreted (bones without flesh, tools without purpose, pieces without the vessel, hints and guesses).

I am getting my house in order: as without, so within. House in dream interpretation is the icon of self. 'House', says

Emily Dickinson, 'that uncanny container'. Some creatures — turtle, snail, pilgrim, refugee — carry their house upon their backs. My 'house' is this archive, honey hive, of papers carried around with me from place to place through half a century. Now it is time to collect the honey from the hive. 'Old age,' my mother used to say, 'is the Promised Land': meaning one could live reflectively, not having to construct a future; meaning a place of milk and honey, milk of hard-won wisdom, honey of time-healed memories.

September 9th 1994. The world going on around me grows curiouser and curiouser: these three items reported on radio in the last twenty-four hours — today's archive: 1. A solemn voice from a BBC science programme describes an experiment. One hundred orphan babies are brought up in silence in order to discover what language they will speak. Result: they do not speak at all. They wilt away. 2. A young man with a study grant is doing a thesis on the Location of the Soul, from medieval theologians to poets to scientists. At Hobart Public Hospital he has had his entire body scanned in search of his soul, results in an art gallery. 3. Magazines worldwide bid for telescopic lens photograph of the Heir Apparent — Charles, Prince of Wales — in the nude, 'the duck' apparent in heavy granulation.

Dear Alice, I am bewildered! I look around me at these Alician fields and hardly recognise them as a human habitation; prefer, like the white rabbit, to take my own timepiece and run tunnelling down underground into the strata of personal memory.

One life has many autobiographies. It depends how one sinks one's shaft of remembering. Now I can look back through this accumulated evidence of my past. I can begin the return journey, the autobiographical archaeological dig, ever mindful of T. S. Eliot's warning lest we have the experience but miss the meaning, his clue that the way forward is the way back. Our lives proceed by experience indirectly, by event and consequence, dates and detail; but the return journey can be only mythic, direct to meaning. The way forward is the way back. We turn what has happened into stories, mythologise them as memory.

Tasmania, Summer 1983. There was a honeymoon, a gateway into a new inner landscape. I began an essay on 'Peopling my Solitude':

> This house faces the sea, the little sea of the
> D'Entrecasteaux Channel, and beyond it Bruny Island
> where sometimes at evening fires blaze, sending up a
> mystery of smoke into the southern skies. The fireplace of
> the house, in its turn, sends up smoke from the dry gum
> and driftwood, aromatic upon the freshness of Antarctic
> summer air. The surrounding strawberry fields now
> picked out, the sheep move in. Here, where we are living
> for the time being in the south of Tasmania, the days are
> quiet – call of plover, bray of distant donkey, sometimes
> throb of tractor, scream of chain-saw among the hills,
> occasional car along the beach road, and, at evening, axe
> chop for firewood, gun shot for rabbit.
>
> In this tranquillity, bread is baked, soups simmered,
> books read, words written, country roads walked and, on
> nights of full moon, landscape and sea shape stilled in
> ecstasy. Our time that is measured by tides and skies is
> punctuated each morning at ten o'clock by the ritual of

walking to the village with outgoing letters, shopping bag and happy expectations — along the sea front, inland past orchards and paddocks to the general store and the garden-gate post office open its couple of hours each day to get mail in from the Down bus and despatch off with the Up bus.

On return home the coffee is brewed, thick farm cream floated on top of each cup, rickety verandah chairs pulled close and letters carefully read. One by one friends emerge from their written pages, the events of their lives staged, their comments considered; they people with their presence this grace of solitude.

I wrote many letters from that place. Several are pulled out of a pile pulled out of a file — 'Judith Wright, Letters to' happily returned to me, as mine to her — a forty and more years' correspondence not sold to a museum. These files are in a cabinet, in a gate house.

Between that honeymoon and now, this house was built; beautiful house of my second marriage, built of mud-brick and stone, so that it rises up out of its land like a Dragon's Tooth, a row of teeth with its outhouses, fleeced with golden light at sunset; edifice of so much love, dream, work, hope — Marcel the builder, Barbara the muse. It is called 'Indooroopilly', a deviation from 'Yindooroopilly' meaning valley of leeches, which it is, in favour of my being a third-generation Indooroopillian, Brisbane-side. Before the house-built was earth and sky with dream between; was creek and bed of creek; was tree and root of tree.

Earlier, this crushed notebook: *Bush Trip Journal 1979* — in hand-written scrawl, red bull dust implanted into the pages.

August 28th 1979. We branch off the Gibb River to
Tunnel Creek. We go underground and for five hundred
metres walk, wade, stoop, clamber our way along the
creek bed under an earth roof. In this damp sweet-
odoured underworld there are pillars, the stalactites and
stalagmites out of rock reaching down, rock reaching up
to be joined; roots coming down from the rock above,
the threads, twines, plaits, ropes of root cabling into
pillars strong as telegraph poles, going on down again
through rock towards some inevitable centre.

Experience becomes symbol, a diary quotation.

September 1994. 'Meetings with Remarkable Women' –
Women's Spirituality Conference at Tialgon, northern
New South Wales. Twelve of us sit in a circle. Each draws
her Tree of Life. Silence, scratching of crayons. Most
silent, I visualise. My Tree is as much below the earth as
above. It rises high, golden and symmetric, a wattle
candelabrum. Branches have been lopped, others bowed
for tree houses, notches of branches not grown (events
forgotten, blissful habitats, 'paths untaken'). Vertical
strokes of gentle rain above, horizontal pools below the
telegraphing pillars of root – generous mercy from
Heaven, deep wavy waters of the Unconscious. The
whole is like a pirouette.

My Autobiographical Archaeological Dig. The return journey.
I make a sample shaft into the first marriage, life before fifty.
Cities, children, art galleries. A page of manuscript:

All June we are in Venice – fabulous city despite postcard-posing at all hours and at all angles and standing accused of sinking into its own watery grave. It shimmers touched by oriental fire, floats on the heat of summer as from a glass furnace glowing in violent skies and mirroring waters. Now, these waters stink, the skies suddenly sulphur forth terrible storms. All morning we browse among the Accademia, San Marco, the Doges' Palace, lace makers, glass works, arcades of fine enamelling and gilding until we are drowsy as bees in a garden too richly emblossomed. All afternoon we spend at the Lido. Elder son is the happiest boy in the whole world when the speedboat driver puts him at the wheel. On the strand a waiter rushes out at this daily small blond boy and says, 'Come and live with me, beautiful boy. I give you everything – peaches, ice cream, big balloons!' to which our young son replies, 'And clean shirts.' The water is shallow, cool, very briny, thick with mussels, shells and an infantasia of minute debris. Paratroopers of cheese drop from a helicopter, bright with a brand name. Each tasty morsel, if not reached in time, sinks comfortably into the bed of the sea. These Venetians have invented all the pleasures of life – opera, tourism, champagne, little boats and the beach. At the ticket box we hire chairs, umbrella, canoe, crab net, pillow, game of Boeee. We sit towel-wrapped, bare-toed, in the sand, salt-breathed, and eat on our laps great steaming bowls of pasta vongole, local version of fish and chips, salad of cress crisper than seaweed, and dishes of wild strawberries swimming in cream. Our daughter wades out, extends her palm towards us, intones in museum guide voice: 'This is a shell from the thirteenth century. Note the intricate indentations, the pigmentation of the veins, and the Umbrian influence in the bottom left-hand corner.' At night we sleep laid out in our beds quiet as the Carpaccios, Tintorettos and Titians there in their dark galleries: wake to the singers of the Teatro Fenice rehearsing as though to their eternal waves of viewers.

There I am, traveller, mother, artist's wife, hungry for life in the strange city, busy at my verbal recording. The way back as the way forward: to have the experience and know the mean-ing: regret a failure to understand: reflection a sweet research. It is not a matter of re-reading the documents of the past, of remembering rightly or wrongly, but rather that in going forward one creates the images of self; in returning rediscovery makes monstrous or marvellous the events at every retelling.

Younger, the little children 'carried Mummy's hand' when we went out to parks or shopping. Sometimes they took a hand in writing letters.

25 Hanover Gate Mansions, London WC1
8th February 1965

Dear Granma in Australia, [This is from Auguste, then nearly eight.]

I've got a new friend on the bus. He has a real boomerang as big as a bed end and is going to teach me to throw it over in Regent's Park. We played wars, Japanese against Americans. My favourite pop song is 'Sweet Baby' by Manfred Mann. We get comics on

Thursdays. We finished 'Lolly Pop' dance at school. The new one is 'Banjo Boy'. Daddy has gone to Vienna so I have to look after the family.

Dear Granma Patterson, [From Christabel, a week off turning six.]

I hope you are having a nice time and I hope your bed is nice and warm. I hope your country is nice and warm. I have new shoes. They are bouncy and soft and made in Spain. I took Honey Bear to school today. I brought him home wearing my hair ribbons. An eagle escaped from Regent's Zoo and we saw it. Daddy got a television set to keep. We made our own from cardboard boxes. I like acting inside it. Daddy has done very big paintings and got them hanging up everywhere. Nice nice Granma. We have got a new game with Mummy in the kitchen when we mustn't say Yes or No. Mummy is the best at it. I say Yes all the time.

Dear Gran-Gran, [Barnaby, then twenty months old, is mind-read.]

They all call me Blinkers. I give them kisses. My nose dribbles. I find all my bottles. I have a ball bigger than me. I laugh when my shoes are taken off. I wake up first. I bang on tins. I carry Daddy's papers. I pull Mummy's nose. I can say 'eyes', 'ears', 'nose', 'teeth' and point to them all. I can't find my daddy. I can find his shoes. I can put my shoes inside his shoes. Daddy calls me Monkey Brains. Here are a lot of kisses.

x   x   x   x   x   x   x   x

My kisses are very wet. My pusher has bells on it. The ducks hear me coming and think it is the bread tinkling.

I get hiccoughs. I blink when I hic. I love my Granma very much. I eat standing up. I make castles out of nappies. I do not wash nappies. I play plug in sink wash wash.

'Mummy and Daddy' were all the time performing on the parallel bars of public appearance and parenting, career and child care. On Friday 2nd June 1961 the Whitechapel Gallery Exhibition of Australian Contemporary Art opened. It brought 'Class of the Fifties' to a new London audience.

Scraps of half-page typed pink quarto diary record.

The Whitechapel is huge and full of paintings, most of them familiars, imbuing one with the trust of chaperoning them to meet an audience to which they are new. About twenty of us go off to the White Tower for dinner. I sit next to Brian Robertson, who curated it all. He sustains me with his great love of describing things. The Boyds, Rowells, Underhills, Keith Vaughan, Prunella Clough, Francis Bacon, Brett Whiteley, Roy de Maistre all there. Bacon sits opposite but slips through our fingers by getting quickly and rottenly drunk. Vaughan seems to think he is in muddy waters amid this Aussie stream. Prunella has much in reserve. Brett wants everything to have a name and an answer — When was I last chocko? Am I preggers? Is art returning to Braque? Is Prunella lesbian? Is marriage serious?

How urgent and irritating the young ones are. Makes me feel like still water, water that reflects, not runs rapids. At this Brian gives me an amusing description of what he thinks I am, something like this: Authoritative, decisive, bossy, not really interested in art, but rather in

writing; poetic, in a blue-stocking kind of way; a bit
snooty, decided to spend my life slumming it with the
artists, putting up with all their impulses and vagaries,
and finally putting them to bed when they are too pissed
to do it for themselves.

The autobiographer throws up largenesses of presences that
faded, smallnesses that grew; is surprised, shamed, humoured,
humbled; confronts the personal changes – rocks around
which the tree has had to grow. The 'dig' is down through detri-
tus of 'ifs' and 'shoulds', and 'might-have-beens' – shards of
intimate exchanges, rubble of half-forgotten people and places.
The archaeologist of a personal life stands back to survey. Strata
and shock lines show up sharply.

Ten years earlier. Here is a word snapshot of blue-
stocking Barbara taking her leap from Academia to Bohemia
headlong on her twenty-second birthday into the arms of
lover, Christmas, a three-decade marriage and the writer's
name of Barbara Blackman. First page of a legible hand-written journal:

22nd December 1950. My twenty-second birthday. I
move into a new year. One of my rare sleepless nights.
Causes never single – fleas, bed hard and falling to bits,
tension of Mrs H's Christmas tea, suspended excitement
at spending tomorrow night and onwards with Charles.
Before 4 a.m. it is quite light and warm. I get up and
wander in my nightdress out to the rock balcony and
down to the road with two children in my arms. Calm of
solitude. Desire for Charles to walk there with me. Easy
to possess the whole world at this hour. At 9 a.m. I set

forth from Seaforth to Harbord! I wore the new string cotton top knitted for me by Mrs H, the flared brown skirt, big straw hat and sandals, and ran up the road to bus stop with leather port and coat and surf bag, J's funny little rag animal sticking out head and shoulders. My friend the postman carried me up the hill. Manly very gay, summery, busy. At a Corso fruit shop the pungent summery tropic aroma of mangoes so I bought three delicious fruit for a shilling each. First time I ever bought a mango. All those Brisbane backyards with mangoes thumping down all night, yellow leaves to be swept up each day. Charles read to me for an hour delicious portions of Gide's *Fruits of the Earth*. I lay straight down to rest, he with me. Lovers cannot lie so straight. We wound together, into a sweet embrace, gave and received in utter unison. We dressed suddenly and ran hand in hand down the streets. Proximity of sea, green vacant allotments, shops scattered. The local pub stands by itself down one of these streets. We hear its buzz a block away, the warm crowded amber buzz of it. The bricklayers have knocked off work and are drinking out on the steps into the gutter. A vacant corner allotment becomes a park where the women sit on the grass with bright dresses. Kids play. Their menfolk carry them out drinks. Chica comes out, a frothy glass in each hand. Cool slow beer sailing down the blood changing the world around us.

What appears at the time to be a series of events in our control is seen on the return as the action of symbols of the universe moving through us making up the story. It reads back like a dream. Those two dream children carried in the half-

awake, those fruits of the earth literal and literary, the winding wound of coupling, and erupting out of it hand in hand,
the amber crowded warmth of those people we were to hive
among in our changing world, in our transforming, the
alchemy into gold. Our life patterns are imprinted on our
palms because when, in the womb, the embryo first divides,
it is the hands that lift away from the foetus whole carrying
the map upon them, the unique divine marking.

I made that leap across a widening chasm. The dark
wings that had hovered over now flew in my face.

> *This growing dark*
> *is slow and brings no pain.*
> *It flows along an easy slope*
> *And is akin to eternity.*
> (Jorge Luis Borges, transcribed from an interview)

Experience:

Brisbane, March 1950. Ophthalmologist's consulting room.
'Optic atrophy . . . rapid decline . . . Certification of
Industrial Blindness. Sign here for pension.'

Meaning:

It seemed to me then that I was being given a life
sentence for a crime I had not committed. Later it was
commuted to solitary confinement with parole and one
hundred lashes a day – the lashes of landscapes dissolved
in vacant air, smiles and gazes buried in blanks, faces of
lovers and children drowned in fathomless clear water;

spillings, bumpings, gropings, uncertainties,
bewilderment.

That was written many years later. Blindness, a shortcut to
humility. Astrologers see it there in the birth map: Taurus rising at 28 degrees. The soul had found the creature unpre-
pared for blindness – a gift whose understanding costs *not
less than everything*.

I leapt forward out of a certificated girlhood: *Bachelor of
Arts, Better Citizenship, Band of Hope, Argonauts* awards: all kept
and framed by a loving mother. This one hangs now above my
washing machine.

Strong in will to strive, to seek, to find and not to yield.
THE ARGONAUTS CLUB
Before the sun and the night and the blue sea,
Number 28 in the Good Ship CASTOR
has stood faithfully by all that is brave and beautiful,
has sought adventure and has discovered much
of wonder and delight, merriment and loveliness,
and shared it freely with fellow members of the
Argonauts Club.
The Order of the Golden Fleece is awarded to a faithful
rower
Barbara Patterson.

A Dig diversion: November 1984. We dismantle my parental
home at the wish of my mother, aged ninety-three and in a
hospice. She was a keeper, not a hoarder – for fear of silver-
fish. We sorted through a neat file of last year's accounts, a
Blackman scrapbook, sepia photographs of unknown Swedish

relatives, a camphor box of my father's letters during his last illness, stacks of my Roneoed university lecture notes respectfully preserved – whereas all my Fifties letters were burned to tidy the house for tenants – and found, secreted among them, a time-yellowed sealed-up wartime envelope – *For the Future* written in a girlish hand. Marcel opens it without hesitation. Now, in our honeymoon days, he used to call me his 'Honey, gold and light'. This, he says, is the meaning of 'Barbara' in ancient Greek. Out from the envelope falls a hank of hair – honey, gold and light, if ever there was – and an inscription that says: *This is the hair of Barbara Ena Patterson aged thirteen years three months and eighteen days. 9th April 1942.* This was the day of Marcel's birth. What moved a bubblesome blonde schoolgirl in the Antipodes on an April day that moved also in a young mother in a small north-eastern town in France?

We know what we do not know. We go by the way that we do not know. The Dig uncovers: layer by layer by layer by layer towards the source: a candle probing into the deep dark forgetting. Was I ever a child frightened in the dark?

Neara Creek via Kilcoy
12th August 1939

Dear Mummy,

I am enjoying my holiday. Jessie has a foal called Jim. We swim in the creek and get watercress. Last night I had a terrible fright. I was having my bath in the bath-house that is an old tank round the back of the house. I was all in the nuddy and in the big tub. I heard a dragging noise on the corrugated iron wall. I thought it was a hose being dragged along outside. Then there was a little sort of clicking noise.

I put on the torch. There was a big black snake around the edge of the tub drinking the water. I jumped out quicker than lightning. I threw the torch at the snake and ran out with the soap. I had to run through the front room where all the men were sitting around. They never caught the snake. Mrs Logan makes lovely cakes. I will write again soon. Hugs and kisses.

Earlier, aged somewhat over four, I had had a stark moment, an immersion in the source. As I sat out on the lawn arranging my dolls in a circle – one of your tea parties, dear Alice – I became strangely aware of myself. I said to myself: 'I am I and no other. No other ever has or ever can be this I. This I that I am only I can know. It came into me as a baby, is the same I as in me now, a little girl, the same I that will be in me as I grow, as a grown-up, as an old old lady, and on beyond that. What happens to this I is the me that other people can see, acting out all this life. So it will be all right whatever happens to me because the inner secret I can never be changed or lost.'

I had discovered the kernel, the essence, with all its nourishing sweetness. From then on I was free to be a witness. Whatever happens, to play the role, take on the metaphor.

Among those framed certificates there is a watercolour *Moonlight on the Water*, signed W. H. P. Caloundra 1931. Smoky, dreamy, shadowy, misty memories. My father, after his first stroke, knowing he had not long to live, gathered up Gurra (my mother) and Boof (me) and took us camping down at Pummistone Creek on Bribie Passage for more than a year with Badtjala people whose land he had surveyed for government departments and whose rights he had proclaimed in *Smith's Weekly*. Stretchers, tent, camp oven, fishing boat. Earth, fire, water, air. I played in the dirt, burnt my hand, long scarred, in embers, fell out of the boat, went nightly to my blanket show of sleep amid clapstick, song, recitation of Tennyson and C. J. Dennis. On my third birthday my mother, merciless, washed my hair in a tin tub. I bawled my head off. The Aborigines laughed and laughed and laughed.

My archive takes me back into the dark age. At the end of a rainy day's excavating, a tiny bookfold card falls out of nowhere. I had never seen it before.

Toowong Cemetery Notice: Burial on 8 January 1929
of Coralie Hilda Patterson, died 7 January 1929, aged 16
days.

This was my twin sister. Here I, the firstborn, began my life as a survivor: entered the poem of life, whose purpose is, after all, simply to witness the beauties of the world, to discover the many forms that love can take.

PART ONE

$\mathcal{M}$Y LIFE WITH JOEY

We met on a blind date. It began well. As soon as I sat down he started talking about the menu. I liked his voice — confident, masculine, solicitous. As expected, he had an American accent, but mild, kind of Bostonian. After all, he came from a prestigious family, although just a young adventurous member.

I felt that if we took to each other, things would go well. He would know how to direct, but would be patient and obedient to my wishes. It was only when he hesitated over the word 'difficulty', making an 'iffy' job of it, that I sensed that he too had misgivings. After all, it was my place to be the nervous one. I put out a tentative hand and a first word — as usual, 'afterwards'.

That was five years ago. Joey and I live together now. He has changed my life, and, as I get to know him better, I have changed a few of his irritating habits. But it had to be a menage à trois. We had to have Mickey live with us to make our life complete. Mickey is a laser printer, Joey my talking computer. Joey is a Keynote Synthesised Accent system voice, attached to an IPX-personal IBM-compatible computer.

Friend Joey switches on duty, headphones or mike, as faithful interpreter; reads out loud the words as we go along or stays silent until asked; speaks to me the traffic signs of punctuation, my computer screen face to the wall. He has a voice that can move from bass to countertenor, from ponderous to hysterical, from pedantry of spelling out each word to companionship of reading whole essays fluently without mentioning commas and periods – all at my command.

He has his own funny little ways of being helpful by filling out the abbreviation clues. For him *Drs* are not Doctors, only drives; and every *inc*lusion becomes *incor*porated, and every *st* is a street. How Bernard Shaw would have loved to hear his play called *Street Joan*.

These jokes Joey and I enjoy together. But sometimes he goes too far, gets out of hand, and has to be corrected. This is done by a 'dictionary' function. By virtue of his New Zealand connection, he spoke very well of the 'Maori' but rubbished the 'Aboriginal' until I told him to put them under the spell of 'Abberidjinal'. Once corrected he abides by my given pronunciation over his own word interpretations, accepts the mis-givings. That was how we got to know that even word-processor designers can make a joke. Remember how, in the book *They're a Weird Mob*, the innocent New Australian is misled into using the word 'arse-hole' for 'brain'? Someone had cheerfully taught the innocent Joey that there were four 'f's in 'difficulty'.

And we are so polite to each other. 'Please wait', he

says, when I have given him a big task. 'Sorry, Joey', I say when I have been silly enough to ask him the same thing twice. 'Bad entry', he says unscoldingly. 'Do you want to hear . . .?' he asks patiently; courteously reminds me 'File is protected' and gives me a second chance, before I delete, saying solicitously, 'Sure?'

But he is not always so straightforward when mate Mickey is involved. He is supposed to report to me what Mickey is doing, Mickey being dumb and given to winking and flashing sight symbols, making faces behind my back. There are times when Joey tries to cover up for him. 'Printer pausing' he says, when indeed, because of internal convolutions, Mickey has died on the job. And there was one notable occasion when Joey was left quite speechless.

It was early days. I turned off 'printer ready' Mickey to save his energetic waiting in the wings until we needed him. He hissed and crackled more than usual on demise. It sounded indeed like water dropping. I put out my hand. It was. I put out my nose. It was not – not water. It was moisture of more maleffluent kind. I pushed my hand up against the soft compressed straw lining of the attic roof, low at this point. I pushed against a lump that began to move away. I turned to Joey. 'Let's hope he's all right. How can we write and tell the insurance people that a possum pissed on our printer?'

Less than ten per cent of blind people use braille, generally those born blind for whom it is the indigenous language, and the 'gorne blind' who have a flair for languages. For most blind people audio format – 'Talking Books' on four-track or standard cassette – is the preferred form of reading. Typewriters and Long Play records were originally devised for blind people. Print Handicapped, alias Visually Impaired people, alias 'the visually disadvantaged', have taken to talking computers like ducks to water.

Like most people with failing eyesight, I took to a typewriter when my handwriting had come to vine and twine its way upon the page with such entanglement, such knots of cramp and scrawl, that friends, receiving letters, too often lost the plot.

When I was young and twenty and Melbourne-winter cold, with a technique of faking more sight than I had, with 'long johns' tucked in under my corduroy slacks, with coward's cold feet for things mechanical and a rogue dog's hot breath to run with the pack of aspiring secretaries, I went each weekday morning for one whole term to Xerco's Business College. There I sat in a row of young ladies, younger than me, fresh out of school, in hand-knitted twin sets and pleated skirts, upswept hair and cuban-heeled shoes. With their blindfold hoods positioned over the high bank of keys, they clattered their typewriters, chattered in whispers. Little did they know what Ruth I was in all their alien corn – that the typewriter was first invented for such as me – such a wondrous object of blocks and tackle to substitute for copperplate calligraphy of fountain pen in human hand.

Those jolly warm-hearted girls who kept losing their fingers and would never make it up to sixty words per minute – so many of them who might have been so good in kindergartens or stewarding on factory floors, but foot-runged now on the ladder towards secretarial superiority – were kind and generous, took turns to sit and read out to me the letters of protocol and architectural set-out sheets, to be typed over and over ad finitum ad perfection. One girl one day – and I could not prevent her dashing headlong into it – read back my typing error 'diffucilty' and blushed; for then, in the Fifties, the four-letter word was indeed guilt-making.

The class instructress, shrill and rhythmic, beat her stick upon the wall. 'Exercise six. Left hand only. Right hand resting. Middle and upper keys only: a-f-t-e-r-w-a-r-d-s. Fifty times briskly. Keep that rhythm. Nice finger work please.'

On graduation day I took the tram from professional to commercial end of Collins Street, there to interview a squad of second-hand typewriters. I fondled them like puppies in a pet shop and carried a full-grown Remington into the boss's office for the paperwork of purchase. He was a grey man, suited and aging. He wanted the going-blind young lady to have the right thing, but wondered, 'Why?' 'Well, to write with – you know, diaries, letters, poems.' The man got up. He paced about, went over to the window, gazed out like a puma from his cage in the zoo. 'To write poems on –' he mused; came back to his desk and brusquely let me have it at half price. Grey puma, I write my poems always for you.

The hands of the blind can see. As the eyes are disempowered, power is passed to the hands. The typewriter empowers the hands to think the words, as the hands of the pianist empower the keys to sing. Joey is my grand piano, after all those uprights – those manuals and electric typewriters.

Half a lifespan after that first Remington, my

performance on a portable electric still gave cause for wonder
– and frustration. My paper fell out unnoticed while my
fingers typed on in rapture, leaving recipients to fill in the
missing words. 'Friends' turned into 'fiends'. CAPITALS
GOT THE UPPER HAND UNBIDDEN FOR WHOLE
PARAGRAPHS AT A TIME. One finger, all unaware, strays
one key to left or right and whole passages slip into code. Pmr
gomhrt. s;; imsestr. dytsud pmr lru yp ;rgy pt tohjy . . .

Technology stalked the faithless typist. It fled me down the
nights and down the days and in a mist of tears I hid from
It. 'A talking computer would give you more independence, privacy, take the strain off withering memory, and
off all those long-suffering friends on demand to be your
seeing-eye readers of manuscript drafts.'
    It was 1980, a first assignation. A black limousine
picked us up – husband and me, suspicions and hope. Two
tall men escorted us as to the bridal chamber. One was the
Company Head unveiling their latest, experimental, newest,
most advanced model of talking typewriter, the other the
Minister for Social Services keen to pioneer technology in
handicapped training. I sat before a dog-couchant-sized keyboard attached to a rearing tuckerbox of inner works, a panel
of buttons strategic between us. At my touch a growling,
whirring voice, from extra-terrestrial zone, pronounced.
Oh, it was an actor's voice to fail any audition; and, moreover, had memory for only one line of script at a time.
Purchase price of eighteen thousand whispered dollars.
    Two tall men stood on either side, cued as for pro-
posal on bended knee, with expectant air for my word of
consent, a hush to hear me take my vows of purchase. Alas,

a slow uncoiling of my disappointment. I shrank and felt my husband's whip hand raised – 'not to be sold a pup' – so made muttered response. Not this. Not yet. Surely I shall have better offers if I wait.

Technology and seduction. Allure becomes imperative becomes authoritative. To see is to believe is to become. 'To have the experience but miss the meaning.'

It was 1982, in a Delhi hotel room. Two small men on either side, my travelling companion and I were surrounded by new silk clothes which these Jain men had made us since yesterday. These eager ingenuous young men, lovers of their city, had taken us out for two nights to meet its foods, its Red Fort pageantry. I offered them a gift. 'Please oh please, let it be the mini AM/FM radio.' I had got it at the airport duty-free. Its technology enchanted them. 'But you do not have FM in Delhi.' 'No, Madam. So this is so good. Thank you. I shall be the only person in Delhi with a radio like this!'

I had a good Irish friend, long in the computer business. He suggested I go to the Royal Blind Society's 'Technology Today' seminar. I went. I listened. 'Technology will go on bringing out talking computers that will be smaller, cleverer, cheaper. But if what is here today serves your purposes of today, it will go on serving your needs, which stay much the same. But your life's time goes marching on.'

It was 1989, and those old cold feet were frozen still. I needed a push to take the plunge. It came in the form of a little outer voice from a wise old woman. This was my remarkable cousin, Olive Sutton, close to her hundredth

year, having lived a full and studious life. She reflected:
'When I was a child they were taking the horse out of the
carriage and bringing in the motor car, and people didn't
want it at all. They were bringing in paper money instead
of gold, and people didn't think that would last either. They
were giving up fountain pens and taking to the typing
machine. Now, you see, a century later, our money is plastic and our writing all computer. And people don't all want
to go along with that either.'

In her nineties, quite impatient with nostalgic reminiscences, she was reading the latest book on sex change
operations and yearned to be taught computers. 'But,
Olive, at ninety-six you are too old.' 'I have been too busy
up till now.' I went to her and I said: 'Olive, please give me
all the determination, persistence and clear-mindedness
you would bring to this task. Let me do it through you.'

I heard again that first faraway beginning echo in my
head. 'Exercise One. Left hand only. Right hand resting.
Upper keys only: q-w-e-r-t-y q-w-e-r-t-y q-w- . . .' I was
'qwerty-fied' to make the new start and that good Irish
friend arranged our blind date. 'This is the man for you.
You'll soon get used to his voice.'

My friend, the philosopher J. P. McKinney, was a great
talker and on friendly terms with those inanimates that
served him well, none more so than his grandfather clock
which he used to wind with weekly Sunday-night ceremony.
Jack was twenty-five years older than his poet wife, Judith
Wright, and died at a good old age. Although he died down
in town in hospital, the grandfather clock, up in the house
on the mountain, did just what the old song says. It 'stopped
short, never to go again, when the old man died'.

For a while Judith kept company with the clock as a silent memento but, being a practical woman, decided to have it repaired. She was at that time as deaf as I was blind, pretty far gone. But we were used to each other. I happened to be there visiting, just the two of us at home, when the clock man came. He had a lot of tools and paraphernalia to unpack and not much to say for himself. Like any good country woman, Judith went off to the kitchen to make a cup of tea and, like any good friendly visitor, I made light conversation. How long had he been at his trade? What's the oldest clock he's repaired? What's his favourite kind of clock? How long a job? He answered but not without certain hesitation and a shuffling and scratching about while he manipulated some tool or other, and then in a voice somewhat clocky itself.

Eventually Judith rattled into the dining room with her cumbersome tea tray and immediately blocked my stream of questions by embarking on one of those long uninterruptible monologues that are the camouflage of deaf people. 'I'm finding out from our friend here,' I chirped, 'all about clocks.' She replied in a schoolma'am manner. 'I think we'll wait for him to sit down to his tea.' I saw the picture. He was getting paid by the hour and I was interfering with his concentration. Eventually the clock gave a striking performance, then settled down to a steady reassuring tick-tock. The clock man climbed down from his steps – the sound that my questions had evoked each time – rattled his tools together, clipped up his case, and then came quietly to the table. Judith poured the tea, serving him in a very motherly way, quite forgetting to give me the usual stage directions as to where my cup was placed.

Then she said, directly to him, 'You make a good job of using that speaking tube of yours. You make it look easy.'

The penny dropped. Tracheotomy tube! We worked it all out in due course and decided to buy a Golden Casket ticket between us named 'The Three Monkeys' — Hear no . . . See no . . . Speak no . . . We didn't win a prize — but the clock went on tick-tocking for ever after.

Talking books are made by professional actors and readers recording in studios at libraries for the Print Handicapped. I was listening to Oliver Sacks' *The Man Who Mistook His Wife for a Hat* on my talking-book machine. He describes aphasia, a form of brain damage brought on by stroke, in which the ability to understand words is impaired:

> To demonstrate their aphasia, one had to go to extraordinary lengths as a neurologist to speak and behave unnaturally, to remove all the extra verbal clues, the tone of voice, intonation, suggested emphasis or inflection as well as all visual cues, one's expressions, one's gestures and entire, largely unconscious, personal repertoire and posture . . . involving total concealment of one's person and total depersonalisation of one's voice, even to using a computerised voice synthesiser, in order to reduce speech to pure words, speech totally devoid of 'tone colour' or evocation. It was only with such a grossly mechanical artificial speech, somewhat like the computers in *Star Trek*, that one could be wholly sure of their aphasia.

Joey, metallic as the sound may be, knows how to nicely turn a comma, uplift a capital, querrilize a question mark.

Speech, natural speech, does not consist of words
alone, nor of propositions alone. It consists of
utterance, an uttering force of one's whole meaning
with one's whole being, the understanding of which
involves infinitely more than mere word recognition.
For, although the words, the verbal constructions
per se, might convey nothing, spoken language is
normally suffused with tone, pervaded with an
expressiveness that transcends the verbal. It is precisely
this expressiveness, so deep, so various, so complex, so
subtle, which is perfectly preserved in aphasia, though
understanding of words be destroyed. This too
becomes clear, often in the most striking or dramatic
or comic way, to all those who work or live closely
with them.

We are 'Homo Loquens', but those with the lack of 'feeling tone' in the voice are a reversal to something more
primitive, more elemental.

Thank you, Dr Sacks. Joey, all is forgiven. I know you
now as an elemental — my familiar, overtones of an alter ego.

One week of Joey-a-go-go, with a patient teacher, and I
returned to cousin Olive and said: 'Okay, we've done it.
Joey and I have come to a firm understanding.'

Nowadays it is quite chattersome up in my attic.
When it's not the radio or talking book, it's Joey's patter
and Mickey's obedient spluttering and spitting out of
pages. Certainly there is much more that Joey can do for
me than I have asked him to do so far. Maybe some day I'll
venture afield into numbers, programs, bulletin boards,

data bases. But, old puma, for the time being, with chop-and-changing away at my poems and diaries, filing letters, recipes and study notes, Joey serves me well. He struts my stage of memory with long interruptible speeches. I do not want him to sing and tap-dance. He is my confidant, keeping secret my stock of dreams, my piled-up failures, my letters sent, unsent.

Technology knocks at the door, trick or treat? 'Joey could grow ears, you know, he could take orders from your voice.' This is a tug-o-war in which I wish not to be pulled over the line. I am on the side of the mystery of words, the feel and weight and place of words, the music of words, the poem of words as part of the poem of life itself. I do not want words desecrated into information carriers, cliché catchers, jargon trappers. I want to feel words in my fingers, measure them on the page, engage their alchemy.

GRANDMOTHERS

By order of geniture I ought to have had two grandmothers. Instead, and despite the mother of my own mother dying when young, I had six – a great-grandmother, a step-grandmother, a foster-grandmother, a grandmother-elect, one only genuine (paternal) grandmother, and her identical twin sister. What an assorted lot they were. What dimensions they gave my childhood. What sustenance their memory gives me as I grow old. With one exception, all of them lived on vigorously into their eighties.

I

Old Granny Poole, because of my mother's late marriage, was aged enough to be my great-great-grandmother. She lived in her pioneer slab hut, built before the Kellys rode, at the end of the twice-weekly mail run on the Toogoolawah road, twelve miles out from the Queensland township of Kilcoy. A four-roomed house of milled timber had been built in front at the turn of the century, a house painted red whose outer cladding had never been put on, so that its struts and beams showed on the outside of single wooden walls. Granny always referred to it dispossessively as 'the new house' and in the Thirties she and Uncle Bill lived on happily in the old slab hut. He had been paralysed all down one side by a fall from a horse many years ago. Granny, black in bonnet and dress to the ankles, prodded her flecked enamel pots on top of the woodfire stove under the flour-bag tea-towels hung up to dry. Uncle would come in from the milking, hang up his hat on the post, wipe his hob-nailed boots on the sugar-sack mat, wash in the tin dish, replacing soap on its spike, towel on its nail, before removing his checkered flannel neckerchief.

The one-room hut was made of vertical slabs. The windows were solid wooden shutters pushed open on a stick. The verandah was built without nails so that the planks flew up like piano keys when you walked on the edge of it. There were two small step-down rooms at the back, the wooden one being the dairy where vats of milk were skimmed and butter churned. The other, earth-floored, was for buckets and tools. A narrow side of this room was partitioned off for Bill.

What comfort of rightness there was in that single room, a sweet sufficiency. Everything tasted good. Everything was true and trusty – the furniture, made by Grandfather Poole, there where he placed it, and Granny's compounds and cures, that would fix anything, up on the high shelf near at hand. When it rained the horses galloped up from the paddock to clatter on to the low verandah, their stable.

As visitors, my mother and I slept in the new house

in the front bedroom alongside the parlour. Granny's bed-room behind it was dark and dank and smelly, locked with secrets. The back room behind the parlour was the grain-store room. Before bedtime we set batches of mousetraps there. At night our corn-husk mattresses crackled at every move, the dog rattled his chains, the horse in the yard kicked over the tin dish, the corrugated iron roof shrank like gunshot – all fearful noises to my city ears. The traps went off like crackers with squeak and squeal. Each time Granny, muttering in her sleep through the thin wall, would call out, 'More mouse pie' or 'Mouse mince sausage tomorrow!' – all of which of course I dared not believe.

The front parlour of the new house, with its hard horsehair sofa and calf skins on the floor, was used on the occasion of visits of parson, government man or not alto-gether trusted neighbour. Then Uncle Bill, in ceremoni-ously clipped-on celluloid collar with studs and polished boots, would stand about looking uncomfortable. Granny, in lace collar and cap, would pour tea in her delicate English tea-set and serve seed cake laid out on starched embroidered cloth, upon the table where ordinarily stood a chiming clock and the two great household volumes. These were a Commentary on the Old Testament with wood-cut illustration under tissue paper of all the robed and bearded prophets, and the Medical Compendium with its amazing colour pictures of diseased people anonymous, blindfolded, and lift-up flap illustrations of the layers of human anatomy, upon which I devoted enormous hours of contemplation.

This Granny was so very old that her very being there made everything about olden times believable. She rocked in her chair singing old English songs and telling the tales of her grandfather's woes at Waterloo with the black kettle hissing on its hob, the big bell to be rung only in case of disaster – snake bite or murderous swagman – hanging above her on the beam, and, beside her, her waddi waddi stick which she held authoritative as a sceptre whenever a swaggie appeared, and stomped on the floor three times at night at the coming of shadows. With her I believed in witches, fairy godmothers, ghosts and hobgoblins. She promised that before we went away again she would see if her goose had laid a golden egg for us. I knew that she would lift the loose floorboard, that her goose was a calico bag and the eggs were her savings of sovereigns. Granny did not believe in tinned food, city doctors or paper money.

My mother brought down on these holidays good sad sensible books like *Seven Little Australians* and *Little Dorrit*. She read them out to us night after night, all four of us gathered close round the kerosene lamp set on the table scrubbed pale and smooth as butter. Town books she might bring, but town butter never. 'It's the rats that give the factory butter its flavour,' Granny would say as she methodically patted her butter in the dairy, eventually setting down the bowl of sour buttermilk eager to the dog. In the year of the big drought mulberry trees were cut down to feed the cows. Their milk, and the chook eggs, went a purplish-pink colour, as did my pinafores, and my tongue. Before we went up to bed, Granny would say, 'It's a long time till morning,' and hot us up a bowl of gruel.

She was the last of them, the three Georges and three Emmas who had settled that district, taking up land at five bob an acre. Her husband was the son of a pre-Victorian Woods–Poole marriage in the Forest of Dean, which, to my word-ripened imagination, contrasted strangely with that bare place of earth among cleared scrub where that slab hut stood. The only flowers were the bunches of ever-lasting daisies, dry live–dead flowers, that my mother and I picked. Once, when the peach tree beside the creek not far from the house was in bloom, I brought in an armful of its blossom. It made Granny cry and she locked herself away for the rest of the day. So it had to be explained to me that there had been another uncle, not paralysed, who had gone out one day and cut his throat there where the peach tree grew, atoning for his despair.

II

Strange that the only daughter of that Poole marriage, the grandmother I never knew, should have spent the decade of her wedlock and given her children to live in an extrava-gance of garden. She married a Swede, a one-voyage seaman so sick from the sea that he spent the rest of his days with his hands in the earth, planting, growing, ornamenting gardens. He was appointed landscape gardener to the Mental Institute at Goodna between Brisbane and Ipswich, and he had an acre or two of garden adjacent.

I hardly knew him, 'a figure lying horizontal in a bed', bald-headed, red-bearded. It was his widow, his second wife, whom we visited on Sundays after church. We would short-cut through the bush from the station and arrive at the white wicket gate to the welcoming bark of Barney. The gate was directly opposite the lattice front door of the high verandah, but to reach it we had to walk a long way, left or right, around two sides of an immense diamond-shaped flower bed, immaculately patterned at every season with a blooming mosaic, while on the other side a line of shrubs stood guard at the edge of the mown grassy verge, close-clipped into shapes of camels, emus, turreted castles, and brandishing cavalry man. Honeysuckle and quisqualis twined over the verandah railing intoxicating with their sweet and medicinal odours the cool interior of the house. Down the wide passageway we would follow grey, muttering Nanny Olson, answering the greeting from parrot in cage in the breezeway between water tanks, the bridge verandah into the big kitchen and back parlour, whose pantry off to the side glowed with rows of pumpkins, globes of strung-up turnips and racks of drying peanuts. The tip-toe honey room dripped day and night, dark and sticky, hectically sweet, cooled by damp hessian, into ten-gallon tins.

Memories are of the things and places of that house rather than of the grandmother — the gravy jugs and rounded teapot in willow pattern, the rose-embossed pitcher pouring warm water into a matching bowl for bedtime washing, the china shepherd and shepherdess fragile and faded on the corner wicker stand in the parlour. The rooms and gardens, verandah and pathways were like, but so much bigger than, my own home. They held more mysteries.

The isolated row of houses, all owned by Institute people, exuded children. At hide and seek we ran winged with pluck into the bee-hive rows, hunched carapaced among the rain-damp ferns bowering the tank-stand. Old Matt stood motionless Napoleon hours while we climbed the camphor laurel tree and made French Revolutions in its branches pelting him with berries of cannon fire. Jumping Jim mowed the lawns by fits and starts – starting off like a bull at a red rag, fitting into a corner to eat handfuls of the mown grass, jumping and laughing on approach. Tree-tall Percy, who had fifteen children of his own somewhere on an island, beckoned us behind the outdoor bath-house in the kitchen garden to tattle us girlies with the petticoat prattle of storks leaving babies under the gooseberry bush. Big Maudie, dress tucked in bloomers, twanged the wires of the aviary to make the birdies flutter, until we ran up and gave her little smacks to make her shriek after us. Such harmless playmates were inmates from the adjacent asylum, free to come and spend their time in the gardener's garden. He always said, 'The vay out of the asylum is through the garden.' I have come to know what he meant. At times in my life when I have been overcome by a welter of anger, despair or misery, seeming to overpower my sanity, I have escaped from the enclosure of rooms, or oppression of city streets, to where I could lean myself against a tree, flatten myself upon some grass, lay hands on a flower or stroke the tress of a bush, and in that presence felt the anguish of the moment diminish as my spirit replenished.

But, in the blown-up image of that Goodna garden of my childhood kept in the scrapbook of my mind, the grandmother is missing, her face obliterated. She did not take me for walks, tell me stories, elaborate my birthdays; she was always busy somewhere else. She understood plants, but not children, so never became that sought-out old tree trunk around which to cling the vines of their trivial confidences. Later, my mother told me she had been a wicked step-mother of storybook proportions; had burned her books and dolls to make her scrub more floors, chop more wood; had locked away her pretty dresses when the giver was gone; had lied to the father that the horse was lame to make her walk five miles to school; had tea-partied the school friends brought home on a birthday afternoon, then beaten her soundly afterwards for giving so much trouble.

III

No wonder my mother ran away as soon as schooldays were over. She got lodgings with the Jonsons, a cumulus family that swarmed in one of those small wooden houses that ladder steeply up the stony hills of Red Hill, seeming to pig-a-back one another vertically, each one braced knee-deep. People from these houses had their own way of staggering zigzag up and of teetering full tilt down, with exactly the right momentum to bring them up short at their own front gate. My mother grew into that family as another daughter, so that I was built-in to its boisterous brood of grandchildren.

Grandma Jonson, stout and barefoot, open-handed, warm-hearted and almost bald, ruled her roost with a raucous voice. In her floured aprons and flowery dresses, she had the attributes appropriate to a country homestead, from which indeed she had been widowed — a voice of a force-four cockatoo that could crackle out gossip and admonitions across to friends and relatives caged in their houses on the opposite hillside, and an inferno of a kitchen that poured forth roast dinners, hot scones, cauldrons of jams, and red-hot poultices.

Her house exploded with squabbles and celebrations. She roused mercilessly at the dog that lay in her way and the hens that did not. From the stingy earth of a rocky perch of garden she raised up prodigious bunches of spinach, rhubarb and mignonette lettuce, exuberant take-home bouquets of zinnia, sweet pea and chrysanthemum. The door was always open. People walked straight in and unburdened themselves – spilling out a suitcase of marmalade oranges, a handbag hold of snapshots of someone's christening, a basket of week-old kittens, a new-learned song or piano piece, a sudden breakdown of tears. And all the time Uncle Arthur, unspeaking and unspoken-to, sat at the far end of the dining table, communicant in a particular gibberish with a mantel radio perched on a special shelf like a parrot at his shoulder, and sibilant with the shuffling of his newspaper Guide to Form. On Saturday afternoons he was 'out', and on Saturday evenings no one was any the wiser. The other adults that pounded through the house – all adults 'uncles' and 'aunties' to us children – were on their way to football, band practice or fishing trips.

Birthdays abounded. Taffeta ribbons were tied on ringlets released from a morning in curling rags, and sashes around the waists of frilled organza hand-me-down dresses all for the sake of hidings in wardrobes or under beds, tug-o-wars down the passageway, stampings round the piano before the sticky surfeit of fudges, cordials, iced animal biscuits and rainbow cake, with the blue castor oil bottle and rattling canister of Sal Vital brandished soon after. On New Year's Eve we were bedded down like an eyrie of eaglets to be wakened at a quarter to midnight, to be given drums, bells, whistles, triangles, tambourines and trumpets; then to be encouraged to make as much hullabaloo as possible to see out the old and welcome in the New Year;

then to have our sleep-sodden stomachs indulged with clinks of raspberry wine and tastes of all the aunties' Christmas cakes, one for good luck for each month of the year.

They ate, they drank, they were merry, for in their yesterdays so many had already died – husbands, soldiers, infants. It was the first house in which I saw adults cry – Granma herself, my own mother, and men too. It was a good safe place to cry, safer than church. Cups of tea and words of comfort were at hand. 'There'll be good times coming.' Recovering from chickenpox, I lay bedded down in a corner under the bubble-glass windowpanes, emerald, puce and amber, well snuggled with rag dolls, comics and packets of jelly beans. At a jerk of coughing, I spilt cocoa all over the lot and was not scolded. It was part of living that much was forgiven. I felt assured from the downright kindness of this grandmother that adulthood, when I reached that far distant unknown state, would be in some ways recognisable, that there would be mates there, like children have, to share secrets with.

IV

Had Gallipoli not happened, my mother would have married into a flatter suburb, into a family where the combination of Swedish sobriety and puritanic religion made for a good temper of order and obedience. She was received into that family anyway. So it transpired that I, in the fullness of time – to use her own Biblical turn of phrase – came under the ministrations of Grandma Hogberg. Believing that it was God's will that childhood should be a happy and improving time, she did her best to make it so.

With her white hair smoothed back into a bun, her gold-rimmed spectacles ever watchful, her lisle stockings immaculately darned, unseen beneath her long dresses that were black with white dots, white sprigs or white squiggles, and neat buckled shoes, she was a very proper, almost professional, grandmother.

Stays with her were planned and looked forward to, the duties and pleasures arranged. She pruned her days and sprouted ours that they might flower together. She showed us children how to cook, knit, shop well at the butcher, make our own entertainment. Black handbag with money purse cautious and honest, black Bible with place markers for morning and evening readings, black shoes in a row for polishing every Saturday morning, black and white draughts set out on the board for play when the washing-up was finished – everything was done well. She would know if we gabbled our prayers or did not rightly make the beds, bottom sheet firm and flat, blankets shaken smooth. Everything was always clean.

Through long afternoons we laid door-stop bottles with layers of coloured sands brought back from a seaside trip, tabbed together paper palaces, pasted scrapbooks, used up all those magazine pieces, empty cotton reels, ends of ribbon that she saved up for us. What was begun got finished and the broken was made whole.

She had been born a Roman Catholic. She had a sister, a nun of high degree, whom we met occasionally, excitingly, so lively in her habit. But grandmother had purified herself through the years, further and further away from dogma and decoration down to the world of the gospels made personal, the Plymouth Brethren humility. She carried her conviction into a contentment with the commonplace in her small flat with its row of pot plants on the balcony, rented cottages for holidays by the sea, and the treat of the long-distance tram ride. She smiled with goggle-eyed beneficence as we changed from neat house dress into newer going-out dress; how could I bring myself to tell her what agony it was for me, a bad traveller, to catch a tram from terminus to terminus, through the city and back again, never alighting, just to watch the world go by?

But children heed with suspicion what is partly told and reach for answers to questions they cannot ask. We got down from the bookcase, while she took a nap, the volume of Nurses' Training lectures to read about childbirth and venereal disease. Animosity between Catholics and Protestants ran high. We were primed to be anti-green because green meant Irish meant Catholic. Grandma had us cut out the green pieces from the boiled lollies, weekly gift in their paper cone from the grocer man. One day we retrieved the green bits from the garbage bin and ate them all at once, then waited to see if we would turn into Catholics.

The rightness of the world she offered us was a narrow enclosed garden of straight paths and weedless flower beds restricted within high walls of prejudice to keep us safe from the ambitious, the extraordinary and the mysterious. It was a garden from which I ran far away as soon as schooldays were over.

V

It was my little Scottish grandmother, my father's mother, who had most hold on me. We were tied by blood, and it was thick braw Scots blood. If the Scots had stopped their wars with the English, then she had not cared to hear of it. She brought out for me the boxes of lead soldiers, the Coldstream Guardsmen chipped of paint and lopped of limb, the Highlanders bright and whole. Tam o' Shanter, the Black Wallace and Bruce and the Spider were all early in my mind. *The Book of Tartans*, exact to clan and custom, was near to hand, the way other people kept the gardener's guide for botanical name and species. She declared on the telephone that she was hungry to see me and when I arrived with my basket of good things, avowed that she was ready 'to eat me all up'. So we sat down together at the dinning-room table, a huge table, and talked for hours.

Her house was dirty, her meals were late. We sat pixie-stooled at her table and talked for hours. It was a grand six-legged drawing table, its woven cloth tasselled all the way round. She fetched down armfuls of books, when I was too young to read, and we made castles out of them, building them higher and higher until they all fell down.

She enfolded me back into the fabric of her girlhood — running through the glens to find earth chalks for drawing on castle walls and under bridges; watching her wax dolls melt on the voyage out from the Old Country, their faces slipping away in the terrible tropical heat; daring to ride the wild horses in ball gowns to abscond through the night to the barn where the red-headed Hendersons were holding a dance. As she talked, she shaped the air with her hands. She sketched, she cut out chains of paper figures dancing, made pen-wiper dolls out of scrap cloth on wishing bone, and, hairy withered bent-up old crone that she was, would jump up to play-act a character in her story or do a few steps of the Sword Dance.

Her house was large but the available living areas had contracted by a process of accretion to a few pools of active space as the rooms silted up with debris of the past. Curtains were drawn across archways to rooms now impenetrable. Walls, cracked and peeling like bark just briefly evident, were upheld by a mass of oil and watercolour paintings, framed photographs, cartoons and picture platters. Chairs were sat upon by years of magazines, archives of Edison boxes, and a conjugation of nasty Scotch terrier dogs, some plaster, some real and snoring. The dust-grimed piano, its antennae of tarnished brass candle brackets thrust forwards, was never shut. Tops of polished tables were unseen beneath stacks of sheet music and bundles of clothes waiting to be mended. Drawers jammed, cupboards buckled, books piled horizontal upon vertical on the shelves, and the huge mirrored sideboard multiplied its multitude – 'How many things starting with B can you see in this picture?' – a jostle of not-quite-finished bottles, jars and cartons of innumerable commodities, liqueurs, liniments, face creams, flea powders, indigestion remedies, white spirits and black unguents. The tray under the ice chest had never been emptied, its ammoniac waters having rotted their way through the floorboards now marvellously nourished hanging baskets of magnificent maidenhair fern in the rockery below.

But Grandma Patterson, spider-wise in this web entanglement of her past, could always unerringly lay her hand on the very thread or page or crayon that she wanted and redeem the whole situation with convincing promise that tomorrow she would have a grand spring cleaning and get rid of all the old things. 'Tomorrow' and 'when our ship comes in' – those were her promises. She was, let it not be forgotten, Jamesina Watt, adrift in third-generation expectations of family fortune when the ship of those lost steam-engine patents would legally come in. Sitting at her windows that overlooked the long reach of the river, balancing the binoculars on the sill, I could just make out the speck on the horizon, our ship coming in.

Effortless from habit and never ceasing in her chat, Grandma would throw together a pan full of those savoury rissoles I liked so much, or an oven full of little queen cakes much too sweet. She measured and mixed by hand, making her hand scooped like a spoon, splayed like a fork, flat, fisted or light finger-tipped. She poured our tea from an interesting Black and White teapot, presumably a pre-World War I distillers' bonus to the wives of regular whisky consumers, and we would discuss the rosy rosy future – places to travel 'when you grow up', a man to marry . . . In her house the answer to that tiresome question so often plumbed into the innocence of children, was not tinker, tailor, soldier, sailor, but rather – proudly, confidently – singer, poet, painter, player. Alas, I disappointed her dreadfully at the piano by hopelessly plunking at notes. Drawing, I spilt the inks. Dancing, I toppled down things from the tops of other things. But I took elocution lessons and could stand forth on the mat, as though on stage before an eager audience, and recite Paterson and Tennyson, a very little Rabbie Burns and a great deal of my own recent translation of the dramas of the Old Testament into rhymed couplets. My father had been a notable C. J. Dennis declaimer in his day. Her oft-repeated sigh to me – 'If only your dear Daddy could be with us now' – was the nearest warmth of paternal embrace I had.

She was then a great age, an embroidery of memories already detached from the fabric of the present. She lived on to over ninety, lived too long. She lived far into that awful forgetfulness, or rather that comfortable animal forgetfulness with awful moments of human recollection. Grown up, I was to her still a little girl, sometimes Bridget the long-gone parlour maid. To appease her and amuse the other old ladies in the nursing home, in my uni days, I would doff shoes and dance in stockinged feet on the linoleum floor a few steps of the eightsome reel and tell them tales of the Highland ball and my latest beau. I spiced the telling with some of those secrets, too shocking for mothers, but a wand to waft these old ones back to the honey hive of their own sweet maidenhood.

VI

That grandmother's sister lived not so long but for a time much closer to me. She was the practical one. I was intrigued to hear Grandma Ayrd's factual account of the events in early days that Grandma Patterson so romantically recalled. Moreover she was the only Grandma to have a Grandpa to match. They were a cheerful bantering pair. He was a naughty old thing and wore a cap on the side of his head to prove it, and she was his Cap'n.

Their territory, commodious kitchen, large leafy dining room over-set with sofas, armchairs and cabinets with a further bedroom beyond, was a kind of green room to the rest of the house where dancing classes for children were held. There, all the bedrooms seethed with little girls in a spillage of school clothes distilling out in a froth of tutus, dressing tables culinary with cosmetics, little feet hardening under swabs of methylated spirits, little heads close-bound with pinned-up pigtails. In the vast living room, devoid of carpet and furniture, its floor polished to a slippery shine, their daughter Alexa, rouged, expansive and spangled with beads and bracelets, strummed and skedaddled on the piano while my cousin Madam Anita gave classes in tap and toe. On the high front verandah the bubs scraped and clattered in the initiations of the shuffle and tap.

I was a favourite, but not a distinguished, pupil. I liked to slip out to the grandfolk to shell peas and eat shortbread with them until the chords of my tune sent me skidding back to the line. Grandpa silver-frosted all manner of shoes, loose-nailing ha'pennies into the instep. Grandma sewed pompoms and bows and star-dusted bodices with sequins. On nights of performances they sat, dressed in their best, in near front rows.

Such were my many grandmothers. Their gifts to my childhood were great. Recalling them now does not, I think, deter me from my five-year-old answer to that tiresome question. 'When I grow right up,' I said to the Rechabites teacher, 'I'm going to be a nice old grandmother.' In 1996 I have six grandchildren by kin and many more by kith.

15 EDMONDSTONE STREET

The time was the end of the Thirties, the place the intersection of Russell and Edmondstone streets at the north-west corner of Musgrave Park in South Brisbane. Ventnor Flats faced the park across Edmondstone, the Vulcan can factory across Russell. Diagonally opposite was an unremembered house, just beyond which was 12 Edmondstone Street, the house of the Malouf family. David was then an infant, seven years younger than me.

That locality of the western end of South Brisbane was mostly occupied by old family houses, mainly weatherboard. As the young of these families flew the coop or the families themselves felt the pinch of the Depression, the verandahs were boarded up and the houses divided into flatettes or residential. Ventnor Flats was a conspicuous intruder. It was bold, modern, concrete, a two-storey terrace looking today like a set of town houses, each with its token front yard and street gate, identical two arches of balcony above and below. We occupied the upper flat farthest from the street corner.

The flat was a long way from that timber suburban house with its gardens and verandahs that my father had built for us and where I spent my early childhood. But he had 'gone to Heaven' and we had come to the city. At Ventnor my mother was trying out an alternative to boarding house life-with-landlady. We were a kind of girls' 'pad' but that word was not in vogue then. We were a suite of five persons female – two senior and two junior business girls and one schoolgirl.

The flat was not large, a string of five rooms with enclosed balcony – that balcony half of which was private domain. From it I looked out over the Park – truly my alma mater to the spire of the church. During the seven years of my girlhood, I came to be more familiar with the twenty acres of Musgrave Park than any other place of earth. For us young citydwellers the Park was backyard, village green, playing field and Wild West – the crucible of childhood.

15 Edmondstone Street was one of the 'Four Stations' of the Park, those four houses adjacent to its several sides in which I lived in these years. The Park was a place for birth-day parties, wet-day games in the bandstand, tree houses, skipping contests, balance walking on high walls, dodging the creepy old metho men, hopscotch on the giant draughtsboard, gang fights, witches' trysts – all the rites of childhood.

Long years, generations before our time, to the south of the settlement of Moreton Bay there was a grassy place known to the Aborigines as Kurilpa, belonging to no particular tribe, therefore a meeting place. 'Here under arboreal edifices named Moreton Bay fig trees, medicines, blankets and rations are given out to the dark people, and they sing their bird-like songs.' The invaders came to this green and pleasant island amid the growing ocean of houses and trade-route bitumen roads. They came in their distinctive uniforms, with survey sticks, and staked out their claims. Each clan, appropriately armed, mapped out a territory with a geometry of asphalt paths, fenced out their separate states and cleared their land flat and bare within. Active or absentee, they owned the Park – the bowlers (male), the tennis players (caged), the croqueteers (female), the draughts players (old), the High School frequenters of barrack school building and playing fields (adolescent), the bandsmen at their highpoint stand (occasional). Sportsmen and schoolmen had taken up the best parts of the Land, leaving the wandering tribes of southside city dwellers to come out by day to walk the dogs or prams, to stalk their dreams by night.

We wilder tribes, we kids who do not surrender to the rules of the game, move among the branches and shadows, the ridges and swamps, a feral wild life. No one ever told us about Aboriginal sacred sites. When the war came and the Yanks invaded Brisbane, the black man invaded our tribal sacred places. Their negro servicemen – 'boongs' – were segregated to the shady southside.

I knew the Park like the back of my hand, the roads where my schoolmates lived spreading out like fingers from it, the pathways like the bones fleshed by the green hillocks and hollows, haired and scarred by the huge dark Moreton Bay fig trees and swampy drains. All these paths wristed out at the fountain exit, with my church, Park Presbyterian, standing on the left and, on the right, that rambling old house where, unbeknown to me then, I was to spend the war years, my days of High School.

At Ventnor we were gentle folk. My four elders were all members of the esteemed Brisbane Business Girls Club and I used to go with them to their meetings in select city rooms where, over tea with sandwiches (asparagus, anchovy paste, curried egg) and cakes (popularly seed cake and Victoria sandwich), esteemed members would get up and sing, recite or play the piano. I used to sit through 'Bless This House' and 'Kerry Dance', 'Rustle of Spring' (with frills), and 'Bells across the Meadow' (with echo), 'The Wreck of the Hesperus' (dramatico) and 'The Lady of Shalott' (pathetique), and was regarded as a 'little old-fashioned thing' who enjoyed such events. My mother simply said, 'No show without Punch'.

We tumble-together of stray people, a makeshift family, lived in this flat without clutter and without elegance of space. They managed the shopping between them in their lunch hours. Butchers wrapped their packages in brown paper and string. A local grocer delivered his box to the back door and my mother dropped in and paid him on her way to work next day. It was the only time in my life that she made up my school lunches. She spoiled me with the modern sandwich spreads in Disney character glasses – cheese and gherkin, raisin and nut, orange and passionfruit.

I had pretty much a life of my own. I came and went by the back door, the narrow verandah and long flight of steps, the concrete path between clothes lines and flower pots, and out by squeak and slam of wooden door into Russell Street.

Arriving home, I dumped my shoulder schoolbag emphatically at the door, that shoulder-brace Queensland schoolbag that left both hands free to swing on boughs, catch balls, throw stones, make mouth-hoot whistles, read comics all the way home: 'Turned Right' into the big back kitchen to fetch myself a clutch of biscuits, a slosh of milk in a Goofy glass to fortify myself for the adventures ahead; 'About Turn' past bathroom, through dining room, single bedroom, double bedroom, out to the balcony, home that I shared with my mother. The striped canvas blinds in the archways left and right were pulled down more-or-less permanently to screen our two beds from the street. It gave a tent-like effect. 'This is our camp, out here,' my mother told visitors. All my wordly goods were stowed in the cedarwood box and bookshelves, that travelled around with us, beside my bed (my father's old resto couch) and in the baskets and suitcases underneath it.

I had a couple of hours to myself before the working girls came home. I peeled the beans, potatoes, apples, left out for me, and soaked them in saucepans, while mono-toning the homework – prefixes and suffixes, similes and metaphors, vulgar fractions and decimals, clauses of the Magna Carta.

My real desire was to earn a penny to buy another bar of Nestlé's Milk Chocolate for the purpose of extracting from its wrapper yet another stick-in colour picture of far and foreign countries for my pride and joy, my Nestlé's *World Wonder Atlas*. My mother paid a penny a story, poem or composition. I became prolific and the production per penny went up to three compositions or ten poems. Thus I embarked on my Great Work of translating the Old Testament, or at least the salient passages thereof, into rhymed couplets. At no extra cost I committed these poetics in lashings of coloured inks and an extravagance of illuminated headings, proud and mindful that Queen Victoria had looked with favour upon the illuminated manuscript presented by the Colony of Queensland on the occasion of her Jubilee, by the hand of my granduncle, Thomas Toye Patterson.

On other days I roamed abroad, skirmished the Park for adventures — a game of tennis to shadow umpire; if lucky enough to have a girl cricket mate, a few swipes with the vigaro bat and ball; if numerous, a full game of cricket across the road as pitch; if left to myself, a private detective mission at breakneck pace and ingenuity, short-cutting between pathways with desperate inner monologue; or the solo ball in the side street, the ball staining the wall more disgracefully at each retrieval from gutter slime. 'Bounce, bounce, bounce, /On the cold grey wall, B. P., /Until a window opens /And a voice cries Stop! to me.'

I had one special friend. Her name was Marea Medis. We were all to the other's all. We walked along arms around each other's waist, heads bent in secrets. We sat together in the same bay of the Moreton Bay fig tree roots and shared our lunches. She was Greek but not totally cousined into the local fraternity — the Trovases, who owned the milk bar opposite the City Hall, the Mitteros, good spellers, Annie Kasakas, who drew elaborate ballroom ladies, the two Frelegus (Consul) daughters who took private lessons from my cousin Madame Anita and danced so perfectly in unison, and the Zapharopolis brothers, sons of Zapha the greengrocer. She came with me to Park Presbyterian Sunday School.

Every elevenses we rushed down to the far end of the South Brisbane State School playground to the embankment to wave to the interstate train as it lumbered out from the nearby station. We waved and waved. Two afternoons a week we walked together diagonally across the Park and she went to Greek School in Russell Street which backed on to Ventnor. No one thought of inviting the alien stranger inside that heavy door, with its peeling painted blue dolphin, to partake of a bit of Greek grammar or dance. So I bounced my ball or sat waiting in the gutter calling out 'Marea, Marea!' just like in the much later *West Side Story*. Then I lost her. She went away 'and I never saw her again' just like it says in the song – the friend of my heart.

By the time the business girls came home from the office, the bird was in the cage. I was dutifully washed and changed and perched in adoration in front of the wireless. This was an altar-piece of inlaid wood veneer with round beacon face, hands pointing to its illustrious inscriptions of radio station call signs, its belly, behind the ornamental fretwork, frocked in fabric of rosy silken thread enshrining the trumpet speaker. A moth had martyred itself within the dial, bruising a permanent beauty-spot over 4IP (Ipswich) and later the silken cloth had borne the wound of my probing finger and, like the rents in my clothes, had been carefully but not too delicately darned by my mother. Acolyte there, I was in a Heaven of my own.

Any privacy in that flat had to be self-made. All the rooms were open for transit, all except the left-side one with closed door. This was a blind box-room, 'the Black Hole of Calcutta', crammed and camphor-smelling. Genn, 'good-hearted Genn', occupied the single bedroom beside it, a sepia, sweetish, still little room. A middle-aged woman, my mother still called her by her surname from the faraway days of their youth 'before the War', when they lodged together at the Lady Musgrave Lodge, the Business Girls Hostel up on the Terrace. Surnames were still used, nicked down to a handier form. Friends and office colleagues might not have known that 'Mrs Patterson's' Christian name was Gertrude. They simply called my mother 'Patty'.

My earliest memory is of sitting on the knee of Scottish 'Aunty Genn', wondrous that her chocolate brown bead necklace never melted. My last memory is of a poor lonely old maid cast up in a hospital bed, bandaged like a mummy, soaked in lotions of medicinal but somehow chocolate odour. The first we knew of that dreadful accident was seeing her name on the front page of the paper. The tram in which she had been coming home from work had suddenly caught on fire and she had only just escaped burning to death in front of fellow passengers. Then, at Ventnor, in her telephonist days, she was chubby, wore spotted dresses and bowler hats; was kind of slow, lagging a sentence behind, and laughing at unfunny places. I once found her slumped in a faint on the lavatory in a fuddle of skirts and stays.

The Juniors shared the double room. One was very young, not long out of school, shingle-cut and tomboy-tall. Her name was Edie Barry and she excelled at reciting poetry, which she did persistently and particularly in front of the mirror. Long passages of Shakespeare, Browning and Wordsworth, all of *Hiawatha* and *The Ancient Mariner* and *La Belle Dame sans Merci*, she had by heart. They became kind of household deities as her enunciation called them into being time and time again. She educated me in vowels and meters and Windsor-knotting school ties. She held me spellbound with speech beginning 'When one looks at oneself in the mirror, one says to oneself . . .'

She persuaded my mother to take me into town on

Saturday mornings to learn Elocution from Mr Harry Boridale, a faded Shakespearian actor, who held forth in an upstairs Queen Street room; two and sixpence a lesson. He taught me to speak King's English, not drawling and drowning my words, not speaking 'slathered in slang like those high school hooligans down below in the Pig-n-Whistle'. Words had to be my way. With loaned tutu and toe shoes I failed the ballet class; at first piano lessons was found tone deaf; was told, 'Go and sing down in cats' alley'. My little Scottish grandmother, however, then in her eighties, made me her star. She taught me the Sword Dance and to pick out a one-finger version of 'Home Sweet Home'. A friend of my father's, unknown, somehow arranged free entry for us to Brisbane Amateur Theatre productions and all music recitals at the City Hall so that theatre-going and concerts became built into my life.

Edie's room-mate was somewhat older and definitely quieter. Edie's clothes were sporty, even military, and she had a kind of rigidity about her, probably brought on by being 'otherwise inclined' but rectified always to the upright. The room-mate, tight-permed and rustle-voiced, wore floral dresses favouring red in that slippery material called Milanese or Ceylonese.

Her rigidity took sterner form. She went without warning into bouts of petit mal, often just as we took our first forkfuls of dinner. She would stiffen sideways in her chair. Her eyes would glaze over. Her hands would wander forth of their own accord. Fingers in the butter. But we were well drilled; with balletic hand movement would sidestep our plates, the salt and pepper shakers, the bread plate, the butter dish, all three spans left and, when the fit was over, three spans right again, and go on eating as though nothing had happened, although, of course, someone had hummed the strains of the song 'Here we go again'. The odd thing was that, in that time of fun and games about book titles – '*Sugar Daddy* by I. Lykim', '*Famous Parks* by Teresa Green', '*The Spot on the Wall* by Hu Flung Dung', '*Rusty Bed Springs* by I. P. Knightly', etc. – the name of this Petit Mal Performer was Eileen Blank.

The cooking was shared but I didn't hang around. I cannot imagine that the poetry streamer would have been 'much chop' with the Irish stew or 'hunky dory' with a Scotch custard, nor that a timewarp from the petit mal would have enhanced the crispness of the fried snags or the obligatory shine and wobble of the milky blancmange.

We sat at the round table that took up nearly all of the dining room and said grace before unrolling table napkins. Afterwards we cleared the table, pushed in the chairs, thus making room to sit down on the soft armchairs crouched behind them, pulled out knitting or mending and turned on the radio serials until cup of cocoa and biscuit time. I brought out my tactile opus magnus, a map of Europe in Plasticine mounted on Masonite, land mass in green, mountains in brown, rivers in threads of blue wool, cities of red beads, square beads for capitals, cotton-wool strips of snow on the Alps, undulating two-tone blue sea. I wallowed in warming and moulding smooth the Plasticine, earnestly positioned the cities, raised the fence lines of mountains, finally pressed in the thin copper fuse wires where railways ran. 'Put your tongue in,' said my mother. 'People will think you come from the apes.'

On Sunday evenings Lux – later Palmolive-Colgate's –

Radio Theatre held us in rapture. We got the washing-up done, all went to the lavatory and got properly settled by eight o'clock and sat quietly as though in a real theatre. The actors in the studio wore evening dress. Some of us sighed, some sobbed in the dramatic places. Sometimes the announcer told us to turn out the lights. We all ceased to see the little room in which we sat and saw instead the drawing rooms, the cliff tops, the panelled head office, the moonlit garden, the storm at sea, in which the action took place. 'Back to earth,' said my mother as the lights went on, 'another day tomorrow.'

My mother was a familiar figure walking to work down Marivale and along Melbourne Street and over the Bridge to her solicitors' offices at the Quay. In summer she dressed always in white, Fugi silk or cotton listav shirt, slub linen skirt, panama hat, two-tone shoes; in winter a two-piece costume in saxe blue or navy. On Saturday mornings I also walked into town, her chattering cub, happily out of school uniform, bedecked in a shop-bought playsuit (a one-piece shirt and shorts in gay patterned cotton). On Sunday she went across the Park to church, sometimes with a sunshade, in a fine cotton frock in palest blue or eau-de-Nil. I went ahead to Sunday School in dresses made by my clever aunt, styled from Shirley Temple, wearing high socks rolled over garters, not Shirley's Yankee ankle socks, and never, never, open sandals like the twins in my class at school, those bold girls with painted toenails, whose mother was a 'Theosophist and played bridge'.

It was Mary, Irish Mary Eagen who came to live with us after Eileen's transfer, who thrilled me. She moved like a butterfly on wings of perfume, danced, sang, had blue

satin ball dresses and paper roses in her hair. At evening I
was her dresser passing her the bows, clips, puffs, sprays;
at morning her confessor, hearing her merry reports of
breathless reels and handsome beaus. Edie, head under
blankets, snorted. The rest of us seem to have no men in
our lives at all. I had no male relative. No boyfriend, sugar
daddy, priest, pursuant father or Mr Fix-it neighbour ever
seemed to cross the threshold.

The motto of my South Brisbane Intermediate School
was 'Carpe Diem' – seize the day. 'Yesterday's gone forever,' we sang, 'Tomorrow we cannot say.' Opportunist or
Buddhist as may be, it suited the makeshift optimism of my
pubescent life. Someone swaps me their indoor bed for the
time I lie with a mustard plaster stinging my chest.
Someone puts damp pads of tea leaves to soothe my eyes
recuperating from the blurring of eye specialist's drops.
Aflame with sunburn I lie on my stomach and someone lays
on towels soaked in cold tea and vinegar. Beset by some
demon I win every prize for which I buy a ticket at any fete,
go up to receive it sickening in a haze of embarrassment;
bring home a gold box of chocolates one yard long, a
plaster-of-Paris sailing ship two feet high, a glass tray with
jug and six drinking glasses with hand-painted poinsettia.

Once I win a newspaper Children's Corner
Competition with a drawing of My Useful Invention – a
marvellous contraption for a 'Getaway with Baby'. It is a
pram with umbrella above, warm stove within, ice-box
underneath, broom behind to wipe away footprints. This
was my first publication, first earned money, two shillings
and sixpence. I bought myself, ironically, an Everyman's
copy of *Pilgrim's Progress*.

There were no other children in Ventnor Flats. No one came home to my place. Two children lived next door with their shadowy grandmother. Their parents, divorced, came on alternate weekends to take them out, came by car. No one I knew had a car.

These children had cubbyhouses in their backyard made of cardboard and hessian bags, like the ones we made as bush fortresses in the Park, only more permanent, with names like 'Piccadilly' and 'Riviera'. In these we tried to make cakes from filched handfuls of flour, raisins, sugar and milk, heating the mess in tins over lighted piles of newspaper.

We had as much understanding of cooking as we had of divorce. Adults lived unquestionably in some other dimension. I doubted that I would ever get there. But I did not seek to find the way. 'All in good time', the old folk would say if you asked, and we believed them.

Occasionally, with a visitor, we might go to Maloufs down on the corner of Melbourne Street and get an ice cream, one of the old aunties scooping it out from a frosted tub. But this was really out of our territory. On our errands we headed off back up Russell Street to the West End shops – 'Special', seven pounds of potatoes for seven-pence ha'penny – or further with rolled-up togs and towel to the Davies Park baths, whence we blondies emerged with hair bright chlorine green.

We plunged into the Park as into a sea, lapping its pathways, searching its flotsam and jetsam for treasure. We sat in hollows on rafts of bark and talked secret things: what sort of 'sick' Gloria with the drunken father really was on her absent days; whether the bold twins were teacher's pets enough to go away with him at weekends. We unrolled dank copies of *Truth* from tree groins and meant to look up 'carnal' in the dictionary when we got home. From the Vulcan can factory we begged old cardboard boxes. These were our wings, our suits of armour, our wigwams, our shields of war, and, most of all, our toboggoning rafts for going down the nearby grassy slopes. If our games were invaded by unwanted kids from down the street, especially if they were young, especially if they were Catholic, and especially if their mothers were la-de-dahs, we would rise up and flap our terrible boards and bring them down mercilessly on fleeing flanks and hatless heads. Our witch cries were exceeding dreadful.

Then, in the middle of it all, on the Third of September 1939 — houses hushed and radios turned up high — real War was declared. I looked out from my balcony and expected to see rows of soldiers come marching up the street. Soon enough they did — on foot and on horse. I too had to help win the War. I stood on the street corner outside Ventnor with a Ten Shilling War Effort card divided into ten by twelve squares and collected pennies, threepences, the rare shilling, from passers-by, solemnly punching a hole with a pin in front of the donor signifying receipt, a pin-hole per penny on the ten-shilling card.

War was serious. I gave up my frivolous ways. The Plasticine map was put far under the bed — where cockroaches found it — and pinned up a map of The Western Front on our dining-room wall. I abandoned the Nestlé's *Atlas* stick-ins and took up knitting squares for rugs for war victims. I left incomplete the coupletting of the Old

Testament — I felt I had to sacrifice something; my arduous training to be a great writer was little enough — and wrote to pen-friends in Army, Navy and Air Force. On austerity wartime brown paper these lonely men wrote back from undisclosed places to this chattersome schoolgirl, who was still under the age of consent when the war ended.

In 1939, when people were nobly giving up their lives, I became addicted to other people's life stories. So my life's course was set, to become one of the last great letter writers, voluminous letter writer indeed, and, later, oral history interviewer, amassing hours of life stories of 'Tall Poppies' for the National Library archive.

On a day in 1988 in my Sydney studio, a woman sat before me. She had crossed my path many times over the past two decades and I had always enjoyed the grasp of her beautiful strong supple hands. Marea Gazzard, potter, cera-macist, sculptor, A.M., first president of the Australia Craft Council, later of the international body, her work world famous, was telling her story. We began with details of family and childhood. Her born name? Marea Ploumedis, born Sydney 1928. We went on to where the family moved to Brisbane, she nine years old. Something stretched at the base of my spine. I named Frelegus, Trovas, Zapharopolis, testing the waters. 'And your name was Ploumedis?' 'We shortened it to Medis.' The thing at the base of my spine uncoiled, leapt to the top of my skull, prickled the nerve ends, exploded in warmth. I gasped. 'You are Marea Medis!'

My long-lost Marea sat before me.

I laid out my cards of memory before her, a shock to us both. She had forgotten the blonde schoolmate who sat outside in the gutter calling her name. I had to draw it all back for her through the mists of time – fifty years, a fortieth of the time since Jesus. She could then fill in that her mother was Scottish, which explained the Sunday School, her father the cook on the Sydney Express, which explained our elevenses waving, also her sudden disappearance when he was transferred to a stationary posting at the Coff's Harbour R. R. R. (Railway Refreshment Rooms). Amazed, we stood up, suffused in that primal warmth. We embraced. Somewhere in that clasp we touched again our child selves, two little girls on the innocent edge of life of which we had both now endured, explored, so much.

We found our footing in that time and this. In the Sixties a house in Russell Street, just beyond the corner shop where I bought my penny Nestlé's chocolates, had become the first Aboriginal hostel. The High School had sprouted laboratory-smelling and choir-chanting buildings at the other end. Musgrave Park was put on the map as the Aboriginal gathering place, focus for action and speeches in the bicentenary year. The old Dolphin House was gone, replaced by a large modern Greek community centre further along Edmondstone Street across from the centre way of the Park. Just the week before there had been reports in the Brisbane papers of skirmishes taking place between the Greek and Aboriginal citizenry, members of both 'in the wars', apropos the hurling of bottles. The Malouf house was gone too, its place marked by cyclone wire holding in place a company car park.

Somehow that all seems like the epilogue of a Turgenev novel. I had thrown open a window on to a past time in my life, showing a panorama enframed, an inner landscape in all its colour and detail full of sunshine, sparking a sensation of dismay that, for this passing period of my life, I was, apparently, entirely happy.

Now that so much of my *Wonder Atlas* life has been lived, I can look back on this opened page of it as on a relief map moulded in simplest forms and a facing array of colour picture memories. At this zenith of childhood I lived in imagination, in the high country of the Park, the hinterland of books. Perhaps I edited out the shadows as my elders used to cut out their own faces from family snapshots. Perhaps there are secrets locked away in the Black Hole of Calcutta of my soul. Adolescence had not yet clutched me in its lunar rhythm of threat and expectation. The sorrow of my life had not yet caught me in its dark embrace. I was not quick at games or deft with brush, but I had not yet taken cover in the joker's cloak. I seem to have sailed in the five-oared boat of that Ventnor Flat without stormy seas. It was my mother's good sense, her great good humour and capacity for friendship, that held us together and embalmed my childhood in content. She gave herself up to me with no more complaint than the oft-invoked wry remark, 'What did God make mothers for?' At night she sat on the edge of my bed and read me several chapters so that I went to sleep in peace with the Park I loved, like life itself, lying out there before me in all its mysteries and shadows.

FOUR OAKS IN THE FORTIES

Four Oaks Private Hotel stood on a corner at the highest point of Cordelia Street in South Brisbane facing the bowling green in Musgrave Park and opposite the oldest Presbyterian church in Queensland. The old rambling weatherboard house, its back end up on stilts, could be seen through the straggle of prunus and privet bushes athwart the low clay-grey stucco stone wall. Its bays and verandahs were blinded or batoned in, not so much for privacy as to make more rooms, or annexes to rooms. On the other two boundaries were the spiked railings and great Moreton Bay fig trees of the State Primary School and the girls' lavatory and science blocks of the new Intermediate School. The High School was visible beyond the football oval. So the big house was isolated, neighboured by day by the noises of playground and classroom, and at night by the railways and shunting yards beyond them. Four Oaks catered for a clientele of decent-living unattached gentlemen, and ladies, three only — my mother, my aunt and me —

maintained in our corner wing to give an air of gentility to the house. We spent the war years there, from Dunkirk until just after D-Day.

There was a wide linoleumed passageway straight down the middle of the house, between front and back doors that were never shut, except on days of strong westerly wind, and probably had no keys. The evening newspaper boy did a quick run through, slipping *Telegraphs* under the doorways of regulars and doing a bit of passing trade with the casuals sitting about on the low front porch or high back flight of steps, and managing three evensong blasts of whistle in transit.

At one minute to six, some twenty-five persons waited, washed and dressed, behind their closed doors. At six o'clock, precisely, the dinner gong sounded. The residents burst like rabbits from burrows. At one minute past six, every chair at table was taken, and argument in progress as to which soup of the day it was: Monday, Windsor soup; Tuesday, cream of chicken; Wednesday, tomato; Thursday, mulligatawny; Friday, cream of celery with sippits; Saturday, pea and ham.

Mrs Cox, the landlady, kept a good table and a clean house. She had come to town from Out West, with three grown-up sons, one lucky, one handsome and one crippled. She had been a station cook and cooked abundantly, with particular reference to the dessert section of the women's pages. Every evening there was a choice 'either or' and every evening for five years I ordered 'fifty-fifty', indulging in such combinations as Caramel Pie with Passionfruit Velvet, Magic Lemon Pudding with Roly-Poly, Spotted Dick with Orange Surprise, College Pudding with

Jelly Delight and, on Sundays, always Plum Pudding and Fruit Salad.

Mrs Cox chainsmoked and lay with her bedroom door wide open to expose her good morals. So prone, she could issue the twopence-a-call key and overhear the conversations on the telephone at the junction of the passageways, or intercept passers-by with remarks. People were known to have missed hearing three consecutive serial episodes by getting caught up in her network of remarks. She was one of those women of whom my mother was wont to say that they talked so much you couldn't hear yourself think.

We females occupied a couple of rooms near a small garden; grew tomatoes, made tea on a little spirit stove, and waged a disinfective war against cockroaches, bed bugs, bad habits and foul language. The men were courteous always. They brought us boxes of chocolates when the going was good, their bad heads and bruises when things went wrong.

Our separate small table stood at a T-shape to their long communal one. Our starched serviettes from the Saturday laundering stayed refolded longer back into the waterlily or fantail shapes and, as rumour had it, our dinners were choicer portions served on hotter plates, unthumbed by cook or carrier.

Minority disadvantage, however, beset us with the bathroom. It was so centrally situated that it had no window or other form of ventilation. Electric light showing through the latticed fanlight indicated occupancy. Large, it contained bath, shower, basin, lavatory, linen cupboard, shaving mirror and bench, so that four or five men could ablute there together at various stations of their matins, with much splash, song and backslap, while we ladies lurked shy in our side passageway, twirling a sponge bag and personal towel, awaiting our moment to pounce.

A hot bath was an interestingly elaborate ritual, best performed on a Saturday afternoon when the brethren were all out at the track or down at the Grand. A slot meter for the gas was situated, logically, vertically beneath the bath heater, under the floor. In order to reach it, however, it was necessary to traverse the back hall, the back steps, the side path, proceed underneath the house, past the ironing table, up three rough steps and then, as the ground sloped upwards, in an increasingly crouched position, over bare earth until, in a supplicatory posture, the offering of a penny could be made to the giver of gas. Twopence provided a wholesome bath; threepence, sheer luxury.

Conscience, or the health inspector, at some stage demanded a second bathroom. This was done simply by positioning a white enamelled lion's-foot bath underneath the house, the foot end under the dripping tap, which was also used for the garden hose, four corrugated iron walls around it, a tat of cloth over a single pane of fixed glass, a three-legged chair for clothes and a nail on the back of the door for torch or candle. The sole cold-water bather in his roofless bath-house, however, was not left out of the party. Right alongside was the ironing table. It stood solid between two tarred posts, heavily bandaged in many layers of scorched-wounded cloth. The iron itself was on a twenty-foot lead from the only downstairs power point, located on a distant post. In the days when irons were switched on to heat up and switched off to cool down, it was as well for the ironer to have an off-sider as switcher.

My mother and aunt, fastidious about their ironing, held court here. Young men sat on the high bench, swung their legs and told the stories of the girl that got away. Older men stood holding up the post, tolling away their troubles. The men over at the wash troughs lathered and lisped, calling one another girls' names. Cups of tea, packets of rocky road, chewies, Minties, Juicy Fruit, bouts of skipping on the sloping cement paths, crosswords, clock patience, rollies, butt chasing and endless endless games of cards, were all part of the show.

Friday night was Buffaloes Night, poor man's Masons. 'For Soaks', they shouted at midnight as they jostled to find their way in through the front gate. Ted was deaf, his wireless always on too loud. The continuous buzz that followed the eleven o'clock close-down of broadcasting indicated that Ted was dead to the world. It fell to me to creep in, thrust my hand through the stag head and antlers that adorned his bedside table and switch it off. Jack the snorer, having been splashed and slapped too many times, was lifted bodily, bed and all, by his burly room-mates to our farther end of the verandah, where he stayed for some months. I could lie in my bed and see through the open door the black soles of feet of too-tall Jack tapping the air to the rhythm of the song with which he was singing himself to sleep.

We became 'permanents'. Others stayed for longer or shorter periods. There were the 'interstates', the 'seasonals', the divorced men who proudly brought their Saturday children to meet us, and the country lads come to the 'big smoke'. There was no garage; no cars. The men two up to five in a room. One blind single room between hall and verandah on our side was known as the 'deadhead's room' because no one stayed there long. There was George who odd-man-outed himself by playing golf, Alan who made only token use of it because he had his lady friend down the road, Mick who was actually seen weeping, and Ronnie who was such a pretty boy that no one dared admit him to the bathroom share.

The wireless serials started straight after dinner with 'The Adventures of Hawi Wing' at 6.30, 'Martin's Corner' at 6.45, and went on quarter by quarter hour until nine o'clock when the ladies made the cups of tea.

'Three gals' we called ourselves — two middle-aged widowed sisters and a growing girl — 'The Three Graces' they called us. Our presence was deemed to keep decorum in a house of bachelor men. My mother and I shared the corner twin room at the end of a short passageway, facing out to the side verandah with its three steps down to the large side lawn. That room is installed in my memory like a tableau and has had recurring presence in my dreams. 'Come into our parlour,' my mother would say hospitably. 'Nothing grand but all clean and paid for.' We shared our intimacy of respectful space, with no room for the injunction 'Tidy your room.'

It was twelve foot square with a window opposite the door, a double casement window, eight panes a side in green barley-sugar glass, each pane a different hue of green and different grain of barley. The camphorwood chest under the window, the 'winter box' in which our woolly clothes wrapped in newspaper and mothballs were stored, with a couple of cushions on top served as a window seat. Either side of it were the bed heads. Each bed wore a Dutch seersucker bedspread, hanging over far enough to curtain off the objects caved beneath – blue rush basket of shoe-cleaning things and circular hat box on my mother's side, school port and skipping rope on mine.

We each had one side of the room. On the right side, beyond the foot of her bed, there was my mother's duchess (dressing table) with mirror, cosmetics, library books, writing pad and letters; then, lower, another camphor-wood box serving as a table. Within were our unused 'belongings', mysterious things I did not know about – packets of letters from my father, from the first sweetheart at Gallipoli, and from someone called Dick; silk garments from the first trousseau, a few kept minute baby clothes of mine, two precious wine goblets, horn jewellery box and crystal scent spray (wedding presents), some lengths of cloth – her hive of wistful memories and broken dreams.

All of these were out of reach because of the multi-tude of things crammed upon the table top: sewing basket, first aid box, bottles of cough mixture, liniments, white spirits, methylated spirits, small packets of senna and glu-cose, larger packets of washing powder and starch, soaps in dish, toothbrushes in beaker, jars of tea, sugar, powdered milk, boiled lollies, honey, biscuits, a bowl of fruit, the china basin in which undies were soaked overnight, and the small spirit stove and its kettle in which our bedtime drink was made.

Opposite this stood my cabinet wireless, that glam-orous piece of Thirties furniture of inlaid wood veneer with its darned satin-weave fabric front; on its top a bridge of four elephants in ebony and ivory in descending order of magnitude, pair of small wooden painted clogs and Big Ben money box, all gifts from pen-friends in faraway lands. Next to this was my chest of drawers containing clothes, a top drawer of handkerchiefs in sateen sachet, carved box for mock jewellery, manicure set, coils of hair ribbons; on its top stacks of school books, pens, inks, dictionaries, atlas and globe, a topple of parlour games, Ludo, Snakes and Ladders and Chinese Checkers. My desk and chair had their spot in front of these two so that I sat positioned between everspeaking wireless and ongoing homework.

On either side of the doorway were, on Mother's side, a quite unnecessarily ornate full-length mirror, swinging in a free-standing frame, and, off stage behind a curtain, the place where our clothes were housed, our shoes kennelled, our holiday ports stabled, and, on my side, the bookcase that had begun life as my father's cabinet wireless, gutted of its interesting batteries and valves, now full of books; on its top my current collection – silver foil from cigarette or chocolate wrapping when I believed a pound of it would buy a bicycle, tram tickets ending in 0 when I believed a thousand of them would buy a dinner set, and postage stamps in bottles – the pre-war familiars of emu, koala, platypus, lyrebird, kookaburra hierarchy giving way to the threesome, sailor-soldier-airman striding forth to victory.

Upon the dull green walls hung the framed photographs of dear departed friends, framed landscape over my mother's bed, seascape over mine. A swinging bulb and lightshade, its socket skewed to take the wireless lead from a double adapter, dangled its push-button switch. The floor linoleum was in a pattern that owed something to the Chinese hexagram. Water rippled below, sky flowering above, here in green, but known in every other colouration in houses of friends. Often on the curly black floor mat between the beds there lay a dog, an old black kelpie, the house dog John, friendly and smelly. The mat also was smelly.

The door of our room was sometimes shut but never locked. My mother sat on the edge of her bed reading, mending clothes, perusing a folded newspaper. 'Gertie,' said her sister Ettie, 'you sit perched there as though you are ready to get out at the next station.' This might well have been true. My mother had had to change stations suddenly many times in her life.

The sisters were quite different. My mother considered Ettie the clever one, herself the plodder. She worked as an accountant to solicitors, her sister as a censor in the Defence Department. My aunt inhabited the first room opening on to the side verandah. She painted the walls cream and put down a floral carpet. She sat back in a comfortable leather armchair, clad in feathery slippers, listening to commercial programmes, chain-smoking and filling in the crosswords to beat the clock, or knitting elaborate garments, a moss-stitch full-length dressing-gown for winter, a feather-and-fan lined with silk for spring. With her high blonde Marie Antoinette hair-do — indeed her own name was Antoinette — and elegant air, she goodheartedly hostessed a salon for the harmless lonely men who were our fellow residents. They came and sat around on the floor, verandah chairs or side steps, smoking and talking the hours away. She boiled the jug, produced biscuits — for the kitchen was locked at night, 'courtesy to the cockies' who liked to feast in peace.

Most of the folk at Four Oaks, like my mother, had grown up in the country and had not discovered the necessity for mod cons. They got along very well on good square meals, flasks of tank water on the corner table, good sturdy cotton clothes, a serge suit and starched collar in the wardrobe in case of weddings or funerals, and a sense of doing the decent thing, basically the old 'Do unto others . . .' and the Aussie version, 'Kindness in a neighbour's trouble, courage in your own'. Life owed them nothing.

In the big front five-bed rooms — ballroom and drawing room in the original grand house — with the furniture all pushed back, men would sit round on the floor playing cards as round a camp fire. On very hot summer nights we all took up our beds and walked. We sprawled out on the grassy lawn and slept under the clothes lines under the stars. We of the fair sex at our time of the month washed our rags by night in a bucket under the garden tap, laid them out on the grass to be gathered in next afternoon sweetened by dew and sun. We were a big bush family washed up on these urban shores.

My mother and I were the only members of the constabulary who went off to church on Sunday. The others didn't want to go themselves but liked the idea that we went. 'Good programme today?' they asked when we came home, or 'Feeling better?'

Mrs Cox and her kitchen were of motherly, generous proportions. The huge kitchen range of the woodfire stove took up half one wall. Sacks of flour, sugar, spuds and oats stood in one corner. The enormous dresser was stacked with thick white crockery. But sometimes a sour mood or 's.o.l.' gave her a bout of 'stiff elbow', which interfered with her dishing-up activity, apt to correction by our concerted demand for second helpings. At Intermediate School (next door) we girls did cooking once a fortnight in the Domestic Science block, a separate cottage over in the corner a few feet distant from Four Oaks' fence. My route to school was, if not intercepted, through a hole in the fence.

Each girl brought home a written list of cooking ingredients for the next day. 'Plain Butter Cake. 3 ozs butter, 3 ozs sugar, one egg, half lb. flour . . .' Mrs Cox's vocabulary did not encompass. For ounces she read pounds and a dozen eggs. I went off to school with a loaded basket. Excused from the sewing half of the class proceedings, I was allowed double cooking. I was also allowed one whole table to myself whereas the other little cooks fitted six to a table with their little packets from home and little mixing bowls. I pounded away at my gargantuan labour. The joy in my pounding heart at Sunday night's high tea, when my big browned cake or vat of jam was laid on the main table, was high reward. It gave me a greater ease at cooking for twenty people than for two. Growing up in this way I never got the hang of how the family unit worked. Actually I don't know that it does.

This was my home for five years, the years between pubescence and the age of consent, then called the 'awkward age'. I was in my budding, opening petals of awareness into adolescence during these war years while Four Oaks gradually faded and went to seed. At first the tennis court had been kept rolled and chalked. On Sundays, while the dumb-shut church had its one live hour of the week breathing in waves of hymns and stills of prayer, and the stray dogs scavenged for scraps and lost balls in the deserted schoolyard, the residents and guests in white shorts and shirts, with borrowed racquets, sat about on the rose-vined trellised garden seats and neat house-maids nimbled down the garden pathways with trays of lemonades and beer.

Then the bank boys got their papers and enlisted; the abattoir boys, seasonally down from the far north, got their enlistments too. Some of them had said on election days, 'Call this a free country, and they force you to vote.' The housemaids jilted their aprons and joined the AWAS. The gardens were dug up for slit trenches in case of air raids. We were left with the one-legged yodeller, the sullen 'consci', and men of undisclosed 'reserved occupations'. Other women joined us briefly – 'reffos' from Riga, Vienna, Singapore. Housemaids did not last long; were 'preggers', 'plonkers' or 'halfo', intolerantly trailed by a wail of brat. Sweet potatoes replaced real potatoes with the Sunday roast.

Yet, pooling coupons, we kept up our good Aussie menu; meat (meaning beef) every night of the week, eggs or offal for breakfast, roast lamb or pork the choice for Sunday dinner. Butter was extended by an equal propor-tion of gelatine in hot water. Fish was kept on choice for Fridays; but generally the Protestants ate the fish and the Catholics went for the meat. Saturday night's set menu, rump steak or tripe and onions, restored the brethren, from their respective afternoons, ready for their big night out, clean shirts and California Poppy hair slick, to the wrestling or the dance. Each morning our lunch packages in brown paper bags with elastic bands, our names inscribed, awaited us on the hallway table, sandwiches made up the night before: ham and chicken paste, Windsor sausage, slim cheese ointmented with pickle, and slabs of cake, left-over plum pudding on Monday, Swiss roll Tuesday, jam tart Wednesday . . . For austerity, as the war went on, Thursday evening meals were cut out. Someone always forgot and was found standing unrequited behind a six o'clock door; was invited to join us at our picnic spread of black pudding and custard tarts.

Mrs Jofeh, late of Latvia, took up her abode for a while in the corner room at the other end of the verandah. She brought from her far and distant parts strange language and strange habits. She could not comprehend Thursday closing so picnicked along with us. She brought black bread, stuff the Germans ate, very tough. Her corpulence was of almost liquid immensity. On days of her venturing forth to social occasions, it fell to me to help her into her stays. Laced tight as a bucket, I lifted and stuffed the yielding flesh into their firm sides, a humiliation and torture accepted with ladylike hauteur. 'Lady Rose' each morning made stately progress down the length of the verandah, pyramidic in a red ubiquitous dressing-gown, hair in turban cloth, carrying, under its draped towel, her turbulent sloshing chamber pot en route to the bathroom. I fed her tall stories about summers so hot that hair fell out and pencils split. She rewarded me, before she left, with a great treasure, a box of tissue-wrapped, icing-sugar enveloped, bitter-sweet Latvian jellies.

Old residents sometimes showed up on leave. I was thereupon despatched all the way down to Stanley Street to get rump steak and take a large screw-top jar to the milk factory for a pint of fresh cream. Other times only the telegrams came, letters from mates following. My aunt's lover, who wore the kilt, was killed at Tobruk. Unthinkingly, some weeks afterwards before my mother got home from work that day, I gave her a letter in his handwriting. Silences were the little deaths that became familiar.

The Christmases got better. Mrs Cox excelled herself with grottoes of fruit and jelly splendour. American sailors shelled vats of peas, boasting of Thanksgiving feasts back home. Beer was handed round in the dining room. The manger scene glowed on top of the piano. 'If' and 'Not Understood', framed on the walls, were joined in due course by 'The White Cliffs of Dover' and 'The Fuzzy Wuzzy Angels of the Old Kokoda Trail'. They also got sadder. Mrs Tuller, a long loose boneless woman, who lived with her husband Fred, a French horn in the orchestra, in the far corner room, played the piano most evenings before dinner. At Christmas she played the carols, over and over. We sang along. The ghosts of missing friends sang with us. Adults, who could not weep, went off suddenly silent by themselves. 'Bad pennies' turned up out of the blue for forgiveness, even once the Far West layabout Mr Cox himself.

The genuine dinky-di air-raid siren went only once. Mrs Cox, one lodger, the church cleaner and I went across to the slit trench in the Park, hunched down in the mud with our chins out at ground level, felt foolish, went back home before the All Clear. My mother and her Business Girls war-worked at weekends room-cleaning at Anzac

House and I knitted pairs of khaki knee pads. On V-day there was a bonfire on the weed-grown tennis court. Chop bones, 'dead marines' and melon skins were hurled into the mud of the zigzag trenches in the garden. Mrs Cox wept. One of her sons had been killed in a senseless barracks accident, one had 'gone to the bad' and had to pay for it, and the other had gone 'that way' with other lodgers. Somewhere I was on the edge of it all with my Argonauts Club certificates and Sunday School medals, my poems and Latin books, old kelpie dog and a terrible yearning for a briefer swimsuit.

We left just before the war ended, when so much else in my inner life also ended. Prices changed. The Four Oaks tariff went up from seventeen shillings and sixpence a week adult and ten shillings for child to one pound (twenty shillings) for adult, twelve and six for child. We moved into a big gloomy house with one of my mother's Business Girl cronies, a half-Haversham woman left over among family leftovers in this high-standing house on Petrie Terrace. My aunt's daughter, my bottle blonde, war-bride pregnant cousin, moved into our room. I visited her there with her new-born baby.

This image of transplantation entered deeply into my psyche. I cannot shut my interior door on Four Oaks and that room. It appears in my dreams. At first I dreamed of being a schoolgirl feeding my secret baby in the bedroom before school, tucking it under the bedclothes, hurrying home from school to find it still alive, hungry, tearful, messy, for me to restore. Or I dream of coming home, a schoolgirl, to find all my things suddenly gone and this young mother turning me away. These images, symbols of new beginnings not properly managed, staged my fears at times when I felt that something new and threatening awaited me in the area where I had thought myself most familiar and secure. Later, at times when I found myself left alone to start another phase of life, I dreamed it as a place returned to after all, filled with all I owned, a trusty friendly place, as though some unexpected fall of Snake, when my Ladder shook me off balance, had landed me back at Go to make another start.

Pupil and teacher: I start school, 1934.

My father, W. H. (Harry) Patterson: 'A good book', 1888–1932.

My little Scottish grandmother: Jamesina Watt Patterson, 1855–1951.

My great grandmother: Emma Dobbs Poole, 1850–1938.

My mother in her garden:
21 Essex Street, Indooroopilly.

My mother: Gertrude Olson Patterson, 1891–1987.
(Photo by Richard Harris, 1972.)

High School Days: 'Horace' and 'Bubbles' in Musgrave Park, 1945.

With Barrie Reid: outside the university, 1947.

With Meredith, Judith and Jack McKinney: picnic at Tamborine, 1955.

With Charles Blackman: in Sydney, 1950.

'The Kiss': in Hugh's studio, Melbourne, 1951.
(Photo by Hugh Frankland.)

Georges and Mirka Mora:
studio at 9 Collins Street, Melbourne, 195– .

A good friend: John Yule.
(Photo by Hugh Frankland, 1951.)

The Blackmans: in Melbourne, 1951.
(Photo by Hugh Frankland, 1951.)

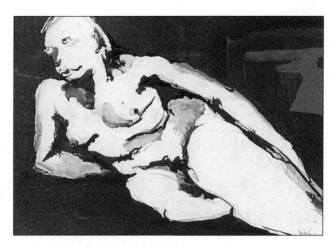

Joy Hester: life drawing, 1955.

John Brack: life drawing, 1954.
(Collection of the Art Gallery of New South Wales.)

$\mathcal{I}$N 1945: 'HOW TO BE HAPPY'

I walk out from the boarding house and cross the road into the Park. I am well turned out in my Brisbane State High School uniform, blazer brushed, pockets bulging, shoes shone, maroon and navy school-tie tied impishly short, black ribbed stockings greening with age, carrying a Globite suitcase. I walk past the bowling green on the left, bandstand on the right, take the left path with the air raid slit trenches on the left all the way down to the oval, the path that in November, examination time, will be hazed with jacaranda blue of fallen petals, the beauty and the anxiety, up to the red-bricks barracks building on the high corner of Musgrave Park.

I have had my mother wake me up in time to hear on the wireless 'Melodies for a Modern Miss', without which my day would be desolate. I have been one of the last to eat breakfast in the dining room, the workers already showered, shaved, fed and off to the tram stop, the maid already setting the tables for dinner, and have listened while packing my books to the ABC's 'Hospital Half Hour' with Mike Connors, the favourite songs of which are 'The Nuns' Chorus', Richard Tauber singing 'The New Jerusalem', Peter Dawson singing 'The Floral Dance' and Josef Schmidt singing 'The Blue Bird of Happiness'. The latest *Boomerang Song Book* is in my pocket, every girl's passport to mainstream. Sometimes I do not leave home until the first bell rings and arrive panting just in time to hang my hat on a cloakroom peg before assembly. This is a state school, academically selective. This is no morning prayer.

Fifty years later my 1944 English compositions exercise book is found. The writing is in fountain pen and blue–black ink, preference Quink because of its fluted bottle and medicinal perfume. The handwriting is spaced and legible, spelling variable, headings sometimes in extravagant script. Marks average B+, term report remark for English generally 'Promising', a comment that intrigues.

At fifteen, my sub-senior year, I have fallen in love with words and prose styles and have discovered the essay as a literary form.

The first composition in the book is 'On Walking'. We are reading Francis Bacon.

Actually I like walking. I walk up the hillside streets and round the Park most days after school with my kelpie friend. I walk up Mt Cootha or White's Hill for Saturday afternoon picnics. I walk red mountain roads and down steep ferny gullies on Crusader camps at Tamborine or Springbrook, singing about Jesus. I write:

Walking serves for pleasure, for business and for diversion. He who walks for pleasure walks nowhere.

He who walks for business walks somewhere. He who walks for diversion walks anywhere.

It goes on for a whole page and concludes:

The chief use for diversion is for cleansing the soul, for entertaining the mind and for clearing the vision. A man who walks, and who walks with unprejudiced intention, alert senses and roving spirits, gains from his walk an enlightened mood, a contentment in object achieved and a relief from the monotony of duty.

The teacher says 'Very good.'

Max Brightman is the English master. He is an old-fashioned man with steel-rimmed glasses and a gentle gaze. He wears a three-piece grey suit with a dozen buttons up the waistcoat, ·has probably worn this same suit for decades. In the playground he wears a grey hat pushed way back on his head. He is overcome with love for Addison and Steele, Charles Lamb, Jane Austen, Matthew Arnold, teaches them with reverence. Years after leaving school, someone tells me of his death and adds, 'I know you never liked him much.' It is remembered how I argued with him about Eliot and *The Waste Land*, let alone *Four Quartets* when it came out. 'But I adored him!' I say and am transfixed that he has died with this misunderstanding and there and then swear to myself that in the future, when I receive such gifts from a teacher, my gratitude will be outspoken.

In 1944 I get bookier by the week. There is a composition on 'The World of Books'. I love books. I haven't enough eyesight to read much for myself. My mother reads to me for hours. They say to me, 'Aren't you a lucky girl to have such a good mother?' – this mother who wanted to be a school teacher, but instead, when widowed, took work as an accountant; now hopes her daughter's eyesight will stay as it is and that, after she finishes school, they will buy into a Circulating Library together. It is a vain hope. I am grateful to my mother for years, for her self-sacrifice, for her reading for hours every evening, Chemistry and Latin as well as History and English. Only much later I realised that in my 'poor sightedness' I somehow fulfilled my mother's dream of teaching. Wasn't my mother lucky? I can just read synopses and extracts in my father's bound volumes of the Twenties, shilling-a-month glossy magazines 'The World's Best Books'. I listen to dramatisations of great books on the wireless, thus peering through keyholes into 'The World of Books'. I write: 'There is no book worth the reading if in it there is not to be gleaned at least one line or one phrase to be carried through life as the silver lining to its clouds.'

I make friends of characters in books and join their language. Indeed the next homework in the book is 'Our English Language'. I leap into this one, begin: 'The other day, as I was reading, I had occasion to take my dictionary down from the shelf, where it sits like a sage among his children, to find out the meaning of the word "pristine".'

From here I work up to a passion.

Words are integral leaves in the tree that is our language. But there are many thorns to spoil the English use and poison those who use it. For now our language is lovely. But today in 1944 it is in bitter danger of wilting under

cruel winds which will fray its beauty. There is cheap slang
that our countrymen are using out of laziness and lack of
learning, gaudy hollow expressions that vulgarise what we
have been proud to call our language. The politicians and
commercial advertisers and newspaper reporters in their
mad cry in over-exaggerated language and blaring
propaganda are distorting my language with the evil
effects of a plague of locusts over a rich cornfield.

I live by daily wireless amid the rhetoric of war and on
Presbyterian Sundays under the preaching pulpit. I elo-
cute. It goes on:

> But I have my dictionary. I am holding it. It is up to our
> nation to hold on to all that it symbolises for it is the
> people who speak our language alone who make it. It is
> our common duty to guard our language against all
> slovenliness and defiling innovations.

I am given to irritating teachers by talking too much in
class. I am chosen from captain to be spokesman to staff.
I join the debating team to overcome jelly knees and
thickened tongue of public nervousness. I discover I have a
spoken and a written self. And I have a secret writing self
and a secret writing-back self. This is a co-ed class, the
academic cream of the state system. In the plenary classroom of forty pupils there are four blocks of twin desks,
five rows in each, boys in the outer rows, girls in the inner.
Boys and girls are too embarrassed to call each other by
anything other than nicknames. I am 'Bubbles'. The secret
correspondent is 'Percy'.

This is R. P. Sheard who joined the school for his senior years, a bright boy pushed over from humble background. Indeed he is the baker's son from the bakery near my religious grandmother's abode. He is red haired and freckled, blushes easily, has grown too tall too soon, wears shabby clothes. This is the year in which boys first wear long pants.

I cannot remember how the passion began. We were too shy to speak but knew we had much to speak about. So we wrote. We never spoke of what we wrote. Hurriedly, eyes averted, our bodies not knowing what our hands were doing, we exchanged letters. At night, alone, and more than once, we read these precious sweaty folded packages, our documents of adolescence, feeling safe in that sexual gap which each sensed but neither referred to. The letters went on for two years. We went to the same parties, picnics, dances. But our lips never spoke of these letters of the heart. Jolly mates, our letters were full of the pain, the shock, the fear, the uncertain discoveries of growing into adulthood. The letters have not survived, nor has the friendship. Somewhere the respect, the gratitude, survives.

There is a composition title that encompasses all that the letters struggle to address, 'How to Be Happy', but the writer's tongue thickens:

We seek to free the gardens of our mind from the weeds of hate, loneliness, sorrow and suffering and in so doing, uproot the seeds of happiness embellished by love, companionship, triumph and generosity. With the lust and determination of a beast at prey, we stalk our happiness in things new and wonderful, but lose our way in the vines and marshes of superstition and prejudice. No one knew more truly than Maurice Maeterlinck what wolves these are that come to us in the sheep's clothing of happiness.

In my sixteenth year life has never seemed more wonderful. I can just see well enough to get by, can goal if not get into the netball team, can run first in the interschool relay team, passing but not having to receive the baton. I am popular. I edit *Everybody's Business*, the class rag which my aunt, a speedster typist, types out seven times each with five carbon copies, and edit also *Us Fellers*, the Church Fellowship's monthly rag. I write copiously to the ABC, Argonauts Club and to servicemen in the field. Indeed I have many different voices.

Us Fellers go camping together down the coast for Easter and Christmas holidays. We have two big tents, boys and girls, a camp fire to cook on, lots of citronella.

On Saturday evening we spruce up, the boys glossy with California Poppy in their hair, the girls showing their suntan from two-piece bathing suits through their midriff dance dresses. We bus or motorbike from sleepy tiny Tugun down to bright-lights Coolangatta. Until midnight we dance, skate, go to movies, eat ice cream sundaes in wide boat glass dishes, dare to steal a long spoon. Then for three or four hours we walk back along the beach. We spread out in a long line, arms around each other's waists, no pairing. And we sing, every word of every *Boomerang Song Book*. We carry shoes and paddle at the sea edge. We break up and leap frog, Catherine wheel, hurl the irksome shoes far ahead along the sandy shore and help one another find them. We arrive back

at camp as the sun rises. We swim. We fill the huge pan with
bacon and eggs. We eat, and then we sleep. 'Youth, glorious
youth!' – a youth of innocence and expectancy, too young
for the war. Young people who never stop talking.

A composition topic is set, 'The Art of Conversation'. I dive in at the deep end. It is now mid-October.
Mr Brightman has put us through *The Spectator*, Roger de
Coverley, *The Essays of Elia* and I have found something of a
personal voice, forgetting lovely language.

Oh it saps the strength and frays the nerves, dulls the
brain and robs the mind of energy; it leaves the body
unhungry for life and the soul unthirsty for company; it
cheats patience and denies courtesy; it suffocates
character with kisses . . . Stop! you cry, What is this? A
Gorgon serpent, some supernatural upheaval, a
nervous breakdown or – ? Oh, worse, I say. What
then? A boring conversation.

I emerge from one with the tranquillity of mind and
elevation of spirit of a dog that has just crawled through
a mincing machine, or perhaps a ship ransacked by
pirates. All afternoon I was 'entertained' (or rather,
'endured') the niceties of gossip. I was plonked in a chair
which after several hours became extremely hard and
the pictures on the wall and the sideboard and the table
grossly uninteresting. My host made polite enquiries
about my health, my mother's health, my contentment at
my present employment, etc. etc. though I'm sure she
did not give a damn about any one of them. And just as
politely and quite as insincerely I enquired smilingly
about hers. If she had asked me how my soul was, or my

bankbook, I would have said, 'Quite well, thank you' and passed on.

Then she embarked upon gloriously detailed accounts of her multitudinous relations and their various ills and their troubles and their faults and their children. We discussed dresses and coupons and seaside resorts and the housing situation and (ultimately and inevitably) the War . . .

Eventually I broke away with a dainty farewell and she said, 'I hope you'll come another day.' I said, 'I'd like to'. But oh how I lied!

Haven't you had the same experience many times? Oh how it wearies one! I came home and read Rupert Brooke all night and went to bed satisfied.

But they are not all like this. I can remember times when I could have cried to leave and enjoyed every small moment of the conversation. I remember an evening I spent 'quietly', one would say, with a friend. We sat and talked – that was all. We began on black markets, drifted to 'shady characters I have met' and I can see myself yet doubled up with laughter, begging almost for a truce, at her golfing experiences.

We chattered long, sometimes lapsing into long reminiscent silences (instead of 'keeping the kettle boiling' with useless babble) and sometimes we yawned extensively and laughed at each other for it.

That was good. You know the deep, soothing satisfaction of it, don't you? Ah, you say, there is Art in Conversation. Not a bit of it. There is no art in conversation: there is art in the conversationalist . . . Character. It is born within us and lucky is he on whom

the Gods bestowed the art. Some are too self-
conscious, others too selfish. Many do not understand.
But I am glad that the world is blessed by many who are
voluble and tactful enough, friendly and comfortable
enough to be masters of the Art of Conversation.

Perhaps there is no such person as a fifteen-year-old, only
a thirteen-year-old and a seventeen-year-old jostling for
position. I write poetry too, lots of it. There is the Spring
Ecstasie and Nocturne Moonlight type which Rita
Humfress invites me to read on air in her corner of the
'Women's Half Hour' – 'our special schoolgirl poetess'.
Then suddenly I hear read out poems of Arthur Rimbaud
and am hit for a six. So I too write surrealist poetry.
Actually it is Swinburne gone surreal. A. D. Hope, then
'Anthony Inkwell' of the Argonauts Club, publishes one in
The ABC Weekly with my heated apologia for modern
poetry. It causes a furore in the Letters to Editor column:
'If a fifteen-year-old schoolgirl wrote this, I'll eat my hat.'
So I write a poem about people eating their own hats.
Barjai – Literary Magazine for Creative Youth, which grew out
of a schoolyard paper there at State High, and is now pub-
lished bi-monthly, prints more:

> . . . *jungles scourged and precipiced*
> *with locusts bearing down to poisoned prey,*
> *of crippled demons cringing at the hangman's rope,*
> *like whirlpools eddying lurid mass of mire*
> *to stinking beasts gluttonised to fat and squall*
> *that rot their bones in desert sands, hounded by gasps,*
> *fleeing, grasped and wrenched to lithe snakes*

> *writhing in the slime of blood spilt*
> *by grinning ghosts in unformed trees . . .*

I get my first review. Max Harris writes five words in *Angry Penguins*: 'Barbara Patterson thinks nasty thoughts'. Worse is to come. Meantime the 1944 school magazine gives its poetry prize to my sonnet 'Youth', which ends:

> *We are not bound by wisdom, have no past*
> *To haunt our harmonies and mould our caste;*
> *We understand not age, know not the truth*
> *That earth for us is not eternity.*
> *We drink our short sweet wine of ecstasy . . .*
> *But o, we shall awake — awake from youth!*

This is wartime. Headmasters stay on well after retirement age to allow young men to go to the front. Isaac Waddle at State High is one such. He signs his name 'I. Waddle'. He is called 'The Duck'. He comes to resemble a duck. Not tall enough to cut a figure of authority, his head bobs, his coat flaps. He models himself on *Goodbye Mr Chips*, who models himself on Winston Churchill. He is a man of science. He teaches senior physics. He believes that science stands for progress in man's destiny and that, conversely, art softens and weakens the human mind. 'Scientia est Potestas' is the school motto. Unfamiliar with Latin, he takes it literally and believes Science is Powerful. He is committed to stamping out poetry in his school.

When he finds *Barjai* in twelve-page Roneoed form circulating among his senior students two years before, he bans it and gives the chief perpetrators — Barrie Reid and

Laurence Collinson – a bad time, a brain-washing that they would certainly fail their Senior exam, wreck their careers, be men of no esteem in public life. (Barrett, as it happened, went on to be a notable figure in the public library field, Laurence one of the first transactional analysts in London.) When he discovers that I am a latter-day Barjaian, ingénue poet, he resumes his humiliation tactics. I struggle with physics formulae, struggle to see the blackboard. 'Miss Patterson,' he says turning to the class and pointing at me, 'is not interested in all this. Her mind is on poetry, her thoughts in higher places.' Then he crashes his duster down hard on my desk spraying chalk dust. My poem 'Mechanical Men' appears in *The ABC Weekly*:

> *I pity men*
> *Who are mathematical men*
> *With mechanical steps*
> *And parts in their hair*
> *Crossing the streets at ninety degrees*
> *Catching trams at pedantic hours,*
> *Men who are congruent*
> *With ha'pennies and centigrams*
> *And build their houses*
> *With twenty-two stairs,*
> *Symmetrically patterned men*
> *With cubical corners –*
> *I pity all of them*
> *Who cannot be free.*

This schoolgirl loves her school and is everybody's friend. On sports Saturdays I go early, cut the oranges and take them down the path for half-time, lay the tables and make the cheese and tomato savouries for the afternoon tea for the visiting team. I am House Vice-captain, organiser of pre-school ballroom dancing under staff supervision in the gym – 'Those who can dance with those who can't. Mixed couples.'

1945 is the final year of school and of the war. In the first week of February the head mistress – her name is Miss Bonna, a name probably derived from the French 'bonheur' (happiness) – presides over a meeting of all the girls of the three upper classes in the gym to elect prefects and Head Girl. I, who have companioned in the new girl, chaired the grievance debate, been M.C. at school concerts, am obvious choice as senior prefect. Duly elected Head Girl, my name is chalked up on the board. Acclamation follows – suddenly cut short by a loud knocking at the door, which is immediately flung open. The Duck, his presence unprecedented at the Girls' School meeting, advances down the full length of the gym, determined, wordless, in stunned silence, picks up the duster, wipes out my name; stamps the duster authoritatively, waddles in silence back down the room, slams out the door.

Silence. No one speaks. The head mistress pats her wig to assure it is in place, gulps submissively, announces in a small voice: 'We shall have a re-election.'

Surely this has not happened. I sit amazed. I sit in shock, isolated in bewilderment. Not one of those girls, not one of them in my form, my hockey team, my Lawson House, says a word. They freeze. I begin to shake. I watch another girl become Head Girl, stand up and be applauded. I walk in trance out of the gym not back into class but, taking hat and port from the cloakroom, straight out on to the Park path and home.

I shin up the wall – on home ground and, I know, in line of vision, across the playing fields of the office window of he who looked through keyholes at Girls' School meeting. Facing his probable gaze. I throw off hat and shoes, open school port above my head letting the books fall out. I strip off school uniform and underwear and, naked, tongue out, arms uplifted, stamp, dance a dervish, on all this cast-off paraphernalia. There is no one else to see me, no one in the house except for the landlady in the far kitchen, no one at the adjacent Intermediate school at mid-afternoon class time, no other neighbours.

I go inside, put on home clothes, bring the stuff in before my mother comes home, go feverish to bed. My mother is good at ailments but not at emotions, is on firm ground with facts but quite at sea with feelings. Next day I am too ill to go to school, with a fever that my mother calls 'reaction' from too much study. Now I take my life into my own hands. I have heard the bell toll and know for whom. I get my long blonde hair lopped into the Maria haircut – Bergman in *For Whom* . . . – wisped to the skull. I apply to join the WRANS, as though I had any chance with eye-sight like mine.

My mother puts me out to graze with a bovinely kind aunt to be restored with nourishing food and rests in the sunshine on the garden chair. This aunt reads only Australian literature; reads me Frank Clune's *Dig*, a saga of Australian history, the Burke and Wills tragedy of messages misunderstood, the moment missed, a personal disaster of universal proportion.

In due course, subdued, I go back to school, have already slipped behind and dropped out of my peer group. Cussedly I keep on Physics but drop honours subjects and any conversation with schoolmates. If they approach, I quote Coriolanus: *You common cry of curs / Whose breath I hate as reek of the rotten fens. / There is a world elsewhere.* My world elsewhere is the senior cloakroom, chair faced to window, back to fellow students. I read *The Rape of Lucrece* to find out about sex, *Love's Labour's Lost* believing it to be about abortion, *King Lear* because I live in Cordelia Street. I ally myself completely with the Barjai group. What need is there to talk to babbling schoolgirls about swimsuits and movies? They can get on without me.

Probably it did not all happen in the same week — the end of girlhood, the loss of innocence, loss of eyesight — but from the distance of fifty years it seems that it did: the triple betrayal. I go again to an eye specialist. He says, cowardly understating, that my sight will never improve and adds with a sanctimonious smile: 'God takes away one gift and gives another. You have a most beautiful smile.' The smile freezes and some part of my heart with it. I know I shall never be able to keep up with a peer group, shall be left behind, left to scavenge, be banished to a secret, subversive, elsewhere world.

I come into breakfast one morning to find the dining room hushed. Someone passes the newspaper. All over the front page are the pictures of Belsen concentration camp, its human cadavers with hollows for eyes. Heart, guts, mind are wrenched out of me in an instant. The child is crucified. I know in that moment why the Jews were wiped out. Nobody spoke up. 'God and the Christian church/ Have left us in the lurch' was a Laurie Collinson poem in the last *Barjai*. I straighten myself for the big world, to be one of the new generation for whom this war was fought, a new generation that must 'Say No to War', must show that poetry matters.

Nevertheless, Wordsworthian upon the mountains, God-striving beyond the church, I go again Crusadering in the August holidays, to Springbrook. One evening the twittering of schoolgirls is hushed. We are told solemnly that an atomic bomb has been dropped on Hiroshima. 'What's for dinner?'

Schoolgirl, I wrestle with the Angels. The dark Angel of Betrayal has severally pierced my heart. The light Angel of Promise has already entered my spirit. I end my schooldays with the 'Promising' defined twofold. The one promise high above and the other firmly underfoot, to hold me upright between Heaven and earth. The great poem of T. S. Eliot, his *Four Quartets*, just published, has enveloped my own poem of life. Its full meaning hovers out of reach. I grasp the tip and I trust my life to its slow revelation. The other I unearth for myself. In my composition on 'How to Be Happy', under its lush foliage of words, the roots are exposed: 'Friends, Nature, Books'. I make no mention of wealth, success, happy marriage – what my mother calls 'being comfortably off', 'being at the top of the tree', 'a union made in Heaven'. I have discovered my Blue Print of Happiness for a lifetime and it never succumbs to doubt: friendships diverse, loyal, full of fun; nature meaning the bush and flowers in close-up; books meaning also music, art, theatre. Lucky girl, thus graced, I step forward hopeful, out of maidenhood, into the Unknown of adult life, its happiness.

ＢARJAI DAYS

Turning corners, heading into mazes, standing under lamp posts, walking on the right side of the road, bumping into brick walls, looking for directions, chasing my tail, dodging my shadow, was how I spent the five years of late teens between two holes in the ground. I walked out of school with a Better Citizenship scholarship and just enough eyesight to look as though I could see. Retrospection juggles the jigsaw map together, the routes taken that got me from Barjai to Blackman, Church Fellowship to Communist job meetings, Argonauts Club to arts degree, dance nights at the Blind Institute to an invalid blind pension of my own.

The backdrop was mother and daughter as flat mates at the Normanby, a small northside district near the Roma Street goods yards and the old hotel, in a house close to the landmark Moreton Bay fig tree at the entrance to Gilchrist Avenue and right opposite a tail-end city warehouse, the emblazoned blockhouse edifice of the South Queensland Egg Board. 45 Kelvin Grove Road was an old weatherboard house, high set front, the narrow right side and front verandahs enclosed with fibro and casement windows, all painted yellowish, the colour of magic lemon pudding, the front lawn emblazoned with insignia of golden privet bush. The passageway had four doors either side, those on the right each leading into a dark bedroom stepping out on to the enclosed verandah kitchen, while the two flatettes on the left each had two doors to two large bright rooms, ours being the front one had also its bit of boxed-in verandah under corrugated iron roof – hot enough to boil the brains in midsummer. Here I set up camp with my father's old dropside resto couch, the camphorwood boxes, battery wireless bookcase and now set of knocked-up bookshelves and a writing table with pot plant.

A hall stand fringed and frothing with pot plants stood inside the front door. At first patter of rain, runnels of footsteps tottered out to back steps and front carrying pot plants to their naturing. The landlady, Mrs de Horne, had known better days, the which she memorialised in her polished 'antiques of furniture' and a war-record husband, a bit of unpolished antique himself. They had carpets.

Behind the second door on the right lived the Jacob 'sisters'. The younger one, with her purring voice, head of hennaed hair that wobbled on a nodding neck, was 'in cakes' at Penney's department store and saved us half-price leftovers if we got there at closing time. The elder was beady-eyed, wiry-haired, stitched-up, voice conspiratorial, snappy, worked high-up in clothes somewhere, held the door half open like a watchdog. Much frying went on within. Occasional pots of chicken fat came our way.

The telephone, a pulpit against privacy that served as monologue entertainment, stood halfway down the hallway. Behind the third door lived little old Annie Stewart. My mother and I took to her, acquired her. Once her timidity, born of ignorance and humiliation, was protected, her suppressed vivacity ran full range, that tenacity that had made her survive treadle-machine factory work, brutal marriage, a squad of children and had got her into a lot of hot water. She was pared thin as a well-worn knife. After I found her stuffing knotted underwear down her front to give her figure some shape, I bought her as a surprise a pair of foam-rubber brassière inserts and left them on her kitchen table. Coming home, she put on the kettle to make a brew to have with the two lemon buns. But she did wear them.

The last door on that side, set into a shadowy recess and close to the back stairs, was the habitat of Josie Flynn, as bold as brass and Irish as they come. The passageway was the byway of visitors, our genteelly closed doors speakers to our ears. Whereas the de Horne visitors were festive, the Jacobs few, 'Stewpot's' (as we called her), upon a wave of reeking fresh baked cakes, a sudden bubbling over of families: Josie's visitors were too many, too male, too late and too given to eliciting her wild outbreaks of tinkling Irish laughter.

The two doors beyond ours on the left led to the 'deadheads' flat, the catchment for a series of violent or furtive couples, the teenage girl who got slowly fat then suddenly thin before doing a moonlight flit with her mother, but not before spilling the beans that she was just shaking the tablecloth out a window one day when he just come up and grabbed her bosoms then quick as a cat in through the window.

The joy was that we had a kitchen of our own with ice chest, sink and gas stove. The stove had a demure wooden door below and a hinged lid above to conceal its true identity and support an embroidered cloth and vase of flowers on top, so that our dinner guests could imagine the meal came out of the air. I took to cooking and produced a real spaghetti, not out of a tin, and for a while kept a ginger beer bug in the pantry closet. Stewpot mostly ate with us. We took an evening pick-me-up, a daily home brew of yeast and treacle, a tablespoon of each stood in a large jug of water for two hours. I went weekly with a billycan and sixpence to the XXXX brewery and returned, shameless and odorous on the tram, with the writhing spongy cream. If stood overtime, the brew became more crusty, dark and potent. Then it made Stewpot raise her voice into all manner of silly songs and a bit of wild dance if we didn't hold her down.

Other secrets took place there, first make-up, first love letters, first lovers, first editing, first friends' soirees, with a tipple of the home brew.

My mother still walked to work, now from the opposite direction, down George Street past 'Let Joe Do It' – she always did – the shoemaker where her own father had taken her as a small child, before the turn of the century, to get her first button-up boots, first button hook; thence past the Law Courts to her legal firm nearby, opposite the Treasury. They were Dickensian chambers. Old Mr Chambers himself, the senior partner, wore little wire spectacles low on his nose and kept alive on whisky. An ominous black crow of a woman called Miss Mann had an office of her own and handled divorces. My mother, the trust accountant and senior, nested in a large office with a twitter of juniors whom she mothered.

She handled the overspending of alimony by Lady Jane on elaborate corsetry and tactfully answered the Henpecked Henrys about the state of the separated wife, and had to count out suitcases of money that had been stored under beds until sufficient for house purchase. Sometimes she brought this home and we sat on the floor and checked the money packages, her count, my count, her count, to verify thrice. Money was a tool in life, not a goal. Each afternoon at three o'clock precisely she caught the eye of the policeman on traffic duty down below to alert him to her crossing diagonally from street door to side door of bank with her strong box of money. First she had to carry it down two twisting flights of dark stairway of Dostoevskian shadows, a routine that never bothered her a scrap. Nor did she read thrillers. She read *The Robe*, *Footsteps of the Fisherman* and ever more Dickens.

I spent time gazing at my face in a mirror knowing it would not be there for long. 'Not pretty,' my mother said when asked, 'nose too large, hair too straight – but not unattractive, a certain appeal.' That would have to do. I woke teenage-late, looked with indifference at the mother-love cup of tea and plate of Marmite finger toast on the floor beside the bed, stone cold. The rest of my life was 'out', out beyond mother territory.

In Brisbane these were the Barjai days. *Barjai* – meaning 'meeting place' – the magazine with its roughly bi-monthly appearances and the group of under-twenty-one-year-old writers and artists published therein and their friends were my hub. I went religiously every second Sunday afternoon to the formal meetings held in the

ladylike Lyceum Club rooms, two floors up in an otherwise deserted building in the heart of Queen Street. Barrie
Reid and Laurie Collinson, the editors, who had begun it
clandestinely as State High schoolboys, were in the chair. I
was, I am told, 'a quiet, observant young woman who
asked serious questions', at first quite overawed by these
sophisticates, untethered by the name 'teenagers' (title of
trivial empowerment). Well dressed, well spoken, very
couth indeed, we listened to invited speakers, had our
afternoon teas and read out our own new work.

Thea Astley, elder, and good-looking in an angular way,
looked down from her height and read pieces generally
crackling and acrid. Vida Smith – whose gym tunic I had
bought at State High and later sold to Evangeline (then Eva)
Burrows with the brown wavy hair – read poems of lyrical
edge. She was like her poems, feminine, slender, graceful,
intent eyes in a heart-shaped face, abundant hair all coiled in
a coronet plait. Patricia Maria Theresa O'Rourke – her real
name – was from Stuarthome, Brisbane's most elegant
Catholic school, where French was the house language. Her
home was the spacious upper floors of the Regatta Hotel on
the river, with a mirage of nun-like aged aunts and penitent
publican father. Her poems were of appropriate mystery and
elaboration. Laurie Collinson personified avant garde sub-
version. He was unprepossessing, as pale and consumptive as
a poet should look, Jewish, homosexual and Communist – a
combination requiring ingenuity of self-expression. He sat
back, authoritative, reading his pithy audenesque poems,
seeming weighty. 'Would the followers of Freud/ Be very
annoyed/ If I did not bother/ To beat my mother?' Cecel
Knobke, also from State High, bulky, swaggeringly serious

with a drawing-room lisp, oscillated between Oscar Wildery of localised wit and eloquent rages about the need for educational reform. He gave a paper on A. S. Neill and Summerhill school.

Barrie Reid was the essential romantic hero, verging on vain – but with a rascally wit. Straight, handsome, with fall of blond hair above engaging blue eyes, he was the helmsman, the front runner, in his soft commanding voice electrifying us with his paper on the artist in the modern world crisis, giving us first taste of the novels of Rex Warner, poetry of Sidney Keyes, imperative of George Borchert, 'Say No to War', or reading his own personal, well-formed poems. Laurence Hope, gentle, impish, Aboriginal in lankiness and hair foliage, brought in a few wet paintings of northern canefields on his return from road gang work there. Pam Seeman, the redhead, well in command of her costume, oil paints and political convictions, brought in her incisive sketches. Joy Roggenkamp, the luscious kewpie beauty, all blonde curls, body curves, baby blue eyes and intelligent sparkle, brought in her sure-handed charcoal and watercolour figures. Edgar Castle, poet from Adelaide, appeared at one meeting, a knock-out in his Navy uniform, and occasionally Eric L. with his cornet which he played in the Salvation Army band. Donald Savage came once or twice, displaying his missing finger, prudently dismembered by an axe at the bite of a snake, poised between his bush work and London success as a designer. One day, as I sat deep in an armchair, balancing teacup, little finger extended, with my hair upswept in a high front roll to match my high wedgy shoes, Barrie told me I looked soignée. I vowed to look it up in the dictionary and look soignée for ever after.

At teatime I wielded the tea-towel in the manner of my mother at the meetings of the Dickens Fellowship, that social life of members of the legal profession. I seldom read my work. Booky Barrie Reid also brought in poems by a shy friend, double quatrains by Alex Lire – a pun it took me years to unravel – one about a sad-eyed Greek schoolmate. 'Small George had/ Painted his grave/ with rainbow colours/ His soul to save/ Thought through brilliance/ His soul would shout/ Though death's heavy hand/ Tore his throat about'. I liked the poem because that George in defeat now served and sketched listlessly between customers in his father's corner smallgoods grocery shop at our bus stop.

As the evening came on and the group became informal towards a Bohemian configuration I took my leave. I was due at the six o'clock Church Fellowship meeting, changing character to most voluble, to give a shock-sharp paper on some Christian mystic, some quotations from Huxley's *Perennial Philosophy*, or the Church's role in the Peace Movement – more erudite than my companions in my greater need to find real substance in religion.

Of all the Barjai guests, two magnetised me. Judith Wright, almost twice my young age, deaf with her awkward off-range voice, then working down at the university as a statistician, read her first book of unpublished poems, and J. P. McKinney, non-academic philosopher, gave a paper on 'emotional honesty'. Both lifted me sky high and thereafter Jack-n-Judith became lifetime friends and sky heroes for me, in the Aboriginal sense. I breathed their book-lined air and plunged into their bottomless questioning at Quantum, the little bush house on the long red mountain road at Tamborine. I loved their wordiness and their quirky humour. They read me Jung.

She of the faraway voice and I of the faraway face did not find our lacks obstructive to the deepening roots of friendship. I would connect with Judith on her trips to town to buy an axe, some kitchen items or clothing at Woolworths, then meet up with Jack at McLeods, a tea and sandwich shop in Queen Street, still the same as it was at the turn of the century, where he, essentially a country man, felt at home, with its marble-top tables, thick cups of good strong tea and clattered-down plate of hot meat pie, an aged Miss McLeod in snow-white sandshoes and snow-white bun, matriarchally serving. The speciality was Victoria sandwich, the thinnest of layered jam sponge.

Barjai put out spokes to a wheel that ground away at the turgid cultural scene of Forties Brisbane — Miya studio, the Aboriginal for 'today', set up as headquarters. The Barjai artists and others, up to twenty-five years, grouped together to hold exhibitions year by year to break through the congealed conservatism of the local audience. Barrie and Laurie wrote fiery manifesto catalogue introductions that sparked the press. Rebellious in our motives, we nevertheless wore our stockings, hats and gloves and hired the ballroom of the temperance hotel Canberra for the exhibitions, a new wave rather than a revolution.

The first Miya studio was up on Wickham Terrace near the Trades Hall overlooking Jacob's Ladder. Pam had it painted clean as a boiled egg and ran life classes and meetings to order. We were young and charged with vision. We loved our city. In high bravado we leapt down and bounded up those long steps, shouted advice or abuse to a fleeing mate. Once hurled a typewriter in its case which, uncaught, went bouncing down and down to the applause of our laughter – all very disconcerting to the onlookers. I bought my first painting, two guineas' worth, a decorative blocked abstract of that Ladder by Laurie Collinson.

We believed in one another. In the way of effect being the cause of the effect, we learned from one another, encouraged one another, gained that sense of authority that makes brave the urge to go beyond horizons, 'returning bronzed as from a myth'. We had come out of a war into the light, not needing the nudge-nudge wink-wink underground of sly grog or dope to smoke. We were high on the prospects of the new world being made.

It was the time of discoveries and losses. My grandmothers were dying. I went out some days to care for my Scottish grandmother, a hairy, bent-over figure lost and lingering, alone all day in the huge dark house. The Scottish terriers had got savage. Outside the front gate, in the suburban street, I stripped off my dress, stockings and shoes, ran the gambit of them with my bundle until safe inside the front door. I scrubbed clean patches in the stale and spilt-over kitchen, washed clothes left standing in buckets of grey water, heated up tins of beans, while Grandma wandered, obdurately ringing at the housemaid's bell, calling for Bridget who had left thirty years ago. She sometimes remembered, heartbreakingly, that I was Barbara, not Bridget.

The religious grandmother faded sedately, rocking to a stop in her chair. She looked so peaceful and completed in her coffin that ever after I have sought the peace of seeing the corpse of a loved one in order to salute with gratitude the beloved chariot that carried the soul through this life.

The grandmother that was a tornado of cooking and scolding lay still and white in a hospital bed, like one of her Christmas puddings tied up in a cloth awaiting its hour.

My mother, who had the art of talking to strangers, met Mrs Hay on a tram. She was a tall old Russian woman, with hair sprouting from her head like a fine white mist, the tattered threads of a once-strong singing voice and long graceful hands. My mother admired her crocheted cotton gloves. She discovered that the making of these gloves, apart from a minimal pension, was her only means of income. She ordered several pairs immediately – sure of gathering orders from among her cronies – and arranged for me to collect them and, for a small extra payment, to stay an hour each week for French conversation.

Mrs Hay lived in a couple of dingy rooms flimsily partitioned off from the end passageway and back verandah of an old wooden high-stilted house on Dornoch Terrace, furnished with the sort of rickety tables and sagging sofas that are given to children for a cubbyhouse. The beds were curtained off, the tables draped and illuminated with little bottle lamps, a picture cloth hanging on the wall. What seemed to me strange then enabled me later to find familiar the rooms I entered in the novels of Turgenev and Dostoevsky. She had a gawky middle-aged daughter, her cousin's child, slow-witted, but with a spark of poetry bright in her soul.

We found we had too much to talk about to fumble

around in the clumsies of schoolgirl French. There was the
theatre where she had sung with Chaliapin, boating parties
on the Volga, Siberian snows through which they had fled,
the street life of Peking – her life before and her life after
the revolution of 'the year –05'. The day's newspaper had
little relevance for her incidental present. She knew the
names of necessary foods, the way into the New Settlers
League, spoke of shillings and pence as roubles and kopeks.
But her life, as she lived it in her château of memories,
materialised still around the few possessions she had kept
from her life-before – a necklace of real emeralds, a nest
of four fine china gold-embossed teacups and saucers, and
an exercise book of her handwritten poems of Pushkin.

Once a week, for her schoolgirl friend, the Russian
aristocrat laid out her cups. The daughter stood preened
between the parted curtains, book in hand, prepared for
her moment to read, giggling a little. The coffee was made
with the frugality learned in the life-after; a saucepan
heated while empty, a handful of dry ground coffee shaken
in to roast, a hiss of cold water added, a simmering and
adding of hot water, three times nearly to boil, twice to
cool down. Suspended, immersed in that long imminence
of coffee, much was revealed – talk of other times, other
lives, of hierarchies and their manners, women and their
lovers, political prisoners and their tortures . . .

When at last the coffee rose in heat and odour from
our wide cups, the daughter placed a hard-boiled egg in
each deep saucer and, on a side plate, a slice of cold buttered toast ingrained with salt and pepper. My little payment for conversation had been recklessly spent in advance
on the luxury of a block of bitter chocolate, the squares of

which we spooned in our coffee to melt before eating. Ada Hay was godmother to my widening life, preparing me for the maturing Australia that the new settlers were giving us.

Another refugee, poles apart, urbane and professional in manner, the art historian, Dr Gertrude Langer, generously dispensed her Viennese culture to the young who found their way to her table. She gave us a foundation for a personal sense of identity and was an attentive press critic. When *Barjai* moved out from the clubroom to host fortnightly public lectures, she was one of the first, lecturing not on modern art but on Chinese calligraphy. This was our Barjai public face in line with the Miya public exhibitions. We hosted other lectures with direct protest. The university did not have Australian literature on its curriculum. We aimed to shame the English department. Indeed, Professor A. K. Thompson later told me that they were in awe of the Barjai lot. We arranged a series of lectures by poets and writers in the Anne Street Presbyterian Hall. Tom Inglis Moore was one of the speakers. He came on after to a backroom Miya party and droned of how he needed peace. Sweet ladies sought to salve his need until it was revealed that Peace was the name of his beloved wife.

Our pranks were the flare of youth, not ostensibly sexual, unconventional rather than antisocial. This was the age before the pill, the days of the more cumbersome and less reliable Marie Stopes pessary caps, bought in plain wrapped boxes from an unmade-up lady in lower Edward Street, who spoke in quiet tones behind an unmarked door.

With a trio of hot-bellied painters up from the South, we walked in file through the long dim sulphur-lanterned piss-odoured tunnel in South Brisbane belting out Bessie

Smith blues, intoning Rimbaud poems to its cathedral echoes. Barrie and Vida took to gatecrashing parties and weddings by climbing up fire escapes, she in hat, stockings, gloves and high heels. We didn't need much money and played with what little we had. At night on the steep hills just beyond the city proper we would spin from the top a penny or a shilling down the echoing descent, then scramble down after it, stagger up and throw again, risking our tram fare home.

Barrie big-brothered me. He gently closed a door behind me and ushered me firmly over the threshold of the one he opened. He took me to one of his father's Rationalist Society meetings. Being a humanitarian seemed a good replacement for being a Christian. I wrote up on my wall: 'Do good/ For good/ Is good/ To do./ Spurn bribe of Heaven/ Threat of Hell.' He took me also to visit Mary Christina St John, whose mystic, rhythmic poems he published in *Barjai*.

Her house was a short walk from a tram terminus, immaculately clean and incredibly occupied. Mary, in simple dirndl skirt and sandals, greeted us formally, with a quizzical gaze and a forbidding air. She had graduated in classics from Adelaide University at a preposterously young age, had changed her name to personify the Catholic traditions and taken on an unlikely profession. With the abundant profits therefrom she had acquired her collections – books in eight languages, chests of elaborate embroidery, cabinets of fine porcelain, myriad pairs of elegant shoes and, above all, the hundreds of dolls including baskets of pobbles-who-have-no-toes and, above all that, her adored companion Edward Bear.

Child-sized Edward St John of the Angels (thus she had had him solemnly baptised) sat down to dinner with us. In fact he said grace. He also listened rapt while she read out long obscure poems, some in Spanish.

She preferred the use of hand towels to toilet paper. Once, when Jack McKinney was drying his hands on one of these, she came up behind him and asked: 'Does it interest you to know that I am a prostitute?' Jack considered. 'Not particularly. But it interests me that you want to tell me.' We walked back to the late-night tram as though a green door had closed behind us, leaving us to our mundane lives.

Barrie also took me to the notorious Pink Elephant café. Its late nighting and dim lighting was all there really was to be notorious about, but for Brisbane that was alarming enough. Frank Mitchell, not yet then a dress designer, had drifted up north in the wake of the war, and drifted round and round the city blocks with soldier Donald Friend one late night in search of a coffee – hopeless! He stayed on, located this small basement room down at the shady Bight end of town and with minimal money set up a coffee-house dive serving toasted sandwiches and raisin toast. He found a knockabout mate in Philippa McLaney and the life of it they made below stairs gave the city about its only glow. The famous tottered down those stairs past the insouciant little pink elephant in a cage brought by someone to the opening night – society people, then a foible of the Sunday press, after-theatre goers and visiting celebrities.

My spinster aunt warned me never to go there for fear of meeting unwholesome characters. She used to advise, 'You must marry a man who sets you upon a pedestal', a puzzling remark because the 'pedestal' was what we coyly called the bedside cupboard that sheltered the chamber pot. Actually my husband-to-be, as coydom would call him, gravitated there as soon as he hit town. One night, when a half-dozen quite proper and harmless people, none of them even homosexually inclined, were sipping and chatting away, two huge thuggy policemen (with hats) off duty came in straight from the hotel next door, and began to throw their weight around with accusations of illicit likker. They dragged off by the hair a medical student, leaving his fiancée to raise the alarm with his notable barrister father. The case caused a great furore. Philippa behaved with grand style in court. The case was won on appeal, the detectives demoted. But it was a pyrrhic victory, for the hallucinatory elephant did not survive.

Our youthful dreams were also being deflated. By the time I, being still under twenty-one, was the sole editor of *Barjai*, the wave of poets had burst into their own thin air. Laurie Collinson and others had gone south to Sydney art schools, others to teaching posts in the country. Dr Duhig, single-handed supporter of local culture with a finger in every pie, had tax problems and was selling his art collection. A fatherly printer, forgiving the lapse in payment for the final slim broadsheet *Barjai* that I had managed to produce, counselled me against burning more fingers. Miserably I walked alone up a Valley sidestreet, somehow ashamed at pronouncing the R.I.P. on the magazine that had ferried our hopes and glories.

We were a post-war generation who cherished

morals while scorning social standards and often found ourselves hilariously twisted between the two. We did not feel life owed us anything, but we felt we owed life much and that the honouring of the debt would quicken us. Only much later I heard the Gurdjieffan prayer: 'Let us live consciously that we may pay the debt of our existence'. We made things happen in the light of our beliefs that it was our duty to activate the world about us, creatively from within.

Barrie, enfant terrible in his saucier moments, was always a pillar of society. He joined the staff of the Public Library straight from school. With a loan from his father he set up the Ballad Bookshop in a little upper room in Adelaide Street, just in from the Edward Street corner, not far from Basil's coffee shop, our home away from home. It provided books not otherwise available, sent up from Adelaide by Max Harris, making it an outpost of the Mary Martin. His partner Charles Osborne, deliberately jobless and universityless, already a prodigious reader and unpublishable writer, managed the bookshop. An on-side distributor's agent gave us a two-day headstart on other city shops. With his sales jackets I ran off to the Parliamentary Library and the Oxley and we benefited from their orders.

All the avant garde books were at the Ballad and other trifles like Boyd pottery coffee sets and small Shillham sculptures. Friends came to talk, sometimes bought books. Sometimes strangers bought interesting books and were not left strangers for long. The Ballad became as much a meeting place as a bookshop.

Charles, looking highly literate, hid his feet in granny's pink slippers under the desk, but, as soon as a purchaser had gone, he locked the empty shop and went out to spend the takings, putting Barrie in a rage when he came back after work and found the lily new-gilded in pink shirt or flashing tie. His vanity was matched by his vivacity, and his wilfulness by his irrepressible wit. The day two-in-ones reappeared after the war, ice-creamy and nut chocolate-coated, he sold two Henry Millers and took me out on a spree. 'Don't drop your stick,' he said. 'Put it in this bin' and deftly directed my hand to a policeman's fly. When Laurence Olivier came to town with his company and his wife Vivien Leigh, Charles gave him in the Pink Elephant his scatological analytic essay on Hamlet entitled 'The Two Queens' and won him as much by this as by his almost direct translation of Leigh into male form. A year or so later he went to London to take up a stage offer.

We sat around on the bookshop floor behind its closed door, sipping out of the Boyd coffee cups the bottle of sherry from our pooled resources, reading the latest publication, the *Kinsey Report on Male Sexuality*. We worried its unimagined statistics like a dog a bone, speculating on the resources of the researchers and our own possible returns. Nuns and priests came in and bought several copies at a time. On the other hand, we Honours Psychology students would have been passed out without any lectures on sex at all had we not protested. As a result we were one day herded rather furtively into a furthest room to be addressed by an embarrassed Phys. Ed. lecturer in the most general terms – such as how many sperm could fit on the end of a toothbrush like angels dancing on the head of a pin. Sorry for him when no one responded to his request for questions, I asked in general if he would say something about homosexuality. He lowered his head and said that if anyone had a problem of a personal nature, he would be happy to see them later. At university, attending evening classes together, Barrie and I welcomed being regarded as inseparable lovers, a mutual alibi, my virginity being also something of a secret shame.

Charles' heart was in music. On Sunday nights he gathered in his own little upper room friends to listen to his playing of 78s on a gramophone in the middle of a bare floor, and gave his prodigious commentaries. I, if I brought one of my famous chocolate cakes, was welcome to his feast. My carpet flew high on hearing my first Shostakovich.

In another part of my forest it was the politics of Russia with which I grappled. I joined the University Radical club, companioned its president, mathematician Alan Roberts, to workers' meetings, sometimes to job meetings at wharf or building site where a bit of skirt got him a better hearing. I lacked political antennae, had not yet heard the pronouncement that the tragedy of the twentieth century was the failure of Communism to come to terms with art. Again I wielded the tea-towel, mothering these ardent young men too besotted by distant social tragedies to remember their own commitments. One election day we slept in and arrived late to the table at the polling booth to find my good-natured mother handing out our Communist how-to-vote papers, albeit with some irony, as well as her own Liberal tickets. Some local social tragedies lay unnoticed. Tom King was the first to marry. Occasional letters, a few poems, had come in from his teaching post out at Dirranbandi. Shy as ever, he stepped

into the bookshop one day with his radiant young wife —
Pearl, already pregnant — full of solicitude and joy. It was
almost fifty years before Pearl could come out with her
own story, *Black Hands, White Aprons*.

By some quirk of circumstance Barrie was keeper of
the key to the Carnegie Foundation Art Library. It had
been set up in the Thirties and was housed in a separate
small building at the front of the George Street Law
Courts. The Ballad Bookshop dispensed the key to students, regulars or visitors. A small scruffy muscly painter
from Sydney, with eyes bigger than himself but no words
to speak of, came regularly to pick up and deliver back the
key. Jack McKinney took up the challenge to engage him in
conversation but elicited nothing more than an Oh or No
or So. He had long eyelashes and a fawnlike grace and by
his prolonged staring at me when he returned the key I
gathered that he had by no means locked himself out.
Indeed he read by candlelight half the night. The Carnegie
chairs diminished in numbers. The seldom used fireplace
was warm at morning. For all Barrie's high-minded
endeavours to match-make me with a series of eligible
young men, each of them poetic, scholarly and handsome,
I incurred his disapproval by being drawn to this drifter.

Laurie Hope had brought him, Charlie Blackman,
north with him after a restorative trip home to his mother
in Sydney, and was his aide de camp, managing to rustle up
a few cold cooked potatoes and battered saveloys cheap at
closing time, from the off-side hot foods shop. For a short
time the two of them got jobs in the kitchen at the General
Hospital, learning the art of opening wide the mouth to
take in a whole plate of dinner in the flicker of an eye,

earning enough to supply themselves with paints, boards and brushes, until he too drifted back home to his mother in Manly.

Sidney Nolan, already 'as great as Picasso' in some eyes, hit town from Heide on the very day Barrie should have done his French II exam. He presented me. But on a trip down to Currumbin beach, when he climbed the elephant rock and I slipped and cut my toe which copiously bled, Sid just rushed past me to the summit. I decided he was cold-hearted. 'No' plunged into the landscape, carried off Joy Roggenkamp to Magnetic Island for the pleasures of painting, climbed Mount Warning to an epiphany of sunrise with Barrie and Laurie Hope and then, hearing accounts of Mrs Fraser, immediately rushed off to discover that island and his vision of Eliza.

John Yule, also up from Melbourne, spent some time with us. His adventurous reading – the surreal *Chants of Maldoror*, the profundities of Kierkegaard, exquisite subtleties of Proust – and his descriptions of the many kindred spirits – painters, potters, philosophers, critics – in Melbourne, not much older than ourselves, already embarked on their life's work, made it clear that we must go south. To Melbourne, to Moscow!

I had supposed that I was a poet. My friend Judith Wright pointed out to me that I was not. I was a person to whom poems happened. Anna Lewensohn, a true voyager, was the only school friend who fared forward with me. Sparrow-sized, mimsy-voiced, sharp-thinking and outspoken, she was trademark Jewish, defiantly romantic and obdurately determined. A Jean Shrimpton before her time, she had refused to wear school uniform black stockings in the sub-tropic climate and hats at all. We went to exhibitions and concerts, ate garlic, disposed of religions and borrowed lovers. Her sister Sarah left home, changed her name to Sue Lewis and went to Melbourne. Anna followed. Two of my uni course mates were soon gone. One, having married a high intellectual, good husband material, found herself, as so many other women of my generation, wife cover for a homosexual life, and suicided with weed killer. The other was murdered under the flowering bauhinias and gained fame in the annals of unsolved crimes.

The post-war energy of Brisbane and our youth was over. By the time I graduated my sight was failing fast. I had fallen into a black abyss of despair; no prospects of being a psychologist, poet or literary person; no veritable Christian faith. I had to jump out into the unknown for myself. My mother in her wisdom accepted all the disappointments I offered her, even the bewilderment of my imminent blindness. She took Stewpot back to live with her in the house of my childhood. When I was young and believed that God answered prayer pointblank, when I was young and taken down to Sydney, that Heaven city, to stay with jazzy Auntie Floss on Fairy Bower, I asked that He should let me marry a man from Manly. And He did. The last book I read with my own eyes I read on the Manly ferry, free-riding across to city and back. The book was Turgenev's *On the Eve*.

PART TWO

$\mathcal{D}$AISE OF OUR LIVES

I had sketched out Daisy, carefully and questioningly, before I ever met her, for I knew that Marguerite Jasmine Hall, that tiny whirl of a woman more than twice my age, was to become my mother-in-law. She became, for over thirty years, a darling, daunting friend.

Her son had erupted into my life with a pace and turn of phrase I had not come across before. He gave me the clue. 'Don't believe a word I say but believe everything I do.' So I gladdened at his neon-lighted lies and let the magnet of his actions draw me ever closer to his soul.

I thought this mother was one of his wilder lies, this woman knee-high to a daisy who ran everywhere, dressed like a doll, smoked a hundred 'coffin nails' a day, threw together meals in a jiff, would bring a tea tray out to the back lawn and do a handstand on top of the teapot. He stabbed into me the notion that his mother thought with her heart and for a blue-stocking like me, an emotional cripple, the one hundred and eighty degree turn of meeting her would be good shock treatment.

She flung open the front door of a little old painted-up weatherboard house stopped short just inside the front fence of a surf-running street in Freshwater. She was wearing the Sydneysider's tots-to-teenagers summer dress, elastic bodice, dirndl skirt, blue-green gingham, high-heeled shoes, hair persimmon pink. Her overflow of welcome alternated with eddies of apology — that the house was not a palace, her gardening clothes no afternoon tea gown. But there was an undercurrent. ('If Chica thinks he can bring home another one of those book-stuffed sheilas to talk over my head, he's got another think coming.')

True, she had every reason to see me as one of those up-sprouts come down in the last shower of rain, but I had my own way of catching on. I had a way of sieving through and sorting out people, where they stood, in categories of my own making. There were the perking class (what my mother called 'people at the top of their tree'), the clerking class (where she herself was), the working class, the shirking class and, beyond that, the lurking class.

For these up-branch classes, 'someone who was in', gently said, meant having a nervous breakdown, gone into a psychiatric clinic, to be welcomed home when let out; but about someone gone to gaol there was tight-lipped silence. For the low-branches this was reversed. Someone or other was always 'in for a bit' and would be back again sooner or later, meantime routinely visited; but anyone who was so far gone as to be seen by a 'shrink' was in real trouble. However, any T. P. I. (Totally Permanently Incapacitated) person was aristocracy in the lurking class. 'They' had to pay you for doing nothing for the rest of your life. My blind pension made me an honorary. 'Being blind wouldn't matter on the game, luv, you'd get tips for it.' The 'four-legged lottery' was the most familiar lurk. Art — cleverly painting a picture in a few hours and selling it to a big nob for a couple of guineas — appealed as a spot-on lurk. There was a meeting ground.

Daisy and I took to each other. 'If you are genuine sincere lovers going faithful, you'd better come home and live here.' 'Here' was a boyhood bed on the glassed-in small front verandah smelling all night of ocean and frangipani. They were an aquatic family, moods ebbing and flowing. As a girl, for a threepenny dare, she had climbed to the top of the Spit Bridge and clung there while it swung up to let a boat pass through. As a small boy he had dived for pennies off Manly Pier, coming up with cheeks bulging to have them tickled out of him by thrashing sisters. But, if I had found him pacy, now I saw he was but a rowing boat to her fast skiff.

Conventional life was something so peripheral to her world that she could not cope with it. For her, it did not exist. Instead she lived in a world of self-inflicted fantasy. An actress manqué, she made her whole life a theatre: not a palace, but a stage; not a tea gown but a quick-change wardrobe. 'Gee, Daise,' said her long-suffering husband, 'how do you think a man feels when he opens his lunch at work and the cake's blue and the raisins all purple?' Suddenly an oriental geisha lady kisses his dirty shoes. 'So solly. Next time olange brossom cake, velly pletty.' The 'old man' melted like butter in the pan. In true Aussie affectionate ironic style he was given this title because he was too young to be their father.

This second husband, Arthur John, twelve years her

junior, adored her utterly with all her caprices. A little boy, he had seen her, the Balgowlah princess marrying a charming prince, and the joy of capturing her for himself when he was nineteen and she a deserted woman with four children never left him. 'Two love birds in their nest.' She slept in his embrace, princessed in a froth of nylon frills, a dangle of earrings, a drench of scent. He was the rock upon which she built her palaces of rare delight, her firm foundation to withstand the shattering of castles in the air.

She is home from the races with a bosom full of pound notes, quilting the bed with them, disappears while a back is turned, gone to the dogs, home at midnight flat-chested with remorse. 'If the cows would run on Sunday, luv, I'd be there too.'

Ghosts and goblins, all the hurts and hopes, churned away inside her. 'I hope you never have to sit and hear your little children cry themselves to sleep for hunger.' 'Sad things cut you to pieces.' 'You just have to go for the good times and see the funny side when you can.' Her life was simply a happening; haphazard, the luck of the game, an unquestionable flow of milk and honey, the spilling of it much to be cried over. She was a pretty woman – flirtatious heavy-lidded eyes, irresistible smile, heavy bosoms, agile thighs, a dancer's double-jointed wrists and ankles, a body for putting feeling straight into action. She taught me so much about love, and sex – the bigness, toughness and tenderness of the heart.

Love was incandescent in her with a flame just out of reach so that she had to walk on the burning coals to keep the warmth. The light of the flame was chiaroscuro on family members with no relief for the subtlety of friendships. Without perspective of time or proportion of significance, the old and re-told gyrated with the recent and reverberating in her monologue drama. People, a bothersome neighbour or eccentric shop-keeper, occupied the foreground by mere proximity.

She had a thrilling up-scale peal of laughter just like the first notes of Schubert's Trout Quintet, and a thousand mock voices for telling stories. But you sat on the edge of your seat ready for when the fireworks or waterworks, tongue-lashings or tears, would heart-burst out of her. This human being could not bear too much reality. Silence undermined her. 'Snake in the grass' stuff. One of her daughters spelt it out. 'As long as Mum can see your mouth moving, you're alright. Talking, laughing, singing, kissing, eating, drinking, smoking, whistling, sobbing – even hic-coughing will do – she thinks you're alright. But if you shut up she thinks you're up to something and she'll come down on you like a ton of bricks.'

She would take a running leap to the footstool in front of the stove that made her tall enough to stir the pot. She could knock up a fine roast dinner or a dish of 'plimsoles' (her word for fine chinese noodles) and prawns, but then go coy and so denigrate it in the presen-tation that it might have been an old dishcloth. Once she called us in to dinner in super-quick time, and there on a freshly laundered white tablecloth were five plates of meat and three veg, cutlery beside, bread rolls between, wine glasses coming into view, all done in coloured crayons. 'Nothing in the house worth cooking.'

At this time I was running on parallel tracks. At roist-erous level I was listening avidly to her stories, myths of what was 'streetwise' before we had the name, stories hitherto kept well under the floorboards. Alone for hours I was limbering up to be a writer. So I used her stories as clay and moulded figures in the forms of Hemingway, Gertrude Stein, de Lautremont, Henry Miller — all handwritten, kept in a big journal thrown into a lowboy drawer. Chica worked all day at the golf-stick factory painting handles, then worked till midnight on our sleep-out verandah painting first pictures — blue skies and green trees with a certain unoccupied air.

One day he came home to find his landscape occupied. A bridal couple came down the forest path and the trees were full of pansy-frocked little peeping people. All glistened, or glossened. Daisy, hair plum purple, danced out from behind her cigarette to say she got bored, so finished it off for him, depicting our wedding day with all the grandchildren-to-be hiding in the branches. 'All just pigments of my imagination,' she explained, and added, 'I got the paint to thin down with sewing machine oil.'

Another day we came home to find the house fully occupied; but silent, no figure dancing forth. I made a pot of tea; nobody drank. She served up the dinner; none for me. Being sent to Coventry was awful, the most frightening thing that had ever happened to me. Eventually the 'old man' spoke. 'Snake in the grass,' he hissed. Another day passed. Then, in a flood of tears, the story came out. 'I thought you were writing a beautiful love story romance in that book of yours and I couldn't wait to read it. Then I found out you were making rubbish of everything I had told you and making me look like some idiot. All lies.'

My parallel tracks had intersected, my train derailed.

An abyss opened. We threw our few things into a suitcase and went up to Central Station, tossed a coin for it, and went south to live in Melbourne. Toss of another coin: he to set up full-time painting, me to set aside my writing. Gradually, patiently, I worked my way back to her heart. Persistently, weekly, I wrote her chatty loving letters until Coventry was burnt out and a new relationship built over the embers of that irreversible misunderstanding.

Within a year or two of our going down to Melbourne we had a letter from her — her letters were always folded up over and over so that they Jack-in-the-boxed out of their envelopes — to say that they had got sick of the bird-brained suburbs and had taken up residence in manorial splendour at the new address, Ashton Park. We visited them there soon after. As park ranger and care-takers of Bradley's Head, adjacent to Taronga Park Zoo, they were quartered in one end of a long building of what had been an early bush hotel, the rest of it being a great drill hall used regularly by Boy Scouts for indoor games, occasionally for dances with live bands and, on our visits, as a gargantuan studio.

These were probably her happiest days. Here she was producer and actor in her theatre. At weekends they manned the kiosk, on stage to the pies and milkshake audi-ence. On unseaworthy days they rang the fog horn. From time to time the police rushed in looking for stolen goods or missing persons, setting alight sensational possibilities. Park duties kept her on the run. She swept leaves, got hot water for picnickers, pushed children on roundabouts, persuaded pairs of nuns to have a swing, left tea trays temptingly on benches near lovers' bowers, arrayed like a stall at the Easter Show the 'lost property' shoes, hats, towels, umbrellas. Handkerchiefs she washed by the score, flotsam and jetsam she hoarded in case the missing legs of chairs or second shoe might swim in after.

At night she strummed at the washed-up piano, dried-out and polished, set up in splendour in the living room. Arthur had once been a drummer in a dance band and they pounded out duets with gusto despite the missing keys and raw nerve wires. Driftwood logs flamed blue in the huge fireplace. Possums and 'chip monks' scuttled along the bank at window-sill level. One rabbit was friendly enough to come indoors. 'That rabbit's got a bit of cat in him.'

Across their bedroom window the Harbour Bridge stretched in postcard precision, its traffic whirring like a fly on the pane. 'All those drones going off to their bee-hives.' She would leap out of bed, crash about in the kitchen and arrive at our bedside like Winged Victory in action, landing a tea tray down upon us, pouring out the scalding brew, drowning a tablespoon of condensed milk into it. If we were slow to get stuck into our mound of baked beans on toast, then she would arrive with new hot bits and, quick as a flash, slide out the soggy from under and slip in the crisp.

It was best to be quiet about taking a bath. Otherwise you would find yourself Hollywooded with sparkling bub-bles up to your ears, an instant luxury of her own concoc-tion, handful of Lux flakes and shake of 4711 whisked to a frenzy, and your elbow room impeded by a bathside line-up of fizzy 'spider' cocktails and chocolate 'fan-tales'. And you were definitely expected to sing in the bath, the gargling high trill notes of Galli-Curci preferred.

I mastered the art of getting on with Daisy — never to say two sentences together that had anything to do with each other. Emotion without thought. No consequences. No argument. Leave the clodhop shoes of logic at the door. It was all done with mirrors. Metaphors were mixed clichés cornered, non-sequiturs the order of the day. Once you got your barefoot balance on this switchback merry-go-round, you were in for a good ride. But for her it had been very often a rough one. She had never cracked the 'they' that made the wheels go round, so she lived in a state of defence. The copper boiling, floors scrubbed, walls bare; no books, no pictures, one toothbrush; all they owned enough to fill one suitcase — ready for a quick get-away in pursuit of a clear conscience.

She came to her son's first exhibition in a swank Sydney gallery armed with a long umbrella wherewith to inflict 'accidental' suffering on anyone who spoke an ill word. She 'didn't go much for the gallery types . . . get more for your money looking at the monkey parade up at the railways.' They would shin up to Central an hour before an interstate train was due in, then take us straight off for a meal at the railway café, Viennese steak (savoury mince on toast) being the homecoming treat. 'Making any money, Chic? Why don't you get Babsy a perm? Hordens have got good suits up there on sale.'

Daisy didn't drink more than the odd shandy. By her own high spirits she stood on high ground. We jitterbugged and bumps-a-daisied into the Fifties. We dressed up, played ping pong with back-turned frying pans and round pota-toes, stood on the rickety chairs for Hyde Park speeches. She had no patience with radio, 'dead heads speaking'. A quiet night was sitting around playing draughts or noughts-and-crosses for worldly gain. It would start with matches and she would lose every time. Put ha'pennies on the table and the winning spirit would lift her. Then she would bring out her big bottle of paper money, torn corners of quids and ten-bob notes she had picked up from time to time, mostly underfoot at the course, jigsaw of lost hopes.

The 'old man' stuck to the idea that you should play life straight. 'Daise, you'll worry the soul case out of me.' One day it did fall out. He was clearing the drainage on a cliff-top path when it came over him. He just threw his shovel into the sea and stood still. Shellshock twenty years after the war, a time-bomb wounding of the inner man, detonated him into anxiety neurosis. Eventually, mercifully, he was awarded T. I. status, a part pension, acceptable reward.

Their dance was over. They succumbed to wall-flowering it out in a beach house up the coast. For a while, hair mulberry puce, she lurked about with the one-arm bandits 'up at the RSL' but gave it up for the occasional frisk with fishing. Mainly she took to the garden. Eve would have envied her. The garden multiplied. Flowers grew in half the time and twice the size. She would heave plants out of their mother earth on a spade, waltz them across the yard and bed them into a new setting, just the way she used to do with the lounge room furniture.

I took the children up for holidays. When the youngest was five and seeming to fly through the air with eagerness to get to the beach to fish, he came home sunburnt and shivering after one long day with his catch of tiddlers. 'Could we have them for dinner?' eagerly, and

'Would there be enough?' ruefully. 'Yes my big fine fisher-man.' She did a Jesus and placed a fish on all our plates. Carefully she had steamed the tiny fish, scraped off the lit-tle flesh, beaten it with fish paste into a batch of mashed potatoes, fashioned various fish, fried them golden for our supper. The little fisherman went happy to bed dreaming of seas full of fish.

She, the generous, the garrulous, whose heart seemed bitten by some tarantula spider of high spirits, sub-sided to the anaconda sedation of the television screen, but generally out-talked it. The old man fixed any little thing that went wrong with Everestian triumph, all for his dar-ling Daise. She fed her Art to bursting point and kept his medicines enshrined like holy relics. 'How's your Art going, son?' – her usual greeting – 'My Art's fine!' But she didn't sleep much, just lay awake thinking over all the griefs and glories of her life, puffing away, keeping up her average.

'Get's a couple of packets of fags, will you, luv?' She was weeding the bed of Shirley poppies out the front. Arthur went off to the shop. Ten paces, turn, wave. Ten paces, turn, wave. At the corner, big turn, big wave. He kept those packets of cigarettes for years. He found her flat on her back on the lawn, gardening shoes neatly together in the bucket full of weeds, her job done.

'I wanted to get her into something good, but they came and took her away just in her old gardening clothes.' Eighty years was a pretty good innings. She would have been proud of us at her funeral. There sat the four of us, Charles' three sisters and me, and she couldn't have wished for a better display of waterworks.

$\mathcal{T}$HE FISH BOWL

Hand in hand, young and brash, eager and confident, Charles Blackman and I — two bits of string tied in a knot — came to Melbourne in January 1951. We came in from the wings, Sydney and Brisbane respectively, on to a stage between the acts, the lights of the heyday Forties dimmed by the post-war diaspora to Europe and not yet illumined by the new generation and the gallery rehab students, into the change of art scene. Quite quickly we sought out and got together with the dramatis personae of the Fifties, some re-appearing from the Forties to rekindle and be rekindled by the newcomers.

I had met John Yule at the Ballad Bookshop, up from Melbourne on a kind of cultural reconnaissance, a cross-pollination of creative growths between the two cities. John, a painter and diarist, was — still is — an outsider, a shrewd observer, a commentator on the motions and motives of people involved. He leaned in the bookshop doorway, looking in to see what might be afoot of fact or fictional interest. The chemistry of recognition and attraction took place between us – talker and listener grasped at each other with the spoken word.

John, balding, shabby, book-carrying, swaggering, whistling his daily monologue, was a tramp, living from kip to kip. I would come in early from my orderly motherly flat beyond the Roma Street railway yards and meet him in the City Hall Square with a breakfast sandwich. He would sit in the sun on the stony steps and tell me the synopsis of the book he was reading – *Joy* by Faulkner, *Cross Purposes* by Camus. Being a lapsed academic himself, he would pat me paternally on to my uni bus as though to a kindergarten excursion, then meet me when the bus returned in the afternoon to adjourn to the Pickwick Inn, a coffee shop up a little arcade with glass-top cubicle tables and impertinent waitresses, to sit for a couple of hours trying not to finish the one cup of coffee we could afford. Occasionally funds ran to a shared plate of raisin toast.

There he gave me a series of lectures on the salons of Melbourne. At English Lit classes I had lectures on the Caroline, Augustan, Romantic poets; at the Pickwick on the Boyds and Murrumbeena, the Reeds and Heide, Jorgensen and Montsalvat, John McCarthy's bookshop, Neil Douglas and his Bayswater garden, the Langley, Coote, Whissan and Smith families, the Meldrum, Bell and Gallery schools. Thus, when I myself entered Melbourne, I was walking on to the set of a movie, having read the book. There was for me then the exquisite experience of meeting the people themselves one by one, set by set.

The runaway Brisbane Jewish sisters, Anna and Sarah, were there at Spencer Street station when we arrived, runaways ourselves with a couple of suitcases, to gatecrash

Melbourne. At the end of a weed-stained alley between tall houses off George Street in East Melbourne, they pulled open a wide squeaking corrugated iron gate. Beyond it was an old disused commercial laundry which they had made habitable. A row of four deep wooden wash troughs with washboard and wood-fire copper set in cracked concrete were in an open lean-to area adjacent to, as in the gold-silver-lead casket stories, a rosy brick one-room cottage (once drying room), arm in arm with a half-sister wooden room (once ironing room) and, cowering behind them, an ugly step-sister tin shed (probably some sort of store-room). Anna had given her brick cottage a folk-story air with climbing rose over the door, pots of herbs outside and pixie cushions within. Sarah's room was something of a maze, her clumps of furniture placed at odd angles to cover over the scorch marks and burn holes in the floor. They fiddled the lock of an internal door into the shed, stark with its corrugated iron walls, concrete floor and bolted paint-peeling door to the yard beyond. We dragged through our bags and loaned mattress. This did us fine for the time being. Melbourne was a bonfire of excitement. We were happy to sleep and eat anywhere.

Many of the painters, students, musicians we met had found themselves derelict coach-houses or lofts around the inner suburbs, got them for a song, and made cosy habitats. So we began to walk the hidden mews, peer over fences. We also advertised in the paper. 'Wanted – coach-house, loft, garage, sleepout or shed for use as artist's studio.'

One reply came from an addressee in Powlett Street, which ran nearby between George and the tram line in Wellington Parade. A baggy bachelor man came to the door of his tall Victorian terrace and led us into shaded rooms nostalgic of grandmothers, hymns, Chelsea buns and cats long gone. He sat us down to be interviewed. He made us tea for company. He insisted on playing us his violin. We kept trying to bring the conversation back to the matter of the studio. He stammered. Finally he admitted it wasn't much of a place really. If only we had come a few months earlier. Another tune on the violin. Perhaps we should leave. No, no, he would show us the premises for rent. Out with the keys with which the front door had been locked behind us. Keys held up to the light, right key selected. Out through the back door, door locked behind us, cat complaining, down steps and through vine-grown trellis door and into a backyard, at the far side of which – behold – we saw, from this different angle, the bolted paint-peeling door of our tin shed. This was now nervously unlocked and we gazed in upon the room from which, barely an hour before, we had removed our things. We looked it over carefully, every bare square inch, and carefully considered its proposed rent of twelve shillings per week, offered ten. Deal clinched, hands shaken. It was ours. He seemed to wonder why we hesitated to make our way back with him through trellis, complaint of cat, chatelaine of keys, dark corridor, threat of more violin, until safely outside into the sunny street – 'A short walk', we assured him, to collect our belongings. We seem to have just lived one of those dreams of cellmates digging tunnels underground, making inadvertent circles and surfacing back in their own bare cell.

Melbourne itself was a shock to the country cousin from Brisbane – so large, so orderly, so close to the sea, so subject to the four seasons. It was summer. We could live partly outdoors with a table set up on the patch of asphalt under the sagging clothes lines, painted on, eaten off, scrubbed daily. Charles painted our door jonquil yellow and, in lieu of furniture, a row of chairs, red, purple and blue, along the back tin wall of the shed. From the Victoria Market we scrounged an end roll of frog-green glossy plastic and curtained this across one corner. From the Salvation Army store we got a primus stove, several dented saucepans, odd cups and bent cutlery, and a couple of mattresses, which, rolled up and tied with rope by day, cleared the floor space and made seats. From Woolworths we got three eating vessels – positioned at the time of purchase between the enamel bowls and enamel chamber pots, probably (in hindsight) doggy dishes, wherefrom we ate our three meals of the day – porridge breakfast, pasta lunch, and for dinner barley soup, with sago pudding, in turn vanilla, lemon, and chocolate-flavoured. The porridge was made partly with milk and beset with globs of brown sugar. The pasta was sauced with oil and garlic and some of Anna's herbs. Raw fruits and salads used the same receptacles.

To get money I went to art schools modelling, Charles went bush, peach picking. He came back after a week with suntan, toothache and friend John Yule. Bad season for the peach. The three of us lived in the tin shed, three peas in a pod, in mini-comfort and maxi-bliss. We read a lot; drank tea. Charles sketched about ten hours a day. John gave us the runaround to galleries, coffee shops, studios and households. But we were living beyond our means, means meaning my non-means-tested blind person's pension and the life class work. 'Out,' I said. 'And don't come home again, either of you, until you've got a job.' Off they went into the hopeful air.

John was first back, some hours later, his tittle whistle heard with gate scrape and squeak. 'Got a job,' he said, as he took up best place at the drawing table. 'I start work tomorrow morning at the private hospital down the road, Matron Spooner, light duties, meals provided.' 'Good boy!' Some little time later scrape and squeak of gate with accompanying footfall. 'Got a job,' said Charles, 'start tomorrow. Evening shift at hospital down the road, Major Spooner, light duties and I get dinner and supper there.'

So their job sharing began next day. Two less sparky men came gate-squeaking home. 'Light duties – run rabbit run!' 'Meals today, stale bread and plum jam – yesterday apricot, tomorrow, let's guess, raspberry or black currant?' They both washed dishes, sloshed floors, emptied buckets and fed Mr Head. Mr Head could not move his head and had to be spooned food between dribbles. That job didn't last long. Too much jam can send you stir crazy. Light gardening replaced it, but in different suburbs.

One evening, after the six o'clock closing at the Mitre Tavern – in Bourke Street uphill from the Post Office and a little way down from Stanley Coe's Gallery – Charles brought some friends home. I was taking the opportunity of privacy to conduct my personal ablution. This was done in a tin tub behind the door, with water warmed on the primus. All too late I heard the gate's scrape-squeak alarm and onrush of approaching voices. I was nude, soapy, crouched athwart the little tub. 'Come and meet Barbara' – the door pushed open. 'Half a mo',' I wailed. But Perceval, handsome, mischievous, lurching ahead on his crippled leg, thrust the door open and came round it. 'Here's a nude,' he called, 'a nude with a pretty navel', and flicked back the shock of blond hair over his forehead. Before I could scrabble for a towel, a second figure came round the door, tweedy and turps-reeking, with hand held out in gentlemanly fashion. 'How do you do? I'm Arthur Boyd.' Charles yanked the table out through the door and threw down on it his pile of sketches. While they were out there going through them, I completed my toiletry and dressed. We all went off to Lilly Bourke Street for dinner at the Lin Nan.

That was one of the great meeting places, especially on Friday nights, when people came to town from outskirt places and Gallery students were finished for the week. Tables were joined together, chairs wedged in, funds pooled. A bearded, bulky man at the top of the table talks noisily, slapping his thigh, thumping the table with his fist adorned with large sculptured rings, making those around him rock with laughter. That's Matcham Skipper the jeweller in from Montsalvat. A tall man, older, hair down to shoulders, is speaking softly, explaining the politics and perfidies of galleries. This is Neil Douglas in from his phenomenal garden at Bayswater to do some pottery decorating with John Perceval and Arthur at the Murrumbeena potteries. Two men at the far end, talking too much to attend to ordering, one stentorious, one excited, are the philosophers Bryan O'Shaughnessey and Tim Burstall, expanding upon their joint thesis having researched the sex attitudes of suburban couples, a new departure thematically for the Psychology Department at Melbourne – possibly even material for the great Australian movie.

A hairy dishevelled paint-stained man with pipe in mouth, feet in sandshoes, comes in one night with Jean Langley, tanned, long blond plait, who draws flowers and children so exquisitely, and sits next to me. He says he has 'dun moochin'' about, wants to forget his army experience, to build himself a mudbrick house and get on with painting. He is working for a chook farmer out at Cottles Bridge close to where, after all, he had been born, working with the chooks in return for a slab of land – pretty rabbit-rutted land it is – but a place to start his sort of artists' colony. This is Clif Pugh. He doesn't want to join anyone else's colony. He wants to start his own to live in the starkness of the bush and paint it. I was not a candidate for pioneering bush life, the hard and happy physical. I saw a lot more of Clif – and indeed he saw a lot more of me – posing at the Gallery School.

Some of these people I meet in other guise, scrubbed up and on best behaviour, at the Sunday afternoon 'arvo tea' soirées of John and Sunday Reed out at Heide. I visited there first in the shadow of Barrie Reid, down from Brisbane; later with Anna, small and dark, wearing that flaring yellow dress we used to call 'Come to Happy Israel'. My dress was a seersucker tumble of roses. We had walked in summer heat right up from the station. We almost stumbled over Sunday hedged into the lavender bushes of the driveway, crouching with secateurs. She was in her soft blue shirt and trousers and spoke with a soft blue voice, as our heroine Gertrude Stein might have said. 'Hello. I'm deaf and you're blind. I wonder how we shall ever get on together?' Actually, I don't think we ever really did. She was such a visual person, and I such a listener.

Cats, gardens, paintings, ghosts, 'French flu': I was on some other side of the tracks, faring forward, rushing into angel lands, treading on toes, pursuing my curiosity down the nights and days.

John Reed was a man I could talk to. He came into the dining room where Sun had the early Nolan Kelly paintings laid on the table, wiping them down one by one with a rag, an old shirt whose buttons scraped the surfaces. 'Hey there – careful!' says John – such a handsome man, in at evening from milking the cow, wearing a kind of shepherd's smock. John was no soft-surface romantic. Sometime later I blabbed to him. 'The painter is like an innocent child running for his life through a fearful jungle,' I ventured out of the depths of my inner romantic muddle. 'Now, now,' he said in a steadying voice. 'I've known far too many painters to go along with that.'

Sunday and John were seldom separated. Ministering angel, or black Venus, as she was, she was earthed in John. They ruled over a kingdom of the aesthetic such as most of us had never known before, a kind of Heaven, where we felt awed and chosen to be guests, whose esoteric rules we were always in danger of trespassing upon. Simplicitas, dignitas, pietas were in modern demonstration in that scrubbed farm house rich with books, paintings, music, and an air of intimacy with them. The Reeds were imperious, courting and cancelling, promising and denying. Poor John Yule never gained entry. Several times he was invited, but, a few hours before the due time, he would be informed by telegram that one of the cats had died. 'The blinds are drawn.'

There was, however, their Open House on New

Year's Eve. Much effort was put into staying sober enough to cross that threshold before midnight, to eat a slice of the home-cured ham, the succulent turkey, the abundance of gorgeous food. We took David Muir there when he was seventeen. We thought him already a brilliant photographer and proven romantic. He had sat day and night at the foot of Anna's bed, when she was almost dying of asthma, and read aloud the whole of Céline's *Death on the Instalment Plan*. We thought him inspired. He was not quite drunk on approach, but became instantly intoxicated with anticipation at the doorstep and hurled himself bodily into the sea of lavender hedge and thrashed about there like a swimmer in ecstasy, doing such damage as made it unlikely he would ever be asked to arvo tea.

At my endless life classes I became aware that there was one eager painter avidly drawing away at almost every evening class – Vic Arts, Bell's Saturday, Ola Cohn's Friday night. An awkward fat boy with small eyes and a breathy voice, shy, inquisitive. He massed hundreds of drawings of me. One night he came and asked if I was free on Sunday to pose for him. It was time to take him home to meet my other half. So it was I brought in from the cold one Friday night Freddie Williams, to the first of the endless cups of cocoa and biscuits over which he and Charles perused and nattered on about each other's pictures.

They decided to have the Sunday 'class' chez nous. This meant I could be soup maker and dish washer as well as life model. There wasn't much room. The two of them had to crouch on the floor working on spreads of board. Both worked violently in enamels. Fred finished first. He ran round and took up a position between me and Charles where he could look over his shoulder and paint another figure on what seemed to be the unutilised sky area of his mate's painting. Then they decided to take the back off Anna's wardrobe and share that.

It was not an altogether male world. One afternoon in a dim coffee shop – the Blue Room in its last days, or perhaps Cinderella's – I ran into Jean Langley and with her an older woman in a fuddle of garments, large blue shawl over her head. This was the mother, Doris Boyd, on a rare visit to town. Some of her pots had sold at the Primrose and she was happily buying tubes of colour and a few new brushes. She carried her own world about with her in a way that made the city seem a Treat, but quite peripheral to that world of which she was the centre. She talked softly, a continuum, about her sons Arthur, David and Guy, her daughters Lucy and Mary, using her mothering names – Chooky, Midgy, Guysy, herself being Pussy – and she asked me lots of questions about myself, a good beginning to friendship. But that friendship would only really begin when I came to her house at Murrumbeena.

I went often. She used to refer to me as 'that nice blunt girl'. I loved her maternal parlour in the Brown Room, a room in which everything happened, sometimes even meals. Merrick, the father, would appear from nowhere, hat on head, and sit playing the piano. Mary, strong and beautiful as a young angel, blonde, barefoot, busy, already married to John Perceval, would come in between doing things with laundry and babies. Yvonne, Arthur's wife, elegant and practical – she had been postered for Land Army recruitment – intelligent and watchful, not always in good books because she was an organiser, was the first to suggest it was long past dinner time. No one seemed to think of doing anything about dinner until night had fallen and hunger stalked. Arthur comes in from the pottery, tells Yvonne to remind him to go and turn the kiln off in four hours time. Doris goes on sitting at her easel beside the fire, rubbing pinches of real sand into her beach scene, and reciting pages of T. S. Eliot. (Fancy actually having a mother who knew Eliot!) Merrick comes towards me like a knightly gentleman presenting a trophy. 'I put it in the bowl,' he says out of some inner kingdom. I look apprehensively into the bowl. A lion with a toothbrush is painted in its base.

Autumn came. We found a forgotten coach-house stable and loft behind an old Victorian mansion in Chrystobel Crescent in Hawthorn, befitting a marriage and a studio. We telephoned a carrier to move us. We did not indicate to the carrier the minimal nature of our worldly goods. A pantechnicon, large enough to take a pride of lions to the zoo, arrived. It crashed the lower branches of the stately George Street trees. By sheer coincidence two visitors arrived somewhat formally, painter Fred and Ian Bassett, known to me from the Inter-Varsity Debating Club, taking this year off from Physics to try his hand as a painter. So they helped us load a rattle of kitchenware, a thud of bedding and lashing of paint boards into the ballroom back of the mighty truck, and, while we were thrown about from wall to wall as the monster turned corners or changed gears, they followed at humorous distance in a very small car.

That stable-loft house, at Hawthorn, to which we were delivered, cleaned out, white-washed, filled with our domesticity below, paintings fresh daily above, with its shabby garden under the huge Moreton Bay fig tree, became for ten years a place of 'life's crowded canvas'. The top half of the stable door pinned back to make a window into the brick-floored kitchen, or out of it on to the asphalt yard, the curve of crazy-stone pathway through privet bush and prunus towards Chrystobel Crescent. Up that pathway, head thrust in over the half door, came many a person to make his introduction, framed like a portrait in the window space.

'I am a great admirer of your husband's work,' said a tall man starchily at one of those drawing-room life classes in the Toorak area — and this soon after his first-ever exhibition, that of the weird little schoolgirls. 'I am an art master at Melbourne Grammar. I would like to meet him.' So John Brack, a week or so later, put his head over the stable door one afternoon after school, very properly attired, like an Edwardian gentleman, in suit, hat and furled umbrella. I had a sudden memory of those turn of the century books with pages cut horizontally in half so that one could make figures of contrasting upper and lower parts. It flashed before me that this figure, whose upper half was so gentlemanly and formal, might, on opening the lower half of the door, be revealed to have the trunk and legs of piggywig or big bad wolf, to confront the artist shinning down the wall ladder like a monkey, presenting lower half first, paint-hardened jeans, brush in hand. Several newest wettest street scene paintings were handed down to the visitor through the trap-door and propped up against sink, safe and cupboard. Some time later he confessed he had a wife and children to go home to. 'My wife, Helen,' he said, in measured tones, 'when she is alone, eats her dinner from a saucepan.' I knew I would like Helen, a woman who was wed to this man of courtesy and quirkiness, yet sensible enough not to incur unnecessary washing-up. I did.

Very different was the husky-voiced overcoat-hunched conspiratorial art teacher that Charles brought home one Friday night after the Swanston Family pub shut, to meet me, or rather brought home to the paintings and whatever stew was on the go. Moreover Len French looked at the lined-up pictures as though they were appearing at the Inquisition. Then he spoke of the overcoat he laid across the back of the chair. 'Best that Sammy Bear had to offer,' he said unappreciatively. 'Not as good as the one I got from him before I went overseas. Wore it two full winters all the way round Ireland, Holland and Germany. Turned it in to him again when I got home and he gave me same as I had paid for it.' That was the sort of deal Lennie liked. 'Sammy Bear Gentleman's Outfitters, Second Hand Clothes' was where all the boys shopped. He showed his appreciation of cuisine barbara by promising to bring me some of his students' work, along with his wife Helen, at the next visit. He taught at the William Angliss Trade School, got as perks the jagged haircuts and breads baked by students – 'Half a dozen loaves. Cut off the burnt bits and the soggy bits and there's a meal or two in it.' Actually he brought us a cake iced 'Bon Voyage to Joy and Gorge'.

The meeting with David and Hermia Boyd on their return from Europe was vastly more celebrative – the fatted calf, no less. It took the form of a mass gathering by spread of word at the Open Country home at Murrumbeena. Open Country was fit name for this suburban-sized lot in suburban setting, but lot where tree was never cut, though much climbed, grass never mown, indeed grass only tuftily grown with all the tramping of feet. The fatted calf took the form of a keg of beer, party altar-piece of highest order, for which we had all promised to pitch in.

David was dark, handsome, voluble, eloquent, a Greek hero figure. Hermia, robed like Queen Mab, was so shy she seemed on point of flight. The mob thronged in the Brown Room. Drinking and talking was well underway. At the centre there was action. Someone got up on a chair, tried to raise his voice above the rest. We knew, yes we knew. Did he really need to tell us so vigorously? Merrick took off his hat and bowed to him. Someone took the hat from his hand and passed it round. We all put in our beer money, gave our all. The man and the chair seemed to melt away. It was at some late sobering hour that the purchaser of the beer decided it was time to rustle up a bit of recuperation. Alas all money was gone. So was the chair man. By deduction from evidence all too sadly gathered, discovery was made that the man on the chair – and nobody knew how he had got there – was talking on behalf of the Communist Party, thence had gone all our money.

The piano was dragged out into the backyard, set up between Arthur's home-built studio and David's cottage. Next day when the dancing was over and the sun was high in the sky, Merrick strode forth and found his piano there, lifted its lid gracefully and proceeded to play his accustomed music at his accustomed hour.

The Fifties were in their stride. The new configuration was taking shape. Group shows, one-man shows,

cross-pollination of the salons and studios was underway.
Wives were bringing forth babies. The new generation of
painters was fledged – youth in flight, that youth of such
certainty without security, such passion without prying
eyes, such purpose without prospect of reward.

Danila Vassilieff made his entry into our scene when
in 1952 the first makeshift Blackman exhibition was
pinned up on the coach-house walls. He stood, hard-
bodied and prescient like one of his own stone sculptures,
in our kitchen, that kitchen which had been the old stable.
We were honoured at his coming. We knew his myth, this
Cossack adventurer who had once eaten the head off a
parrot in the frenzy of a sword dance, had loved women
mille tre, was still teaching painting to schoolchildren, up
on the Murray now. He brought me a posy of flowers,
bowed like a courtier at their giving and thereby dismissed
me from the conversation. *Sois belle et tais toi*. He had wise
things to say to the wild young painter. He stood with his
back to our good German combustion stove, set under the
old chaff chute, and said: 'I've been up to Sydney . . . met
friends I had known twenty years ago . . . now all
achieved their lives' ambitions . . . shockin' thing!'

$\mathcal{L}$IFE CLASS LIFE

The shock happens the first time. You feel this must be a dream, the kind you cannot wake from. This is really me — sitting here without a stitch of clothing on, naked, motherless nude, starkers — up on a dais in front of a room full of unknown people. It is real. It is true. What would the neighbours say, your dear old grandmama . . . 'Shocking, shocking!' Then you become real. You are no ordinary undressed damsel. You are a statue in flesh and bone, a landscape in anatomical form, a still life in living state, a traditional life class model.

My father died when I was three. 'Daddy's gone to Heaven.' But I saw his clothes still in the wardrobe. He had gone to Heaven without them. A great truth came upon me. Angels are all nuddies. So, artist's model, I sit here in birthday suit, in angel suit. I sit here as anonymous as on an operating theatre table. Only my shape matters, my solidity, my corporeal substance disposed in structure of limb and torso, head and haunch.

This first life class was at East Sydney Tech. The

teacher was a quiet man hovering about his students, speaking in reassuring sotto voce to me to set the pose, Godfrey Miller.

In those few months I lived in Sydney in 1950 I posed for quite a few classes, for Datillo Rubbo in his studio full of Italian vowels and Umbrian light; for Desiderius Orban in his turpsy studio at the Quay; for a young John Olsen with friends in a garage at Waverton; for Yvonne Audette in a swanky Rose Bay house as all twelve disciples in her travelling scholarship entry; for Thea Proctor and friends in a high Victorian studio in Grosvenor House. This was one evening after a day's sunbaking nude in a friend's courtyard. I had a fiery blushing bottom to show for it. 'Never mind,' said Thea. 'Don't sit on it, dear, just let's mute down the tone' — and she dusted me delicately with a small and scented powder puff to a rosy hue, a paler shade of madder.

When I took up modelling full time in Melbourne, I was no novice. I had come to enjoy the role. It suited my independent spirit. I posed, I got paid. I honed my love of solitude into a skill of still performance. I had meditation thrust upon me and sat contorted into what I later recognised as yoga poses. I listened to the master of each class as he went from board to board, drawing each student towards his own way of handling pencil, charcoal stick, conté crayon or paint-dipped brush. I learned to draft my pose to fit the purpose of the method. I took a craftsman's pride in arranging the pose to suit the class, holding it for long periods without moving more than a breath, or repositioning into quick-change poses like stills of a movement. I kept a coded notebook in which I planned my repertoire on standing, reclining, sitting on stool, on chair, on tussock, on mat, my backs, fronts, sides, always the different planes of ankles, knees, hips, ribs, wrists, elbows, shoulders, head, the planes inclined, counterpointed, reciprocated. I was left alone to use my imagination. I got to know the styles and teaching methods of the prevailing art schools. I met a lot of painters and got to understand the workings of their studios. I was making my own mud map of this territory of 'the art world' to which I had been given in marriage. I found my own niche in that exciting world of Melbourne art in the Fifties.

There were three theatres of life class in Melbourne: firstly the Gallery School in classic academy style still with some postwar rehab students among the throng; secondly, the city and suburban techs running more commercial art courses; then the private, mainly evening, classes of particular masters, societies or dilettante groups. Sometimes an artist hired a private model for his own work. Early in the piece I was lucky enough to meet up with Joan Britten, long-time model, who showed me the ropes. Our shapes and lives were so different that we took to each other at once. Joan was twice my age, tall, lean, tanned, lazy, a figure from a Tropic island. She lounged about happily in a sunny upper room in an East Melbourne terrace house become residential, cooked on a landing gas ring; was well served by a corpulent French chef who brought her home spatchcocks, lobsters, lemon meringues, and dragged her mattress down on the floor to stop it squeaking. She was an Irish–German mix and read me lengths of Joyce, especially *Finnigan's Wake*. We fully booked ourselves into Tech and Gallery classes then swapped about, benefit all round.

Gallery School had tradition. Students spent a couple of years there studying painting under professional painters with intention to become one themselves. The gallery itself opened at ten o'clock, classes began at the gentlefolk hour of a quarter past ten. I came in through the revolving door at the main entrance, had a word to the familiar guards who also spent their days in silent pose. Past the screens of Blake etchings, a different one peered at each morning, then out through the 'No Entry', to the marble staircase to the studios above. Some days I entered sharp at ten o'clock, thick scarf wound about the head, fresh from visit to the City Baths a block away for indulgence in a grand sixpenny hot bath and washing of my long blonde hair, to sit and dry my tresses before the scratching oil heaters while the students casually arrived.

The first Monday morning was spent in setting up the pose that would be the subject for the ensuing fortnight. Everyone, all dozen in the room, had to find their particular spot on the floor with aspect to satisfy their need – a move to better suit one inevitably led to dissatisfaction of another – canvasses primed, palettes laid out, Barbara pigments replacing Joan pigments. The walls were impasto with a random dung patina of wiped-down brushes and thick with paintings by students from the last hundred years. Three banks of eyes watched – the portraits from the wall, the students at their canvasses, I from my fixed point. I looked also into the past of childhood remembered, the present of shopping list and possible weekend party guests, a future of great paintings, coming not from these before me, rather from a secret painter left behind at home in the coach-house loft, painting twelve hours a day but one of no school, he who was referred to in those days as 'Mrs Blackman's husband'.

The master painters – William Dargie, Roland Wakelin, Alan Sumner and Murray Griffin – had their own studios further along the passage from which they emerged periodically to tutor their students in Still Life or Life studios in the way of a doctor perusing his ward of patients – paintings in states of emergency treatment, steady progress or revival tactics. Dargie once said quite audibly to a student with reference to my small breasts, 'They may look like pimples, but do try to plump them up in your painting'. I toyed with the idea of bringing him in the foam rubber bosoms that I used to wear tucked into my swimsuit. Griffin seemed always to erupt, hand clapped to forehead, as from a Dostoevsky novel in search of epiphany. In winter I sat between two heaters – and that burning curiosity for life that stirs my blood kept my inner being also warm.

It was the custom at Gallery School for students to work up a sketch into a completed painting over the summer vacation, these to be exhibited in a bay of the main gallery. In 1952 the rural idyll produced by Clif Pugh, Barbara lying blissful in a sunny pasture, gave rise to rumours about how I had spent my 'last summer of happiness'. 'Far too nice a story to be denied' was my stock answer to any such speculation. However my darling mother-in-law Daisy, unacquainted with the art world, came home from the exhibition highly indignant. 'They gave first and second prize to that skinny little dark girl' (my friend, indeed bridesmaid, Anna) 'and only third to you – and you've got much Lovelier Legs than her!' Miss Lovely Legs was the cinema circuit beauty queen title at that time.

Architects at the Tech had occasional life classes, awkward with embarrassment. 'All problems of form are solved in the human form. Every shape is balanced, every line fulfilled. By drawing the contours, elevations, facades of the human form you learn to draw all that you will ever encounter.' These age-old words fell on spirit-level ears. There were also costume classes which I disliked. They were less anonymous and paid less. However, in my first year I was endowed with an elegant, romantic, full-length pink wool-de-chine nightdress, a wedding present, far too beautiful a garment to wear to bed where, in any case, as on dais, so in sleep. Robed in its drapes, I graced the dais many times. Some years later my aunt, that whiz of a dressmaker, made me a summer dress that was much admired. Sleeveless, with squared cape collar and box-pleated skirt, a good sculptural shape, its seersucker material in checkerboard pattern of navy striped and green circled squares on white ground. The effect was a precursor of Op art, forebodings of Bridget Riley. It was a popular design hazard, requested year after year for final year students' costume exam, even though I got thinner and it stretched baggier.

Once the cartoon actually happened. A young man gave me his seat in a crowded tram. As we stood together to alight at the stop for the Tech, he said innocently, 'Oh hello, I didn't recognise you with your clothes on.' The tram moved off looking over its shoulder in dismay. The incident is reminiscent of an experience of my Scottish grandmother over a century ago. As a photographer's colourist she had worked for days on a portrait, peering intently into the features. In her lunch hour, out in the street, she happened to see the wearer of the face walking toward her and, spontaneously, she bowed. The man's face reddened, beyond her pigment, and he sought to have her arrested for soliciting.

Many lunch hours were spent going by tram or train from Tech to Tech, with railway platform lunches. At Caulfield there was, for all its modern institutional building, a homely air. Here I was invited into the staff room and took up the role of honorary tea lady. One member of staff, Len Williams, in that first year, deliberated whether to send his brilliant guitar-playing seven-year-old son John over to study with world-famous Segovia in Italy. Gladly he did. A 'mature-age student', Marie Buesst, frequented one class and brought her patient obedient labrador with her. On several occasions when I was indisposed, he proved a good understudy, obligingly taking up his pose on the dais absolutely unmoving until he heard His Mistress' Voice. I was always, on close acquaintance, scrounging old clothes for paint rags and superseded telephone books as palettes for my housebound studio husband, who was amused one day to find himself wiping down his board with Marie's husband's underpants, Tristan Buesst being then the Chairman of Trustees of the Gallery.

Ben Croskell at Caulfield was probably the most humane and humble teacher of all I met. His love was lithography and he spoke so eagerly about it that I evolved one of my great schemes. By now in the thick of the eager young painters in Melbourne, I decided lithography would be good for them all. I arranged for Croskell to mount a Thursday evening class at Melbourne Tech, an evening when I worked a sculpture class there, and rounded up the boys for it – Charles, Arthur Boyd, John Brack, Fred

Williams, Harry Rosengrave, Tate Adams and Len French. Moreover at each 'rest', robed in my customary Japanese kimono, imperial gold dragon shimmering on its back, I strode one floor up and checked that they were all present and lithographing industriously. Much burgeoned from that seed sown.

At that sculpture class I posed on a roundabout dais, a standing pose offering three-dimensional interest. The students stood all round at plinths shaping their wet clay, also moving around. Sometimes a clay cold hand, direct from shaping mass of thigh, axis of shoulder blade, would land questioningly on my warm and unsuspecting flesh. I felt like the girl in the Beatles song – I worked my 'sixteen clubs a day', meaning often weekly six days and five evenings.

My sweetened memories are punctured by a diary entry recently rediscovered. In 1952 we had been staying up in Queensland for six weeks and were due to return to Melbourne life.

I had gone to bed sad to tears at the thought of becoming a model again, the idea repulsive to the point of impossibility. All night the green taffeta eiderdown kept slipping off. I dream: I go in desperation from one life class to another trying to pose. Every dais I mounted was green, and began to soften and swell until it was a great slippery cushion. If I did a standing pose, it was like trying to keep my balance on a great back of some restless animal so that I kept falling with the clumsiness of a faint. If I sat, then I sank further and further into the mossy marsh of it and pillowy hills rose up around me until I was quite out of sight. The students got angrier and the instructors very stern, my poses more ordinary, more of a failure. Reclining, I gradually rolled off on to the floor. With every pose the tension caused pain, such as a difficult pose causes only in the last few intolerable minutes.

Friday afternoons, Saturday mornings and afternoons, I worked for George Bell at his Toorak house school. The separate studio building took up all the backyard of an ordinary suburban brick veneer house. Fee-paying quality students came.

George was a bulky bull terrier of a man, dogmatic, prejudiced, self-styled sole authoritative conveyor of modern art to Melburnians, scornful of the Max Meldrumites and the Montsalvat Jorgensonians, utterly contemptuous of the John Reed Contemporary Art Society artists, particularly pejorative towards young upstarts who had the temerity to set themselves up as painters without benefit of art school of any kind. 'Mrs Blackman's husband' didn't warrant a mention other than as some aberration that misled this poor lady. 'This poor lady' was nonetheless his preferred model because of 'the range of splendid poses she gives us', and was herself tactful enough, over those hot Saturday lunches shared with the master and his wife, to steer the conversation to his favourite and safe subjects, map reading and home winemaking.

Roger James at Swinburne was certainly the most dramatic teacher, given to extravagant elaborate withering speeches intended to discourage and deter his students from the path of art. Avuncular, he would make a brutally honest assessment of their work in Edwardian accent and stage whisper. 'You know this drawing is utterly dreadful. Look as I might, I can see no glimmer of hope whatsoever. The line, the shading, no sign of any talent or intelligence anywhere. I don't know why you drag yourself along here week after week.' He would then move on with similar encouragement to the next victim. 'Why do your parents allow you to come here wasting your time and their money? Don't they know about knitting mills and jam factories – or even babies?' Of course he himself had never had anything to do with such things, had probably done his drudgery in some repertory theatre. Given his lapses in punctuality, I was familiar enough with his style and students to start them off. Sometimes I would even monologue his most familiar speeches just to make them feel at home. One day he came silently into the room and let me carry on. 'Really no need for me to stagger in at all,' he mused ruefully. My being late, however, irritated him. I lived five minutes walk – or gallop – up the road but, when the ABC radio 8.45 a.m. book reading of *Little Dorrit* was on, I had to hear each episode through. 'For God's sake,' he would say, 'I'll get the book and sit here and read it to you myself, if only you'll get yourself up arrayed on this dais in time, to encourage these dreadful lazy people to lift their pencils.'

The triangle of room for dressing, created by the positioning of the dais across one corner, was equipped with rickety chair, perhaps a nail for the gown, a broken piece of mirror, a tat of floor mat on which to stand, a rail strung with cast-off curtains to provide both variety of drapes and screen. Every item was of cubbyhouse scrap and ignominy. Even so, it was constantly pillaged so that the triangle space awaited the model like a bare cell. Once I took revenge. In the opposite corner of the studio stood all term a table cluttered with jugs, paper knife, books, ornaments and wax fruits, its green cut velvet undercloth, although dusty, for me highly useful as a cover. I took it. What a furore. I had vandalised the term's painting still-life tableau. Impossible, when I honestly restored the green cloth, alas now laundered, to replace all those significant objects in exactly their former position. The painter I lived with often painted jugs and fruit and tablecloth, but he got the job done all in one day.

Sometimes I was posed as in the three on the Mount of Olives – me between Homo and Hobo, skeleton and cylinders-cubes-spheres block man both mimicking my pose. The model as problem of space and form, the model as impersonal anonymite, the model as mute in the room's conversation, all conspire to make her human entity out of sight, out of mind. Students evaporated instantly a class finished, abandoning the poor model, her human beingness quite overlooked, left her struggling into her numerous layers of winter clothes behind her modest screen while she heard the front door slammed closed, locked and bolted.

At the private classes, I enjoyed the company, made some friends. Ola Cohn hosted Friday evening life class, people coming by invitation, word of mouth recommendation. I loved her house utterly. It had originally been the headquarters of Cobb & Co. coaches, its spacious cobbled courtyard on to Gipps Street in East Melbourne. Ola had made its large stables below and spread of low lofts above into accommodating studios and private living rooms. She was a big flourbag of a woman, healthy as bread, strong as a millstone, working at her figures indoors and out with the abundant confidence of a housewife making her loaves. Stairway newels were carved. Headstones marked the garden graves of successions of birds, cats and lizards. She welcomed me one day by asking my advice about a boy figure whose genitals were then in her moulding hands. 'Do you think I should crisp it up a bit?'

Everything at Ola's was, like her generous self, larger than life-size. The dais was higher, the combustion stove chunkier, the chairs wider, the cats huge. A happy humming atmosphere prevailed. Afterwards she served cocoa and biscuits for those who liked to stay.

The life studio backed on to a small lane and had a door through which Ola pushed her garbage bin. One night my husband slunk like a shadow down the lane and noiselessly mounted the bin to peer in to see if the pose were ending and wife ready for collection. A strong hand grasped him. Police took Peeping Tom in tow. He did seem too young and lurky to really have a wife. Loud knocking awoke life drawers from their dreams of creation. Presented at the door, husband, recognised by Ola, was invited in like a visiting prince, but his escort coldly forbidden to set foot over the threshold or cast an eye within.

The venerable Victorian Artists' Society had their Victorian palace of a School of Arts in East Melbourne. Here the Vic Arts had its old worldly air. People went there for whom painting was a lifelong hobby. Sometimes others gravitated there for whom life class was a peep show. Their uninitiated manners were soon obvious.

Cessation – as for the Hallelujah Chorus on the Stock Exchange floor – model bade to robe up, intruder to leave. One evening a last-minute stand-in model modestly wore a blue bathing suit. This embarrassed the regulars. Len French at his donkey worked away ignoring the bathing suit. However, when he looked up, he saw that every other drawing wore a blue suit. Furtively he rolled up his work and silently stole away. Fred Williams turned up everywhere. He did stacks of life drawings, a source of wonderment to the plumbers who one day burst drunkenly into his studio over their workshop, footprinting their investigations.

The model is an enigma to those outside the art world. On visits home to Brisbane my occupation was never mentioned, and archived letters of the time have no reference to it. Others saw it as bread-winning casual labour, but nothing like an art form in itself. Within a year I decided the five shillings an hour pay should increase and, for the first time, used the press for my purpose. The photographer leapt to the bait, in for the kill of a nude pictorial. I grasped a blanket around my shoulders and refused to smile for the dickie bird, saying 'This is not a smiling matter'. The photograph story came out 'Bare Wage for a Bare Model'. The hourly rate went up.

Husband Charles never drew me as posed nude. In the late Fifties he was invited to contribute to an exhibition of nude work. He asked if a drawing of a baby without clothes was eligible.

The intimacy of the life class is sacrosanct. I had the reputation of being remote, the ice maiden's daughter, the intellectual, often because I was unable to meet the gaze of another. My sight lack kept me distant. I was the model for whom the artist's work held no interest but for whom the right to do his best was my raison d'être. In fact the good model does speak to the class. She speaks in a silence of eternal form. She depersonalises her body to allow it to be personalised by the painter. She becomes one with all those patient unknown women who sat before painters and became Madonnas, Venuses, Madame Olympies. They transcended name and identity and transformed into images in art. They offered their present moment to the gaze of the painter who transfigured it, in the light of his past and the presence of his love for his work, into a metaphor that passed on to the future. The model is integral to the painter's understanding of his art. She is the focus of the student class, the portfolio of the mysteries of form. Her own content is her secret. The body is the noun, her self the verb, the adjectives all the painter's. The model has in her power the levelling of the spirit of those who draw her, to heights or depths. Yet it leaves her un-possessed, free to her own thoughts, private in her teem-ing solitude.

$\mathscr{T}$HE GOOD SHIP MORA

The ancient wisdom of the enneagram — that diagram of two interlocking triangles within the circle that graphs the interiority or magic power of seven, the number of becoming — demonstrates that for a creative act or new configuration to take place, there must be an element of the unknown entering in in order to animate the known elements. So there we were in Melbourne in the Fifties, the current of the new wave of painters, in confluence with those active figures of the Forties art revolution who had not been swept away by the end-of-decade diaspora to Europe, needing some steering, some ship in which to sail, some destination of intent.

Europe gave them to us, movers of the new force, disguised at their arrival as a salesman for the new Continental Chicken Noodle Soup and a Parisian seamstress. Georges and Mirka Mora had come from the heart of that war-wounded Europe which we in our protected isolation were only slowly coming to understand. Both Jewish, Georges had worked in the Underground, living

on grapes (for which reason he never ate fruits or took
country holidays thereafter), smuggling people out to
Switzerland and later managing camps of displaced children. Mirka had fled by night with her mother from Paris
and spent her girlhood years hidden in the forest, emerg-
ing a mistress of invention untainted by formal education.
Postwar, they frequented the Parisian theatre world but
yearned for a new life away from the presence of dark
shadows. A toss of a coin brought them to Melbourne,
Singapore's loss.

City dwellers, they rented a basement studio with
low upper room at number 9 (Paris end of) Collins Street.
Years later they found a letter, 'Smike to Bulldog', in which
Streeton writes happily to Tom Roberts delighted that he
too would take up a studio in Grosvenor Chambers which
he had bought. Much later Mirka found a photograph of
Streeton leaning upon the mantelpiece of the long-familiar
fireplace at Mirka's Studio in number 9. But these prevailing illuminatory ghosts remained unknown to us in the
Fifties.

Sunday Reed discovered Mirka, directed to this
maker of original costume by the music critic John Sinclair
with whom Mirka, in joint shyness, had shared a sofa at a
stranger's soirée. 'Down at the end of a dingy corridor and
steps so dark you fall down, sitting with an infant playing
on the floor and surrounded by waves of cloth and pins,
beautiful as a young fawn.' Sunday never wore the dress
that Mirka made for her. Instead she hung it on her wall
along with the paintings by Nolan, Tucker and Sam Ateyo.
She and John sensed an acquisition to the 'French flu' that
pervaded Heide after their end-of-Forties sojourn in

France. By this time Charles and I had met the Moras in the company of John Yule and his French mistress Edith and I asked Georges naively after his first foray at the court of Heide, 'Are there such people as the Reeds in Paris?' 'Of course,' he said with an unfamiliar urbanity. 'Lots of them.' I had much to learn. I had not yet encountered the Verdurins of Proust.

Georges was off to Adelaide with his two suitcases, one containing his continental square pillow without which he could not sleep safely, the other full of the packets of the new 'Continental' comestible. So it was Mirka who ventured to the suburbs, to our coach-house in Hawthorn, in the company of her close small friend, the infant Phillippe. She had an immediate affinity with Charles and his schoolgirl paintings, almost leapt into the picture plane herself, leapt out into the world of their new founding with the idea that she would at once turn her studio apartment into a gallery and exhibit them. This should happen in a few soon weeks, when beds and things were moved to the room upstairs or to the tiny kitchen two steps below and walls painted – all this despite an official first Blackman exhibition, of schoolgirl paintings, scheduled to open at the most prestigious city gallery in a few weeks time, and her own second childbirthing.

Their urgent impish rule-breaking spirits flared up together. A spark was struck, audacity to have two shows of the same subject one straight after the other, one up front, the other decidedly underground. After a few days of elaborating this wild plan, we all realised we had to smooth it down for Georges' approval. He was adept at taming Mirka's enfant terrible escapades. Charles and I circled nervously outside the Aladdin Gift Shop corner telephone box at the due time to phone for his decision, fearing that he might be, after all, the prototype Jewish businessman with only token gesture to the presence of art. Our doubts were blown away. Georges, as ever after, grasped and elevated the daring idea, while grounding it in his realistic caution.

So in 1953 Charles Blackman burst upon the public scene with two shows, one in May at the Peter Bray Gallery, one in August at the new Mirka Studio. Most Melbourne galleries then were on 'do it yourself' lines, most attached to furniture shops, so attachment to a couturier's was not so strange. But Mirka, with her flamboyant dress, 'sharming axont' and invitation to coffees and cake, her desire to meet new people and naiveté of response to them, was something quite new.

One good spark ensures another. Mirka's Studio became a centre of gravity (and much levity), the place of exhibitions, meetings, parties, dramatic moments, tableaux vivants, plots, confrontations, improvisations, last suppers, diagnoses and prognostications, exhibition after exhibition – vortex of our marvellous lives. Endlessly, endlessly we sat around on those two steps down into the telephone-booth-sized kitchen. Saturday after Saturday Georges carried in cases of 'cheapest and best' Agostino wine. Ping after ping of doorbell admitted the unexpected welcomed visitor.

The dramatis personae of the Fifties was drawn on to this new stage, the overture struck. I was moving into my life's role of catalyst, the stepping into an empty space with a certain feeling engendering something new to come into being. We were an Underground needing to surface. A second wave for change, a re-firing of the Contemporary Art Society, was called for. The exhibition of modern art brought to Melbourne from Europe by Basil Burdett just before the war threw into action the momentum of the Forties. Now this after-war European sophistication of the Moras thrust into focus the artists of the Fifties.

Georges and Mirka offered us new sites. They were happeners, not owners. They had lost families, home, land of birth, friendships, memorabilia of youth, and lived in the focus of the present, its possibilities. Georges never personally owned much more than that pillow, a change of clothes and the bedside book he was reading. Good food and good conversation, that was his stock in hand. He hosted endless discussions in the awareness that politics – not just the party politics of government, but the politics of time and event, opportunity and action – were the pivot of civilised life. Bails Myer once said of him that he was 'a man who made Melbourne into a city'. Certainly he 'grew us up' as assuredly as Mirka never let us escape our child-hearted spontaneity.

So the new C.A.S. foundation meeting in 1953 happened at Mirka's Studio, a calling of the clans. The elders, John and Sunday Reed and Danila Vassilieff, stepped into this new venue from their formidable past, once more unto the breach, and took office on the new committee. With them came John Perceval, Joy Hester, Arthur Boyd, Neil Douglas and other veterans, Barrie Reid and Laurence Hope from the Brisbane Barjai, Clif Pugh and other rehab Gallery students, migrant sculptors Gunter Stein, Julius Kuhn and Clifford Last, and the new runners Laurence

Daws and Erica McGillchrist from Adelaide, Bob Dickerson a Sydney ring-in, Ian Sime with his new language of the abstract and precise wife Dawn, odd balls and evens of the new exhibitors, many, many. All crowded into that expectant room. Some who were asked held back, waiting to see if it were kosher before stepping aboard. Others like Len French, suspicious even of his own shadow, always stood outside looking on. I magnetised inevitably into the position of Treasurer, incurring for years endless hours of office, lengthy telephone calls, inflated crises, celebrations of success.

It was the insistent belief of John and Sunday Reed, perhaps the most important ingredient of the era, that art sources not only from the creator of it but also from the audience that demands it, a subtle fermentation between the conceiver and the receiver, those who encourage and those who take courage to create. Artist and layman always carried equal weight in the Society, men and women equal power.

That was how it was in our young lives. We worked flat out, the painters on the job twelve hours or more a day, those with jobs half the night. I worked as a life-class model doing classes, in term six days and five nights a week. On Sundays I wept because my husband would not stop working. Time was boundless in youth that flung us out of bed before dawn to walk for miles through streets to reach the Victoria Market as stalls were set; youth that stretched our nights discovering each other's thoughts till we could delve no deeper. We quilled our questions, read one another's favourite books, loved one another's minds. We moved by leaps and lulls. Laurence Daws as herald burst into one party night in '56, cleared a path to the gramophone and changed the dance. Haley's Comets sounded out loud and clear and we rocked around the clock for parties ever after; in late '62, he and Brett Whiteley burst into our London terrace house and charged straight to the television set – 'It's all happening' – there were the Beatles express delivery arriving over the horizon.

Mirka's Studio became a home away from home for us who were used to the studio being the centre of the habitat, meals and children fitting in among and around, reek of paint and turps intermingling with soups and boiling nappies, viewing of new works taking priority. Mirka, who had brought four canvasses of her own from Paris, never stopped painting amid it all, even if, at ping of doorbell, hair was combed, easel bundled into back lavatory. Our studios were generally as big as the rest of the house put together and their supplies devoured at least equal share of the family income. We were a generation who married early, aware of the gaps in the lives of those before us for whom the war had kept marriage at bay or precipitated 'mistakes'. A woman was 'on the shelf' if not married by twenty-one. Most of my new wife friends had several babies before they had that key of the door – babies born in bed-sits, makeshift backroom flats, converted lofts. Sales of paintings were rare. Swapping was more common. Painters showed spontaneous admiration and fellow-feeling for each other by swapping shirts. 'Shirts off!' became a term of salute.

Right from the beginning of the decade we women wore a new garb – jeans, T-shirts, Roman sandals, bought for two and sixpence off a board at the markets, and wide elastic belts. We ironed our jeans to a shine and soft-starched our cotton shirts. I myself kept an array of splendid wide-striped, embroidered, tartan, tricolour ribbons for my ponytail. Alanah Coleman, a shocker, was the first to wear zip fly jeans. Everyone – except me – had a sewing machine and whipped up a swirling party dress from cheap cotton, gingham or ticking, corduroy or pinwhale, padded skirts common where central heating was not. We knitted. I cut out an ad for a continental doona, sold at just one place in Preston, cost eighty pounds, and dreamed of owning one, one day. We slept under a mound of half a dozen second-hand blankets, often overcoats on top. Bessie Smith sang to us of love O careless love and aprons worn up high. We knew the names of the three best abortionists in town and for their cost of thirty pounds, the hat was often passed around. The wisdom of the women decreed the Grattenberg ring, known affectionately as 'the wedding ring'.

Few photographs survive. Not many of us had cameras, let alone home movie devices. Some had old cars. Arthur Boyd's Dodge had its tyres stuffed with straw the day he went into Tye's to collect his Dunlop Prize and was hand-cranked in Bourke Street to start up for home. Almost everyone had a telephone because talk was of the essence. Before we could afford one, I used to go out for the night to a quiet phone box at the other end of Chrystobel Crescent with a kangaroo-high stack of pennies to make calls at fourpence a go. A friend of a friend cracked the code for making free calls through a roadside booth in Albury, but the fault on the line soon made its presence felt and was corrected.

As a gallery Mirka's Studio was not large. One short wall was given over to the entrance, steps down and steps up, the other to head-height windows, the two long walls broken by fireplace and back door. There was room for about twenty pictures. On occasion, double banked and rafter hanging, it impacted twice as many. The C.A.S. erupted with its 1954 alternative Royal Tour Exhibition and put Mirka's Studio on the map. 'The mother and father of all our angers and frustrations', the Menzies-mediocre art establishment, staged an exhibition at the Town Hall as part of its celebration of the visit of Our Queen, parading all the dead wood of the art landscape. We retaliated. Everyone put up toughest and best works and architect Jim Birrell brought out a bold glossy catalogue proclaiming protest. Mobs came, mockers and discoverers. Namatjira defected to us – but flanked by two plainclothes men.

Group and solo shows followed one after another. Celebrities joined us as openers – Larry Adler, Hepzibah Menuhin, Malvern Douglas, Sally Gilmour, Isaac Stern, Gene Krupa. After openings we partied on into the night.

We made theatre. Aroused by morning coffee odours, those who had slept over, dossing willy-nilly on cushions and mattresses, blinked into blurred reminiscence, took up positions of discourse. My arms of Morphe happened one night to be those of an innocent young architect to whom I had been trying to explain the difference between bisexual and hermaphrodite. He wore oxblood shoes and, after a few red wines, sported a rosily luminous nose. Now he was rubbing the one and looking for the other when my husband accosted him. 'You slept with my wife last night?' 'Well, yes, no, sort of, nothing like –' came stammered reply. 'Did you fuck her? Yes or no?' 'Absolutely no.' 'Then you have insulted my wife. She is too attractive a woman to be treated like that. I'll have you put on trial.' Thus began one of our prolonged mock trials, everyone present being given a role, accuser or defender, judge or interrogator. These trials went on dead-pan for hours, an improvised hilarity, often with spur of the moment costume. Newcomers were allowed no conversation that was not relevant to the hearing. Someone who burned a cigarette hole in a rug was up on trial for arson, someone appearing with a new haircut stood accused of impersonation with intention to spy.

Sometimes the Mirka Studio entourage went on circuit. On Sunday afternoons Gertie and Klaus Anschel, the handsome Viennese couple who kept The Little Nut Shop, the best confectionery in town (and later kept one of the best craft shops in London), held open house. We decked ourselves out, sat in their elegant rooms, discussing the plays, concerts, exhibitions, playing chess, dancing out on their deck, flirting, eating the meals of wieners and sauerkraut, meatballs and noodles, that they bountifully cooked. Sometimes we took cushions and went out in rowing boats from Studley Park. Neil Douglas the potter always left any party early, his homeward sack slung over his shoulder, in time to catch the last train to Bayswater, back to his garden.

At our first visit there we felt, on that long walk up from the station, that we were chasing the wild goose through cow paddocks and barley grass until, as though at some magic sign, suddenly the garden was upon us – in through a wicket gate, into a tree of life that caught you in its branches, its blossoms and leafage, its arcadian perfumes, its undergrowth pelt of spice leaves and small flowers. Neil loved to be come upon by visitors, burrowing or kneeling over among the foliage or stooping to scythe his grass, deft as a barber. The bosoming mounds of lawn were formed to enfold and rivulet the rain, when it fell, in many directions, for this was a waterless garden and for him it flowered in all seasons. For Neil, landscape and foliage patterning were paintings already and he drew the painters' attention to them through his vegetative eye.

His house, discovered like a face hiding behind tumbling tresses, was a little old Lutheran church covered with draping vines, once derelict at this end of his mother's farm. Inside it had the tree-trunk smell of drying herbs and scrubbed wood. His infant children, with hair as pale and curly as the Shirley Temple locks of woodwork shavings, played quietly between large decorated bowls on the low shelf, one of nuts and one of eggs, indigenously hammering the one but not the other. Neil, tall, home-grown, elfin in poise of movement, voice ground soft, played the old organ, made sage or peppermint tea, concocted a meal out of whatever he could rustle up from the garden eked out with barley.

Neil's garden became our weekend Eden. We swarmed up from the station or landed in droves when people had cars. We lay sprawled out in the sun, peering into the secretive shadows, crushing aromatic leafage between fingers, reading poems, unveiling intimate parts of our lives to one another, arguing, nibbling away at pungent herbs. The children tumbled among the pottery teapots and cups. I drank, and had pointed out to me the painted tail within the cup lead down into a rat at its base.

This garden oasis among the pasture paddocks seemed by its intensity of detail somehow huge, like a drop of water under a microscope.

One day Fred Williams, Hal Hattam and a few others scrambled through to the paddock and set up a game of cricket, the Lysterfield Hills calm in their distance. Both later painted it. Once a whole Mirka Studio Saturday night arrived the next day noon, twenty hungry people. The small wheelbarrow was trundled out and all hands to the dig to pile it with potatoes. Mirka proposed a parsley soup, parsley gathered not by sprig or posy but in such armfuls that the winter doorstep mass of bush parsley was all uplifted. Such a tasty, rustic soup resulted.

Momentum gathered. The C.A.S. grew large, hired first Tye's, the largest city gallery, and then, the next year, persuaded Preston Motors to give over their street corner plate-glass showroom for the exhibition. In the Forties Bert Tucker had once got one painting into a Collins Street dress shop window. Now the city had the whole C.A.S. in its midst. Ralph Richardson opened the show. Grist became yeast. Joy Hester and John Perceval came back on to the exhibiting scene. Arthur Boyd came back from a visit to Hermannsberg Mission with a new dream, the black man and his bride. Mirka went professional and opened her own café in Exhibition Street.

Terrace tables with gingham cloths, *très Parisien*, were put out on the footpath. Each time the Council ordered them removed. Mirka got the first espresso coffee machine in Melbourne, a Gaggia, and from it a black eye at first use. We, who had enjoyed the bounty of her cooking for so long, now came and paid, and stayed. Madame Otier from

Georges' Underground days came on scene and gratefully served below. The soups normandie or onion appeared hot in lidded pottery ramekins. Pâté, coarse country-style, fresh mayonnaise, duck in orange, creme caramel, dinkum homespun French. The room above was 'family only' where we could take wine, every night a birthday. The C.A.S. meetings were held there. Gradually they became stormier. Pigs is not equal. Barrie Reid and I put out a broadsheet, he informing the Fifties' members of the feats of their forebears, I discovering – foretaste of oral histories – that the painters who argued so convincingly with thumping of table, raising of voice, were less wordogenic on the printed page.

Some paintings sold – to bigwigs – and the Gallery of Victoria actually bought a Bob Dickerson but took a nervously long time to pay, during which I censored Bob's 'punch on the nose' letters of demand. Among ourselves we knew that a lot of the paintings were good, but nobody in wildest imagination contemplated a latest model Mercedes car, one-man show at the New York Museum of Modern Art, sales to the Tate, high-price sell-out exhibitions and celebrity status, London houses and whirlwind European trips as a possibility in ten or twenty years time.

We scratched about. The news that in Japan an artist could get a part-time job and could have all his work photographed at State cost, astounded us. We Blackmans paid thirty shillings a week rent for our coach-house, used the City Baths, had water from an outdoor tap. John Brack, a most respectable and well-spoken person, applied for a housing loan and was rudely refused by a bank manager who explained that a loan to an artist was out of the

question and added consolingly that not even if it were
William Dobell himself – Dobell at home and Picasso
overseas being the everyman concept of a modern artist.
Arthur brought his tax return papers round to our coach-
house – I being treasurer and presumed intellectual – to
ask, since this was his umpteenth year of income below tax
level, whether he ought to add 'Will try harder next year'.
I was considered 'a woman of independent means' on
account of my blind pension.

Sunday Reed, when she saw a convincing gush of
paintings, would insert a small gift of money into the
works. We went off for a trip to Queensland early in the
piece with one such gift all spent on a plumber's leather
bag packed with tins of Dulux enamel. Charles sent back a
couple of dozen small paintings on board from Stradbroke
Island as evidence of need of more supplies. An answer
came, quoting the wisdom of Sweeney, then a child of
seven, who had remarked on their unpacking, 'Just practising, Sun,' and with injunction to 'lick those paint tins
clean'. The letter was on finest rice paper, no cheque. We
back-tracked to Melbourne, Charles to odd-job gardening,
me to the life modelling.

I took myself off monthly to two apparently secret
societies, the one partially and the other totally, uncon-
nected with the 'art world'. On chill Sunday nights, through
half-deserted streets, persons in overcoats carrying knee
rugs made their way through a side door of a church hall in
Chapel Street into a muttering retreat, there to be hosted by
Alex Berry and Kevin MacBeth into the thrill of contemporary music. They played records got in from America. Young
Barry Humphries was among us but our avidity was for

My Blackman image: detail from the Blue Alice, *1957.*
(Collection of the Art Gallery of Western Australia.)

Generations: my mother with Auguste,
me with Christabel, 1959.

Childhood: Auguste with Daddy Bear, 1960.

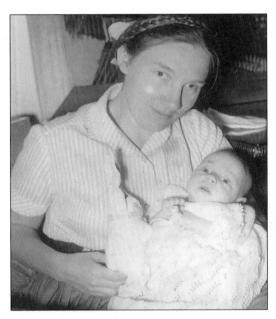

Motherhood: nursing Christabel, 1959.
(Courtesy of Queensland Newspapers.)

Charles Blackman: Barbara and Auguste, *sketch, 1957.*

Barbara Blackman: at Folkstone, 1963.
(Photo by Axel Poignant.)

Charles Blackman: at Folkstone, 1963.
(Photo by Axel Poignant.)

Family: outside 8 Southwood Lane, Highgate, 1963.
(Photo by Mary Boyd, Lady Nolan.)

Family: inside the house, London, 1963.
(Photo by Mary Boyd, Lady Nolan.)

Family posed: after Paris, Sydney, 1972.

Auguste and Daisy: Christmas Day, Sydney, 1974.
(Photo by Robert Walker.)

With my typewriter: working on Certain Chairs, *Sydney, 1968.*

listening not talking. To join the other group I was permitted to use the Scotch College private tram stop at Kooyong, thence to stumble up the path to the Association Hall, to fumble into a chair at meetings of the Guild for Professional and Business Blind, a mainly male affair. Occasionally the lady novelist Mary Mitchell joined us, formidable in her height, black apparel and stiletto umbrella with which she penetrated all obstacles. Ringleaders Hugh Jeffrey and Neil Westh, both teachers, honed me in on the courage and comedy required in our lives. Both groups, like the C.A.S., pounded away at closed doors.

Books were my craving. Charles read to me incessantly. Sometimes others: John Brack, when I was laid up with a burned foot, called in on me on the way home from school, and read me Beerbohm, Chesterton and Belloc. In mid-decade I found my way to talking books and the unlocking of doors to an inner life of my own. I was exploring my blindness, that isolation, that life sentence for a crime I had not committed, and chose for my first books *Penguin Island* and *The House of the Dead*. At the end of the decade I won my own personal travelling scholarship when I reached the UK talking book library.

The Mirka Café and the Preston Motors exhibition of the mid-Fifties were first steps before bigger strides, individual paths. Georges left the food company and bought into the Eastbourne Café in East Melbourne, a plain menu for its working-class local regulars, within cooee of our first tin-shed habitat, and, as it soon happened, the 1956 Olympic Games. He got a liquor licence for their duration but waited a couple of years for a permanent one. C.A.S. meetings were now held in the after-hours café.

The wisdom of Sunday Reed was that 'artists shouldn't have wives' and, on hearing of my first pregnancy, she endowed Charles with train fare and enough money to escape to Sydney, and then, upon his return, with baskets of fresh farm eggs, for use in his tempera painting, 'but throw the whites away'. Georges, however, gave Charles a regular evening job as a short-order cook at the Eastbourne, plenty of take-home leftovers. The Alice in Wonderland paintings, with their iconography of tables, chairs and teapots, woman changing shape, emerged with subtle tempera lustre. A couple of years later, a greyly lavender well-polished lady from the Society for Amelioration of Hardship among Indigent Persons of Talent and Scholarship knocked at our stable door. I held in check our eighteen-month-old child. Charles in his loft above stretched out on the floor, ear to a crack. After a lengthy interrogation, she gave me a promise that fifty pounds would be forthcoming to pay outstanding dentist and doctor bills and something over for a little pusher for the little one. Alas, her spinster tone of benefactress tinged with redress as, with due words of gratitude, I showed her to the door and, in something like defeat, she observed: 'And am I to presume you are yet again in a certain condition?' Joyously I was.

Georges, now president of the C.A.S., was in his stride, John Reed keeping pace. It was time for the Society to have its own Gallery of Contemporary Art, to mount survey as well as group and one-man shows. A warehouse in Flinders Lane was found, two upper floors of it. We moved in with a familiar procedure of cleaning out and wall scraping. Peter Burns, long-time secretary and visionary architect, long outgrown oxblood shoes, was given free range with the transformation. He cornered off the office space with panels of tinted Perspex, a new material, and proposed a wild and wonderful solution to the dreary old brick walls as hanging space. A metal lattice mesh in interlocking panels would skin the wall with an illusory grey shadowy form upon which paintings could be easily clipped and moved about.

The opening exhibition was an act of faith, a 'gift'. Each artist member presented a major painting for sale for support of the gallery. It was a splendid show. Doc Evatt, an old Reed friend from the Forties, returned from his stint as President of the United Nations (for part of which time painter Sam Ateyo had been his secretary), was to be the opener. Hopes were high.

All was ready. Hush of expectation prevailed. Almost time for the guests to arrive. A thud on the stairs below. The sandwich woman, carrying the tray of little cocktail offerings, had tripped, the cargo tipped. All was righted just in time. The Evatts came early to make survey. Just as first guests arrived, however, there was an ominous unanimous rumble from the walls, some last-hung painting being straw to the camel's back. The lattice did not hold, the panels came unstuck, the metal buckled. Peter, as on the deck of his ship, ordered all friends to the walls. We press our backs firmly against the quivering panels, forcing them to stay in their locks, while smiling expansively at arriving guests. We were magnificent. As the last guest left, we sagged – and the walls with their burden of paintings sagged down upon us.

John Reed took his place in the venture as gallery

director, reappearing out of his country ivory castle to be a city man again as in his lawyer days. At a committee meeting, with Capricornian practicality, I had asked, 'John, as director, are you prepared to sell a painting you do not like to a person you do not like?' 'Of course,' he said, in his 'down, Bonzo' voice used to the dog, 'it is part of the job.' On that first night, when David Wynn, a winemaker on the glamorous fringe of culture, came up to him to purchase the Charles Bush picture, he replied (in the Mr Grouser voice of 'Toy Town' in the beloved BBC Children's Hour), 'You ought to be ashamed of yourself.' Nevertheless the Gallery thrived. The shows went on; including the original Sid Nolan Ned Kellys, the first Blackman Alice show, the Perceval Lerderderg landscapes and the first of Boyd's Black Man and his Bride, a show by Bill Dobell who came in person, standing frail and famous in the middle of the room as long as he could bear it, and one by the newly dis-covered primitive Belgian painter and opal miner Henri Bastin, who stood a pot of brushes in place of the usual vase of flowers and subsequently made me a 'feel picture' out of string and bobbins.

Balancing this widening there was a centring. A pocket of painters took to *plein air*. As Sunday painters at Williamstown, an unsmart bayside suburb, they set up easels at the dry docks in somewhat removed homage to Turner who had lashed himself to the mast to experience storms at sea before he lifted his brush. Wives and children picnicked. The public gazed. One member of the public approached Arthur and plied him: 'Are you painting a pic-ture?' 'Do you come here often?' 'Do you like painting?' 'What do you do with them after?' Arthur replied monosyllabic with the patience of fly swatting, then went silent. Member of public approached Charles and got immediate swift reply: 'Piss off!' Member of public approached Perceval who parried. 'Would you like to be in my painting? Then stand way over there near that pier – and don't move.'

Charles never came to grips with this painting on the spot. At home he painted on paper a huge *bateau ivre* out of Williamstown, a contradiction that so annoyed Perceval that he lunged to snatch it off the wall. He was deflected – side-swiped by me wielding stool – and it was a first purchase for the Melbourne Gallery from the Gift show.

Times were changing. G.C.A. shows got major reviews. The National Gallery of Victoria got a new director, Eric Westbrook, who took our measure and mounted Perspective Exhibitions of local contemporary art. Enthusiasm grew with success. An Australian Museum of Modern Art with permanent and current exhibitions was now our goal, the transformation of Melbourne into a city with contemporary art sophistication. We had good shows and growing audiences. All we needed were the backers.

Georges' urbanity led us forward. 'We invite the most important businessmen in Melbourne, the *crème de la crème*. The others will follow. Just one prestigious event, not a splashy fund-raising dinner – bad taste. With our quality of work and our confidence we shall raise a lot of money from businessmen used to handling big projects who understand such things. You will see.' The day came. All the 'photographed living' were there. Dubonnet only was served with oysters, smoked salmon and rare roast beef. Speeches were made. Right things said. The spirit was rising in the room. John Reed, as director, came forward and asked for generous donations and himself pulled out his founding cheque already written and showed it – one hundred pounds. That was worse than all the walls falling down around us. Not a thousand, just a hundred – the one wrong word, gesture of someone too long out of the real world of finance. The effect was a trivialising, a touch that turned the balloon to lead. Shame and disappointment: the Museum at one damp spark fizzled into amateurism. Dick Seddon, then the chairman of the National Gallery Board, had been offering Georges every support but had to report that the hoped-for backers did not take a hundred-pound museum seriously. Georges tore his hair but no good came of it.

With the dispersion of C.A.S. members having shows in other states, other galleries, some travelling abroad, the centre gained centrifugal force. Tension flamed between figurative and non-figurative painters. Words flared. 'Faces have had it.' Tachism was a facet of abstract art. 'The Tachist Emperor has no clothes.' The Sydney virus of American-import abstract non-figurative painting was spreading south. Up at Clif Pugh's ever-expanding mudbrick mansion in the latest courtyard or inner dining hall built around a rock, or down at Arthur's first own-home at Beaumaris by the sea, or in the opened-out, glass wall on to flowering garden, house of the Percevals at Canterbury, discussion mounted, focused, became militant.

Art was about people, the human condition. It was more than pleasurable picture plane decoration. Figurative painting must take a stand. Seven 'brothers of the brush' took oath on it: Clif Pugh, David Boyd, John Perceval,

Arthur Boyd, John Brack, Bob Dickerson and, the youngest of the pack, Charles Blackman. Their argument needed an articulate authority figure as philosopher spokesman. Bernard Smith got the job. A movement took shape and name – the Antipodeans. They closed ranks and prepared for action. A manifesto was drafted. They laboured as on holy writ.

We wives went to meetings at first but, as the plotting of the outbreak Antipodeans Exhibition got serious, were refused entry because of our irritating habit of feeding babies and making commonsense suggestions at the height of the proceedings. This led Helen Brack to dub them 'The Secret Seven' or 'The Brotherhood of St Bernard'. We preferred our mother talk anyway.

John and Sunday stayed mostly at home, invited selected guests to Heide-style dinner and quiet fireside talk about the state of art, the lives and deaths of the Siamese cats, the dispute over Sweeney having to eat white bread at Geelong Grammar, and were the first to get a television set. Danila died. Mary and John Perceval, in their large solid Victorian house at Canterbury, found themselves a few doors away from the gynaecologist Hal Hattam and his elegant vivacious wife Kate – an immediate affinity. The families merged to become an oasis of daisy and lavender cottage garden beset with small blonde daughters, dinner tables of good roast dinners and robust talk. Hal presided over all our birthings and himself took up painting and took office on the C.A.S. committee.

Word came of Nolan's first show in London and the interest of the great Sir Kenneth Clark in work from the Antipodes.

The definitive Antipodeans came out with their mighty show in the middle of 1959, not at G.C.A. but at the largest available exhibition space in town, the gallery of the most hidebound old guard, the Victorian Artists' Society. Mattewilda Dodds, the black American singer, opened it. It was undeniably a demonstration of major painters producing major works. It was, however, accompanied by a manifesto – so dangerous and unnecessary that the brotherhood blushed individual denial of the hand that signed the paper.

Each of the Seven had seen the show as the beginning of a new movement. The shock was the recognition that it was the grand culmination of that decade of feeding from one another, visiting one another's studios, spurring on and outstripping themselves to heights of creation that now brought each to that point in his life where he was acknowledged proven, henceforward professional. All the paintings sold: maintain a trademark of excellence.

The climate for contemporary art was changed utterly. Professional commercial galleries sprang up in all the capital cities. Patronage of travelling scholarships brought on a diaspora. The Helena Rubenstein trumpet blew five times and at each blast a painter left for Europe, as from some farewell symphony. Georges became a professional restaurateur. At his now-licensed, newly named Balzac, with Perceval ceramic angel sculptures on the walls and David Boyd carafes carrying the wine, our Rubenstein departure was celebrated. We drank. We cheered. We danced – Mirka on the table seducing a most figurative bread roll. The good ship Mora had brought us to port.

PORTRAIT OF A FRIENDSHIP

I

I met Joy Hester in May 1951 soon after coming to
Melbourne and saw her for the last time in August 1960 a
few months before her death. For most of the intervening
time I lived in Melbourne. In that vital decade of my life,
Joy was the most vivid person, an amazing, abundant, reck-
less, irreverent consumer and creator of life, and a close
beloved friend. Joy was an utterly passionate, loving, tor-
mented creature, and what she was most passionate and
loving about was the ordinary life, the ordinariness of life
that was to her always extraordinary, a world of miracles
and wonder. She did not desire; she received. Whatsoever
drop of water fell upon her or grain of earth landed on her
doorstep, she put under the microscope of her great eyes
and imagination, and saw it as marvellous. With that
blonde hair, those huge orbs, those lips full and trembling
with words, a certain way of thinking from the hip, she had
no hope of passing for ordinary. She did great drawings and
some paintings, wrote moving poetry, but art was not

uppermost on her list of life's pursuits. Mothering and domesticity enthralled her. Art was somewhere on the list as one of the absorbing facets of life and the understanding of it, the giving back of it, that she threw herself into. This is not to say that she was not absolutely conscious of herself as an artist, and wholly professional in the way she went about it.

That first time I met her was in a scene so often to be repeated. A group was sitting around over a late lunch in the back parlour of Mrs Smith's Aladdin Gift Shop on the corner of Glenferrie Road and Chrystobel Crescent in Hawthorn. There was a front parlour behind the shop but this was reserved for the stacks of pictures awaiting frames or framed pictures awaiting collection. Picture framing was the 'back room' life of the Aladdin. Son Martin was the framer, the draughty two-storey back shed his place of manufacture.

Sitting around the late lunch table were inevitably the painters who had been promised their urgently needed framed pictures for nine o'clock that morning. It was an atmosphere of suspense and animation. Joy was in charge of the animation. Her theme was the incontrovertible evidence that the earth is flat, and to demonstrate this she was firing oranges across the table and letting people pick them up as they fell to the floor. She had an answer to any rational argument put to her. Rationality was the last thing in the world for which she had respect. To her it was abundantly clear that nobody really lives their life in any rational way. So why should rationality be assumed to run the God-made world? In the middle of all this a baby awoke and she opened her shirt and put it to the breast, transferring her ashtray from table to bundle top of baby, and having to respond in mid-flight of argument, from time to time, when Gray called out, 'Joy – tit!' to indicate that in her vehemence she had positioned her nipple way out of reach of their suckling babe weighed down by ceramic ashtray. She was quite gorgeous. I loved her at once.

Exactly a year later Charles and I, not quite married but generally known as the Blackmans, moved into our coach-house loft at 45 Chrystobel Crescent, halfway between the Aladdin and the generous house and family of Martin and Rosemary Smith, Martin being the brother of Gray, Joy-n-Gray living at that time up the country at Hurstbridge. So they were generally rushing for the late afternoon train or capitulating to the wine flow of fate and bedding down until next morning. Charles and I became honorary Smiths, Charles even at one stage working as Martin's assistant, an activity that involved our hovering around on Saturday until almost shop-shutting time in suspense that Martin would remember and would have some money to remember with. We were woven into the comic and tragic dramas of that family, the convivium of what was, in effect, Elsie Smith's salon.

It was clear that Joy and I were on the same wavelength. We were drawn to each other like magnets, would talk at once across a crowded room, always having something urgent and trivial to tell, an incident to embroider, something read or overheard to elaborate. Joy and I had a great friendship. It was about the wonderful ordinariness of life – household things, children above all, dirty, earthy and high to Heaven things; so much fun. She never held back. She was unrestrained in her contempt for those who did, who dissembled, manipulated, stitched themselves up in safety jackets.

Joy was the greatest of story tellers. Her stories were endless, hot-blooded, hair-raising, apocryphal, unstoppable. Sometimes one just had to put one's fingers in one's ears and pray for amnesia. 'Only names, places, events, dates and dialogue have been changed' people would say. 'One of Joy's stories' was a common phrase among us for something outlandish, over the top. It was the place she knew best. She pitched her life on the outer limits of possibility. After all, that ten years of my knowing her was the ten years she defied death and outlived all medical prognosis. Hodgkins disease had her by the throat, but she danced away from that deadly grip with every other atom of her body and pinpoint of time. She drank in life, every offered glass of it, and took strength from it. Her imagination burst out at every tangent and curve of human contact. She did not switch off until every drop of life had been mercilessly wrenched out of her. What we have left are a few jewels that crystallised, a few drops of her uttermost being that condensed in the form of line or word, the few drawings and poems, those haunting faces of love, of loss and longing. These stories in images are there also in her letters as they were in her talk. But Joy herself will remain chameleon as in life, evasive, out of reach, a living brilliance of which so much that was marvellous, monstrous and magnetic evaporates when historians, academics, biographers, and feminists, try to catch hold of her.

Snatches of her childhood came to light in her talk. She was a bad girl at school, all that wild Spanish blood firing up; was once locked into the school tennis court where she ran round screaming and throwing things to show she would not be caged and tamed. Another time she wrote S H I T on the headmistress's door. Detectives came to the school, into her sewing class and asked each girl to write down clearly in block letters THIS IS IT. Joy knew what It was all right and wrote in left-handed disguise, then next day stood by with shammed indignation and watched another girl get expelled. On return from a nature study country excursion, investigating roots and leaves, the mistress Miss Warren stood up as the train approached Glenferrie Station, ordered the girls to stay sitting, knees together, and, as the train crossed the overbridge, suddenly flung aside the doors and leapt out to her death.

Then there was 'How Joy Hester became a blonde'. Determined to avoid the daily agony of having her long knotty hair brushed out and plaited, she got hold of a basin of peroxide bleach and dunked her plaits in one after the other to turn them blonde so that her mother would shear them off. Instead her mother got more peroxide and blonded the rest. So, of course, she went on peroxiding – something pretty popular in the Forties.

In her teens she met Danila Vassilieff at his exhibition, made her way into the art world and during the war married painter Bert Tucker. In the time I knew her, in her life with Gray Smith, she never told stories about Bert-time in Gray's presence, a great editing discipline – although burnt toast was always a joke, hailed as Burnt Tucker.

My friend was the Joy of the Fifties. With our spouses we made a gleeful foursome. Joy had a splendid vulgarity about her. She was ten years older than me, had sprung the coop and been around in the Forties, had worked in factories and on the taxis (as telephone girl), and been out and about during the war when servicemen painted the town red – years when I had been tap-dancing my blue-stockinged way through high school and Bible class, university and youth intelligentsia. But the street people and workers she knew were the people both Charles and I had grown up amongst. We spoke the language, knew the taste of it, and, like Joy, knew when to draw down the shutters. We were, after all, four wounded people with inner cores of violence prone to erupt into anger or despair – Gray with his epilepsy, Joy with her cancer, me with my encroaching blindness, Charles with his psychic childhood traumas – and we saw each other through dire dark nights, licked one another's wounds in a way that made our own seem trivial – a room half wrecked after a Gray fit, swollen glands that made walking hard for Joy, a black eye where I had collided with furniture, Charles' survival by flight from a nightmare of abandonment. It made for great warmth and lightness of being among us, an infectious sense of fun.

When Joy's cancer was first diagnosed and she was given a death sentence ultimatum, she gave her infant son Sweeney to her friends John and Sunday Reed to bring up and her mother willed her share of property to the boy. Then that unbelievable extraordinary thing happened, her meeting with Gray Smith, a love to the power of restitution. A year or so later, in a Sydney hospital, without her pre-knowledge, she was aborted of twins 'for her own good'. This authoritarian aggression, rape of her womb, was an extreme outrage, a crime against the essence. She pledged herself to stay alive to replace those two children. Peregrine and Fern were the result. That profound transference of love that fused the two halves of Joy-n-Gray was the deep well in their desert of death and violence, the poem coursing through them in unison. In their presence I felt that fathomless tenderness, the strength that love gives to the shattered, the safe and solid substance of it, and in their separation, often on visits to town and family, the threat that regressed each to tooth and claw.

By 1952 Joy-n-Gray had moved up to the hills beyond Ferntree Gully and had got a house on the Macclesfield Road at Avonsleigh. Early in 1955 we went up to visit them for a weekend and ended up renting the little cottage over the next paddock and staying six months. We pooled our small resources, talked endlessly, read books together (Clune's *Wild Colonial Boys* and the Somerset Maugham omnibus); Charles painted prolifically on sheets of paper spread over a table, and Joy took to painting herself, one of the few times she really painted as distinct from drawing. In late summer there was a bush fire quite close to us. The line of fire on the horizon exploded the pine trees one by one. We rushed for cleared ground. She pulled out sheets of paper and painted furiously.

She and I had life classes. She would be already talking flat out as she came over the crest of the hill, rolls of paper and spilling ink in her hands as she stooped through the fence. 'Life drawing is to the painter what love is to the poet,' she quoted. Gray also painted and wrote poems. I was writing a weekly activities column for the children's page of the *Argus*. Joy was back on the exhibiting scene that year, as was John Perceval, showing work at the Contemporary Art Society annual exhibition held at Preston Motors Showrooms.

It was a wonder that Joy got the paintings done at all. We were 'impossible' together. We sat and talked for hours, sat over breakfast until lunch, over lunch until tea time when we had to walk over to the next farm for billy cans of fresh milk, the farm of Leonard Mann the novelist. In the morning we read the *Herald* Missing Persons column, de-coding and making Russian novels over the lives there glimpsed. After lunch we got serious about doing something that would make money. So we got down the thick volume *The Great Australian Chook Book*, which detailed every known breed and disease, Joy describing to me in lurid detail the accompanying illustrations.

Indeed we got quite deeply involved, all of us, in the chook world. That Joy painted dignified golden hens at this stage was no far departure from reality. Chook yards were built, chooks bred, and a great money-making plan evolved for the Christmas market. Joy, in one of her costumes as an ordinary respectable country farmer's wife, had promised to fulfil an order of fifty or sixty dressed fowl for Christmas Eve to a delicatessen in Belgrave.

It was a stinking hot Yuletide. The day before Christmas Eve we sprang into our four-man choreography. Charles chased up the chooks and tied them to a branch. Gray slit their throats, cut off their heads and brought them to the out-house laundry. I kept the copper boiling, dunked and plucked. Joy gutted, washed and laid them out, complete with epaulettes of lemon thyme and parsley. The trouble was, we did not have cool room or refrigerator. The heat went on all night. We put them in a meat safe with bowls of water and fanned the water. By next morning they had a certain piquant odour. Nevertheless we packed them in cases and Gray and Charles in honest farmer guise make quick authoritative delivery of same, picking up cheque. I cleaned up the bloody mess. Joy took the telephone call from the irate delicatessen owner, who cancelled his cheque forthwith. ('Not a word to John and Sun.') It was all a great fiasco. We sent him a solicitor's letter. His solicitor, to cap it all, in his reply, reprimanded us for our illiteracy in referring to the said poultry as 'chooks' instead of chickens. We had not kept even one 'chicken' for ourselves. So we had another penniless Christmas — potato omelette and cabbage salad, jolly good fodder.

We were poor, but we were good at being poor. It gave the simple things a glow, the lavish things a sense of the absurd. Art was always a contour of our lives but the focus was domestic. Joy sat at the kitchen table one day and vehemently wrote down a List of Things I Never Want to Do — Travel, Sport, Fashion, Interior decoration, Flying, Skiing, Car driving . . . I think that going up in an aeroplane with Joy would have been an interesting experience; going up a spiral staircase was amazing enough. But she liked making cottage cheese and growing vegetables. 'Us cottagers are cheesing today.' The house had been a hideaway abortionery and Joy regarded her gardening success to foetal fertilising — 'strong male cabbages and sweet girly spuds'. Moreover, as neither of our husbands were good lavvy pan emptiers, she insisted we shit as often as possible directly into the garden. She would look with intense observation on the product, as rapt as at a Picasso portrait, a curiosity and analysis quite new to me.

Sometimes we went off to town together, stopping at the little corner shop where the buses changed, to doll ourselves up with a one and threepenny string of pearls, one white one smoked. Joy said that it was how you wore them, not what they were. She would tell people fingering them lovingly that they reminded her of her grandmother (which family heirlooms were supposed to do). Generally town came to us. Carloads of friends came out for the day on Sunday. They brought cheeses and sausage and other delicatessen delights. We made huge cabbage slaw salad and offered wine. This wine had to be got from the pub and kept for the day, no easy feat either way. It was generally decided that the 'coolest' place to keep it was way down the creek, well separated from our eager grasp by steep slopes of blackberry bush. But, sad to say, it happened that sometimes late of a Saturday night when the decent modest reasonable couple of bottles we had kept aside for our own good cheer were emptied, four figures went crashing and thrasing their way down through prickles and precipice to retrieve cool cool flagons.

Next day the least scratched and scarred had to journey to Paradise, the nearest watering hole, a town but town-no-more, just a pub marking the place where a branch rail line had ended, a pub moreover licensed to serve only bona fide travellers. Joy rummaged out the most extraordinary hats and scarves and patent leather bag to render herself credible as a long-distance traveller. And this had to be accomplished on the Sabbath morning before the visitors arrived, to save face. 'Better a saved face than a shamed face.'

Our other great scheme for visible means of support — we were all dead serious — was that we would look after the children of the rich while they went trotting off on grand gallery tours of Europe. We would give these little people, for months or a full year, wholesome food and healthy adventurous country life. Gray was set to build the swings and slides, Charles to give painting classes. We, without electricity or 'facilities', let alone faculties, nevertheless proceeded with brochures but got no further than experimenting our 'holiday home' with Mirka's two sons who survived with tales to tell.

II

When Charles and I went up to Brisbane in the winters, Joy and I turned our talk to letters. Reading her letters now, forty years later, I am filled with joie de vivre. They really are written-down talk, sketch-book fresh with moments seen and felt, and spinnings-off into the surreal, spared of punctuation, full of her mid-century turn of phrase. She burned all my letters and almost everything she valued in one of her rages against going 'gentle into that good night'.

We both enjoyed the company of children and I used to write to little Peregrine as well.

Peregrine loved his letter all to himself and unlike other [people's] letters he gets they interest him and he can think about them. he says he is going to write to you. Sometimes he gets a letter from an aunt or what, and he loves getting the letter, but then some odd sort of mood sets in on him, bewilderment of some sort takes over. He really can't think why he got the letter and a silence takes over — but your letter stimulates him to a great lot of chatter and excitement.

Part Two

Again,

> its rather funny your letter to peregrine telling him to
> talk to the letter box and tell it, 'it wont be long till
> you come back' is rather a joke because peregrine is
> staying with rose for at least a month, and can see him
> (as always) taking it very seriously and carrying out
> your instructions to the letter — and much to the
> bewilderment of the neighbors, they will most
> probably witness the extaodinary daily event, of a little
> boy talking into the mouth of a letter box, as the abos
> inniciate their young by breathing the myth from
> mouth into mouth . . .

I sent Peregrine a present.

> Barbara, you're little jumper to peregrine is lovely I wish
> I could wear it myself I think its lovely the only thing, it
> won't fit him but Fern will love it if you won't be
> offended — but it won't fit her yet but I think it will next
> winter. Isn't it lovely! We had a good laugh because its
> the sort of thing I do if I knit a jumper — but it is lovely
> and it will fit Fern next winter thats providing Fern
> grows! She seems to have stopped and everyone says
> 'shes tiny, isn't she? dainty really' and you can see that
> look in their eyes, and I'm afraid I do wonder sometimes
> myself — I mean after all midgets do happen — still we'll
> have an eternal doll if that's the case — Fern has her first
> doll and is very funny, and the doll has no name (because
> another suspicious thing Fern doesn't do is talk) . . .

I have known Joy to get set up to paint and then, because Peregrine asked her to make a picture of a horse, drop tools to go and look at horses. So we went for a long walk over the hill and came upon the skull of a dead horse. We sat down and had a wonderful time taking all the dried-out teeth out of their sockets in the left jaw and replacing them in the right just to see how it altered his smile.

Joy's raves jostled with her rages. That year we spent some winter time at Mt Tamborine in Queensland with the McKinney family and I must have described the little daughter's budgie in a cage. She wrote back:

Have not been able to get down and give the little nest the once over but will soon. I wonder if your pure white towel still hangs on the line as an emblem of 'here lived a good housekeeper' and Persil Whiteness is the only White . . . Terrible awful thing (perhaps I'm getting terribly ancient or some thing every thing seems to be a 'roaring up' – you know these mad old dames whom nothing pleases) But STILL. I have a pet and everlasting hate. Budgies in cages. The name "Budgie" and the whole blanky get-up – from the man who first caught and tamed them to the terrible awful horrors of parents who indulge children in this love of false nature in the false raw – awful!! and the little mirrors! and the ladders. Oh its awful!! . . . God the poets of _today_ – the very symbol of purity of movement and moment – freedom every thing a poet can think to symbolize a bird – surely is that symbol – Catch him put him in a cage and there we have the refrigerator, Surfers Paradise, and Birds heaven all

rolled into one in our hand neatly tabulated — teach it
to talk — and lo! we have an image of ourselves — So
I'm an old maid? Who cares, I'll never let it pass —
those sweet nattering things in the gum trees — heavens
surely its easy enough for children to see birds from
their back door — Tell Meredith if she looks she will
see they make nests — Now she can't let it out, the
other birds will kill it but she could pass the buck and
take it back to the shop and look into the sky and see
the 'bird world' in its untouched pure form — She
might even see god — better than Sunday School you
know. Her mother writes poems they tell me. She
writes them but she can't live them . . .

Meredith's mother was Judith Wright.

It was singularly Joy who gave me the courage to have
children. Blind people were not expected to take that step.
The Royal Victorian Institute for the blind had only one
book about maternity in its library. *A Manual for the
Management of Nannies in the Nursery*. Other women were
very circumspect about letting me handle their babies;
deposited them tentatively on my lap when I was securely
settled, and hovered close about. But when Fern was a little baby, Joy would just fling her at me and leave it to me
to feed and change her, trusting simply to my common
sense. 'You and Charlie have got to have babies,' she would
say. 'It's part of living.' She made it sound easy and, as ever,
I believed her story.

Motherhood was raison d'être for her. She hated,
loathed and detested homosexuals, beyond all reason; had
bouts of rage to go and tear 'Sunday Reed and her harem

of homos' limb from limb, having worked herself up to a ferment that her son was being brought up to 'be a bum boy'. Somehow she got hold of the information that boy prostitutes in Amsterdam were sat on greased pegs for hours to make their arseholes more delectable. She got it into her head that Sunday was peg training. She concocted the scheme of doing a pile of the sad-eye drawings for Sunday to ooh and aah over with her at the fireside while Gray nicked off and cased the joint. Such schemes soon blew over.

One day when we were plucking armfuls of dock, she stopped in mid-air to say, 'I am lifting my arm exactly as my mother lifted hers. You feel it after your mother has died, all the time. She is inside me just like once I was inside her.' She told me that Max Meldrum kept his mother's shrunken head on his mantelpiece. We both loved the idea of primitive tribes who smoked the corpse until the mother shrank to doll-size and could be carried around.

She loved children's drawings, X-rays and photographs.

One of those mad photograph people caught me on the hop the other day. I was expecting a 'mother' from the M's club when a strange woman devaporised on our back doorstep and turned into a saleswoman for a photograph co. "Under <u>no obligation</u>, madam, we just come on Wednesday at 1.30 p.m. and photograph your children. If you don't like the prints we send you, you're under <u>no</u> obligation, madam. Shall I say 1.30 p.m.?" – Of course I'm a sucker, I just can't resist people on the doorstep – I always feel that once life goes that far, as to present itself ready made on my

home territory, I'd be tempting fate in some weird way –
Of course the kids were wild with excitement at the
prospect, not quite knowing what a 'photo man' could
be, Peregrine washed and donned his town clothes at
about 11am and Fern of course (who is now his second
self) had to follow suit – exasperation point was
reached by all of us by 2.15p.m. the kids glued to the
window refusing to give up hope – then seven feet of
the thinnest shyest stove piping arrived wordless and
blushing but in some extraordinary way a wow! with
the kids Put pennies on his head and teddy bears etc.
Peregrine roared his head off – Fern was enchanted to
speechlessness. Anyway not one word did he utter to
us, when I asked him the price of the photos, he
blushed and said he didn't know. For 25 minutes after
he left Peregrine and Fern sat hand in hand (in front of
a sheet we'd hung up for the occasion) posed in exactly
the same position as the stove pipe had put them – end
of the story was another man came another day with 8
small prints and told us the price of the photos. We
bought just the prints after much haggling – we
wanted them they were so lovely.

John and Sunday Reed had known Joy since before the war
and made her an habitué of their home. They seemed to us,
who had almost no money – no grants, no dole, no rich
relations – to live like royalty and be very wealthy. In hindsight they were probably not as rich as we thought and they
did try to hand out money sparingly to a good many
promising and penniless people. Joy had a highly ambivalent relationship with Sunday Reed. There was that

magnetic side of Sunday for the painter whereby she 'seemed to see your paintings before you painted them and lead you up to them', a communion at great emotional depth with the mysterious creative inner being. This Joy responded to ecstatically. Then there was the other side of Sunday – the altogether missing Monday to Saturday side – that seemed unaware of ordinary life, which was infuriating. Sunday elevated the artistic creative process out of context, used to say 'Artists shouldn't have wives' and act accordingly. Perhaps they threatened her role as muse.

Joy, being artist and wife, became a kind of alter ego. Together they could be at the heart of the heart for each other for which the doll Gethe was inner sanctum. Joy always said that secrets were those things that *could not* be told, therefore there was no question of 'keeping' or 'telling' a secret. But, for all the intensity of the love between them, the trust involved in their being the 'two mothers of Sweeney', there was a treacherous abyss. Sunday saw the heights reflected in the depths, but Joy must crash them together to make visible the spark on the horizon.

The two women clashed. Sometimes it was emotional: Sunday, having spent an hour tearing Joy's heart in strips and rubbing in salt, gently picks up a stray spider on a leaf and takes it magnanimously out into the garden paradise. Sometimes aesthetic: Joy rebels against the Reeds' emphasis on personal aesthetics. She deliberately does not shower in the morning but, at breakfast, ostentatiously begins a sentence, 'When I was in the shower this morning I thought . . .' Mostly about money: Sunday asks Joy to hang out a load of washing. She finds a ten pound note left in a pocket. She knows this is a plant, a deliberate test of her honesty. She takes the note, assured that deceit is more dishonourable than dishonesty. The Reeds had a parsimonious way of handing out money in prescribed or deserved amounts that could be infuriating. In my teens I had a landlady, Mrs Cox, who used to say of her errant bush husband, 'I wouldn't wipe my arse with his five pound notes' – a dazzling statement I supposed hypothetical until one day Joy-n-Gray, suffering humiliation beyond endurance, did just that.

In December 1956 Joy wrote from Mount Martha where the Reeds had rented them a holiday house for the summer.

We are having a very serene time here. The beach is very deserted only one other couple, perhaps a fishie or two in the far distance and father brooding little cliffs with she-oaks and banksias whispering in the breeze – the cliffs are a deep rose madder and very crumbly and I crush it up and paint with it – very organic, eh? – but a lovely dryness its like the colour of the old fashioned 'attar of roses' rouge my mother wore when I was a child and strangely smells just the same – there is a lovely nuns walk all along the top of the cliff just like a Fragonard – but so unlike a Fragonard – tea-tree meeting above and a long tunnel walk all very dark like walking into one's childhood . . . very virginal. So different from the Aussie bush which I never feel _is_ virginal – even in what is called virgin country – it holds too much age and its form is tattered – but the ti-tree is so very different, and there is no grass beneath, only layers of undisturbed and unfermenting leaves, a sort of less than dust quality –

Mornington is a very resolved township divided into
upper rurals, sea picnicers and Captain Cats — all quite
at home with one another and the old township, which
is very old, but everything is new and holding the age
within its heart — the sea here, is not any part of the
bay I know — though of course I have been here often
before by car for day trips — the worst way to see
anything is in a car — because one only <u>sees</u> it — hate
them! I would like I think to live here one day its so
peaceful but then by the time 'one day' came perhaps it
would not be so — but I think its the unchanging thing
that makes the peace here.

   We live in a ghost town all the houses are shuttered,
and owned by people who only come down here at
Christmas times — the beach has all boat sheds along it
but no one comes yet to take the boats out.
Occasionally a lone boat-shed painter scrapes away at
the old paint to the rhythm of the sea — all very solid
and all very settled and cared for and never lonely
looking — only there is so much an atmosphere here —
at the beyond of the sea front are all the old 100 yr old
farm houses on the grand old scale — a broken
windmill and hand-made bricks glowing on the grey
sandy soil — and plenty of fat lazy sheep well fenced
and cared for. I have just found out that tape recorders
cost £240!! — and have no more paper.

She wrote again:

It would be lovely to have you on a picnic — on the
beach in the noonday sun — the sun beating down, the

grog seeping in, the tide ebbing out, and all the
tinseley things tinkling in our mass minds . . . Come
before the Christmas rush in the joggy old Frankston
train then in the bus — another hour. We would so love
to be with you at Christmas.

That Christmas was not so much memorable as an inerasable
memory. I was six months pregnant. The Reeds were coming down on the Day bringing Christmas with them. Joy and
Charles made drawings for Christmas presents. Our food
more or less ran out a few days before. It was one of
Melbourne's freezing Christmas Days. The husbands decided
to 'be men' and go for a swim, and Gray to be heroic and
actually dive into the waves. They spent the food and fares
money in the pub and walked miles back. Gray was shud-
dering and Joy in fear and anger gave him the last of the
children's milk warmed up in a glass. His teeth chattered
and he bit the side out of the glass. Kids bellowed, adults
swore and some best-dressed calm was only just established
before the opulent car drove smoothly up to the door.

Out came John, Sunday and Sweeney in special day
new clothes, beautiful baskets and beautiful bundles,
turkey, ham, presents and lastly Elsie Smith. They, being all
well breakfasted and lunched, set about slow-motion
preparations for the beautiful feast in decorative array,
while we felt the pre-dinner drinks fizz like imminent fireworks in our hunger-ridden bellies. Plates and beautiful
plates of foods, untouchable, were carried in. Then it was
decided to give out the pressies before feasting. By this
time Joy was hyped, Gray surly, Charles hysterical and me
weepy. Charles told yet again the story of a childhood

Christmas amid a family throng when little Charlie, so little and squeezed in between bustling aunts and bulging cousins, was overlooked and not served any dinner at all. He declared that ever since he had never felt any hunger at all on Christmas Day and settled for drinks only.

The Reeds' presents were expensive and generally useful. Joy was given a rather large bottle of beautiful French perfume. Joy was much given to rage about people who saved things up, kept things for later, shrivelled away in the process. So now she squirted herself with perfume from head to foot; then me, then the children, then everyone in the room, then the cat, the next door cat too, and the curtains from head to foot, and, I think, also the turkey, until the bottle was quite empty. This extravagance was recorded forthwith in Elsie Smith's familiar slurred moralising mutteration which was now well away.

A blur set in. The Reeds persisted in regal presentation. Eventually we did eat. I was craven, cunning to get as much more than my fair share as I could. Joy twirled round and round with the cake giving it out to everyone too, children, cats and curtains. Somewhere in the further blur, decent gratitudes and greetings were given as the car drove off leaving food behind it.

This lavish provender was to last us until they came again at New Year. We arose next day to find our Mother Hubbard house fairy-godmother filled. We behaved like the ravenous barbarians we were. We tore legs off turkeys, slashed hunks off the ham, ate brandy butter thick on toast, made a whole meal of Christmas pudding floating in cream, drank beer for breakfast and liqueurs for lunch. We had a wonderful party, but it didn't last long. Shame beset us. We

tried to conserve remnants. We blamed one another; concocted all sorts of excuses to prevent the New Year visit —
outbreak of diarrhoea, chicken pox, Barbara's needing utter
peace and rest, painting not to be disturbed, etc.

Hunger made things worse. Joy and Gray had one of
their terrible fights, chasing each other round and round
the house, through windows and passageways, tripping up
and kicking, grabbing and slapping, hair pulling and biting,
while Charles tried to tear them apart and I to talk them
out of it. Eventually they plunged off to their bedroom to
sleep it off. We chose the cowardly way out, packed up and
caught the bus home, a self-defence they thoroughly
approved, indeed found quite inspiring. Joy told a sorrow-
ful tale about being robbed of all the well-saved food, not
neglecting to infer that the rapid departure of the
Blackmans might be a clue — and all the children's presents
too! Of course the Reeds arrived, regal and resplendent,
utterly forgiving, with formidable replenishments.

In mid-1956, when I had begun my first pregnancy,
Charles his first Alice paintings, Joy wrote:

Dearest both of you, your news is astounding! fantastic!
and lovely! I can think of no person more suited to be a
'mummie' than Barbara you are my pet childologist —
which is some rare being who knows how to write
letters that children like to read . . . we have always
thought that if we were both killed in a train crash the
children would be happiest with you two — Charlie of
course is like a fairytale in himself. Let me congratulate
you I think you are both very very clever.

She wrote to me, in hospital labour ward the following April, in a ferment about a name, not mentioning at all her first one-man show for a long time that was then running.

Perhaps 'IT' will come at Eastertime — very very lucky that is supposed to be! Then you'll just have to call it 'Bunny' — Bunny Blackman, rather nice don't you think? and it could be a boy, a girl, or an 'it' with that name — Why not call it Easter Blackman? I've never heard of anyone being called that except Strindberg wrote a book called Easter. Anyway, it would be a terribly symbolic name, incorporating the holy trinity sort of thing — or you could call it Daisy [for Easter daisy]. Gray suggests Egg, would be topical, not only because the government is dumping eggs and so is Barbara, but also it would suggest industry and wealth — also a hard exterior but soft at the heart — and no one could ever say an egg was 'yellow' all through — very white in parts!! Also it suggests and symbolizes life — the continuousness of same — and would never (when it got older) be called a lousy b-----d — the first thing that would come to the enemies' mind is you rotten stinkin egg! . . . Also Gray says you would be putting a yolk round your neck . . . Well I've taken a ticket in Tatts and called it Hatts — I won a hat in the raffle at the U. M. C. [Upwey Mothers Club] meeting last week — nice little number in natural velour. I'll wear it to the christening!! Tell Charlie to drop me a line. I forgot — Charlie who is reading this drop me a line . . . Poor, dearest Barbara, I hope everything is all right and not

too many hitches at this late date but knowing you, its
bound to be quite sensational.

It was. The babe was born a boy by Caesarean section near
Easter and named Auguste, partly after Strindberg, partly
after Augustus Caesar.

My mothering began but, unlike Joy, I never made it
to the Mothers Club.

How is Alice going? Is she still moving the images?
Talking about images you'd love the Mummies Club up
here. They're a pack of very rare pieces I'm thinking of
enrolling John Brack as a member to take the minutes
I'm not president now as I sent in my resignation –
formal like – but the meetings are not only bun and
cake feasts of the most delectable kind and in the most
fantastic abundance!! but the types! whacko! We play
games, charades, and carrying cigarette papers on the
end of a paper straw and tearing down to the other end
of the room sucking for dear life – Try it, not as easy
as it sounds. I get the giggles – unforgivable! Then we
raffle things and raise funds. Surprising how much
dough they take in – lets raffle something! Oh as
Charlie says 'Mothers are Marvellous' – especially
when they 'club up' – at what level does the world
function? Its all so mad, crazy, but one feels its the
backbone of a nation – spineless . . . To them the
world is wonderful – I s'pose it really is you know, the
thing is to get a spirit-level on their works, and find
out how it ticks.

Joy big-sistered me. Sometimes she signed herself Helpful Hints Department. She told me about cotton singlets under baby's woollen ones, and not to worry about the baby becoming bandy because they had wonderful corrective exercises nowadays. Later, in 1958, when I was disinclined to come back to Melbourne with two infants to the coach-house with outdoor lavatory and no bathroom, she first sent instructions about Sani-seal indoor toilet, and then advised strongly my renting a suburban house with safely fenced garden, saying that I could adapt to it and sublet half of it for two-thirds of the rent to 'congenial company'. The letter ended abruptly: *Someone is knocking at the door. Life is very hectic in this suburban routine.*

Home life for Joy had always been hectic. She immediately put up the decibels in any house she entered. She did not regard ghosts and poltergeists as hectic, and cultivated their company everywhere. She had so many — the horseman who rode up to the door with an urgent unspoken question then disappeared, the young couple looking for something in the rubbish tip down below, the one that rattled cups on the dresser, the one who shut doors — all part of her entourage. 'Ghosts are no bother. They have such trivial minds.' The wallowing pig was more tangible. She called it Elsie after her mother-in-law.

By mid 1957 Joy's disease had worsened. She was at Heide and had got her hands on the Reeds' typewriter, which she used rather like don marquis' archy, lower case and no stops.

a couple of weeks ago after feeling on top of the
world, and had at last shaken off the accursed exema,

. i was suddenly smitten down with pains in the tummy,
and had to go to bed feeling absolutely wretchedly
sick, went to the blanky doctor — only to find i was in
the grip of hodgkies again — glands in the tummy and
huge spleen etc. and have had to have a transfusion,
my blood was so low, and immediately had to start
that cursed deep x ray agin for three weeks — so as
john had picked me up, to take me to the hospital (and
waited for me just as well) because they gave me the
transfusion then and there and i was so sick by the
time i had had that, and blood counts at another part
of the hospital, then the deep x ray the same day, at
another part of the hospital, and then the chest x rays
at another part, and saw two different doctors at two
different parts of the hospital — i came out the front
door (i had so innocently gone in earlier) just a piece
of pulp! so john, who had been waiting hours for me,
whisked my lump of a body out to heidie, and sun put
me to bed, and then rang rose and arranged for her to
take the kids and then sent poor tired john up to
upwey, to collect clothes gray and the children (all a
bit bewildered by this time 8 o clock at night and gray
had expected me home for lunch, so plus bluie and
cat, we are all in melbourne . . . my news is vetted a
bit, as i am not allowed to worry and sun is treating
me with kid gloves and i am in bed and only hop out
to hop into the car to the hosp. for treatment. thats all
the details — but really, is not as bad as it sounds, and
am having the most wonderful rest and have read
myself stupid.

She asked me to find out all the dope I could about my cousin who had just died of Hodgkins.

> Perhaps no one in the family knows the answers, often people dont, nor do the patients. they just accept the overall explanation and do not delve . . . i am just the opposite i feel the more i know, the more measure of control i have in the affair — and the more i am able to help myself. and the doctors cant tell you — its all on inner knowledge of oneself and what one can glean from others who have had it.
>
> Dear Barbara your letters I swallow and digest whole. I love them with their many codicils and ask your (legal) mother what a codicil is . . . So as you see, as always when life looks darkest god sends wonders to tell you life is not what you thought it was and ones ideas are only ones ideas on life and very very limited like you and Charlie getting August who will make dark clouds sometimes for you and you will find they are only ideas and that August is a wonder and so is life and so I am a very lucky girl to have so many people who love me at once and thank you for your love because you two are my wonders also. Can you buy me that newspaper photograph of you and August?.

III

Over the years, as my sight declined, I gathered about me typewriter, talking book and tape recorder, all of which Joy loved.

> I do hope you are over the worst of the bug by now. I
> can just see you all rugged up in your little cubby hole
> with all the machinery — your typewriter has lovely big
> capitals hasn't it? I loathe these little modern
> typewriters that look like a museum of modern art
> production the print, I mean, its so fashionably small
> and compact and air-conditioned looking . . . I envy
> you your machine. I just adore typewriters!

My capitals leapt in the air due to my inept pressure on the
shift key. But — beg, borrow or steal — we wanted a tape
recorder.

> I thought of you, when I went to see my doctor the
> other day — and he said as all doctors do 'Would you
> mind slipping your things off' in spite of the fact that I,
> anyway, never have the sort of 'things' that slip off —
> always a hell of struggle to pull 'em off and straggle out
> of them — Still I thought of you as I waited in the damn
> cold surgery wrapped in an inadequate blanket waiting
> for the doctor to come back and wondering if the b-----
> were having a cup of tea with his nurse, when I espied
> on his desk, of all things, a tape recorder!! Natty little
> thing just like a suitcase — well I was a little surprised
> and wondered what the h--- a doctor would need the
> tape recorder for, and thought would I make a hurried
> slip <u>on</u> of my 'things' and a more hurried slip <u>out</u> of his
> rooms — and slip over with the booty to the Blackmans —
> when at long last just as my mind was nearly made up
> in walked the doctor! I must say I still think of that dear
> little brown case sitting on his desk and think how easy

it would have been if you had been outside the window which is on to the street.

During her wintering recuperation, I wrote to tell her I had met my first tape recorder at Lucy Beck's where her brother David Boyd was using it to write a voluminous autobiography. I, however, had just produced a wan girlish gigglesome 'What shall I say?' on it and told her of my shame. She had had much the same first experience at Heide where Barrie Reid had a tape recorder on loan from the Public Library to make poets' recordings. Joy explained how she had groomed her voice for the occasion.

> I practiced and practiced and discovered that for ones
> voice to sound like ones voice one has to project it — to
> stand apart from it — as actors do — and create another
> voice which is not your normal speaking voice, but
> becomes your voice when recorded — it's all very
> strange and a new world which is involved to some
> extent in the theater — but not 'theatrical' — and cannot
> be theatrical if it is to be a success — So somewhere in
> between, the 'I' that is 'me' — stands in some
> recognisable form — this to be perfect would need a lot
> more practice but we only have the recorder for 3 weeks
> . . . As far as you and I are concerned it is a wonder you
> cannot help but write the only trick is to learn how to
> use it — mechanically — and then you write your Barbara
> into it . . . There will be no stopping you . . . I am
> determined to get you writing because you don't know
> what power you have with words.

In late September 1957 the taped performance took place while I was up in Brisbane. She somehow sequestered the disc and smuggled it up to me.

They did not go back to Upwey. The Reeds bought them – or rather their children, in lieu of the Elwood flats left to Sweeney by Joy's mother when Joy seemed on point of death – *the sort of house children like to grow up in* at Box Hill, easy bus-trip distance to us at Hawthorn.

Eventually I got a tape recorder with backing from the RVIB (Royal Victorian Institute for the Blind) for my project to record the voices of artist friends. Joy showed me how to project, deepen timbre, purify vowels, emulate great actresses of the past. Our great day came. A beautiful reel of virgin tape was inserted. We read our poems. We performed quite magnificently. We laid down at least an hour of archival recording. However, overlooked in our rapture of vocal intent, an altogether strange pussy cat had infiltrated in under our feet, slipped a little paw up under our noses, twitched a piece of slippery silvery tape and, all the while we put voice to poem, had made herself a wonderful woven nest of tangled tape. 'A lovely lovely nest!' Joy said it was. History's loss. 'Well,' we said, 'only practising. Better next time.' No next time ever happened.

I left the typing machine and the magic box with her while we went to Queensland the following winter.

No I haven't taped yet. We have absolutely no money at all, so stay away a long time and something might break for us before you get back and I will at least be able to have the thrill of switching it on – still I'm not unhappy about that. I love having it in my bedroom –

the children say it's a TV set we don't use because it's
lost its legs.

She went on two-finger tongue-wagging to me nonetheless. She wrote of friends, paintings, reading, futures.

Mirka's show opens today and Georges and Mirka are
on tenterhooks. Mirka now eats steak with ice cream
with chopped parsley on it in all the best restaurants
and goes everywhere in space suits. She is going to have
music concrete playing all the time at her opening on
the HiFi even through the opening speech by John. I
wonder –

She read Caitlin Thomas' *Leftover Life to Kill*:

. . . as a person one could not obviously be with her for
more than half an hour without kicking her or
something, but that is all so much better to me than the
wife of Jean-Paul Sartre who has written a book called
'The Mandarins', a very much hailed book, and the word
genius floats not very far away, and she is supposed to be
the great woman writer of france today and all I have to
say is heaven help the french. a duller less humorous,
damn dirge without any relief from a tedious sort of
'realism' which to me is never very real anyway.

She loved the typing machine.

I am now back in my glorious girlhood of mechanical
annunciation – or the freedom of mind and spirit by

Jack Remmington — it is lovely lovely — and i hope you stay away a long long time, and I write a book and wear out your typer and my aunt meets her maker and makes me an heir and i will beget you a noo typer as this one will be put in the museum, like Elbert Hubbards Diary. with a little epitaph beside the machine Joy Hester was known as a woman of character and strength, and always liked to have the last word, and it is in tribute to the foibles of this strange and lovey woman that we, the literary trust of australiana have deemed it — this machine — was never to be fingered again by any humanitarian, great or small.

The death of Joy's mad old aunt happened in my time. She had been an art teacher but Joy had not kept up with her. She lived in Camberwell. The police contacted Joy when the aunt was taken away. For years she had lived alone and unvisited in her little house. The bank manager alerted the police that the little old lady, behaving queerly, had been coming into the bank and taking out hundreds of pound notes with increasing frequency. She had been worth quite a bit. The police found her living like a little bird in a nest, sleeping and defecating in rooms heaped with newspapers in which all sorts of things were buried, packets of tea and sugar and biscuits. In the grate were heaps of ashes, demonstrably the wads of money. Locked presses revealed stacks of unused drawing paper, boxes of virgin chalks and pencils. Joy got armfuls of the drawing equipment, but none of the money and certainly not the house.

Christmas 1959 was her last. We went over to the Box Hill house for breakfast. Fern, who was then about five, fed two-year-old Auguste in his pusher with shiny golden mustard on a tiny silver spoon from a pretty fluted bowl beside the leg of ham, and nearly blew his face off. They then went on to dinner at the Aladdin, the house being now taken over by Martin Smith and family, while we went to Murrumbeena to join the Boyds. The end of the era had been closing in around us ever since the Antipodeans' exhibition in August. Arthur Boyd, the tribal elder, and family had already gone away to live in London and we too, six months later, moved out of Melbourne to live in Brisbane.

As we departed, we heard that Joy was again out of hospital but terminally ill. We gave up hope of seeing her again. Long-distance interstate telephone calls then were an extravagance, or an emergency. But in that last year we had 'a friend in the telephones' and had long illicit late-night calls which left no room for letters. However, in August Charles won the Helena Rubenstein Travelling Scholarship and we briefly returned to Melbourne to receive the prize. I went out to visit Joy for an hour. She was a brave but beaten creature, coming to sit with me, shivering, walking with a radiator held in each hand. She told me that she had moved towards Catholicism; also that the little pink cake I had so obligingly eaten with my cup of afternoon tea was considered by her children to be inedible because they had alternately carried it to school and home again for a week. There were no farewells. She had already surrendered and was enveloped in love. We had our Christmas 1960 in Brisbane in the shadow of her death and left straight after for London and another life.

PART THREE

POETICS OF FAMILY LIFE

> Our memories are encumbered with facts. Beyond the
> recollections we continually hark back to, we should
> like to relive our suppressed impressions and the
> dreams that made us believe in happiness.
>
> (Gaston Bachelard, *Poetics of Space*)

As a family we had ten abodes in the three decades of the
Blackman marriage. We two who became five flowed on
diverse currents into these different harbours. These
habitats were walls, rooms, windows, stairs, doors that
assumed for each of us personal and different poetics of
space. For painter, writer, child, cat, teddy bear, the
focus in kitchen, studio, play room, corner extended out
into activities and adventures. These houses are remembered in all their dislocation and distortion, are revisited
in dreams, revoked as containers of stories.

When the health inspector visited our first home, the
white-washed sparsely furnished wooden coach-house that
we had brought into being from a derelict pumpkin of a

back shed lumber room, he said approvingly: 'Jesus Christ was born in a stable.' The nearest neighbour in the big house, who gave us an electric lead until we could get connected, seemingly also approved of the upstairs loft activity by referring to the slight, aproned figure who burned the midnight bulb as 'Good on you, Rembrandt'. The brick floor of the horse's room, now a kitchen cosy around a good German stove, was kept washed clean as a river stone, and the interior small coachman's and harness rooms had no-good Masonite paintings nailed to their splintered floors and enamelled bright blue and yellow, a kind of Dutch interior simplicity.

The outside was also our abode. Much time was spent there, hanging up clothes on the lines across the asphalt courtyard, spreading floral cloths on rough tables in the wide garden under the huge Moreton Bay fig tree. Cats enfolded themselves in cordial shadow play of our domesticities and later, towards the end of that house's decade, babies and their needs filled every corner, echoed at garden level the birds in the tree, traffic beyond the old unwieldy wooden gate. When the first babe was born, we got indoor running water, which, however, ran only into a concealed bucket. By the time the second babe joined us less than two years later, most of the household objects had climbed on to shelves high up the walls out of infant reach and we had laid the bookshelves down to hold a double divan mattress as our sleeping place. Some nights I only half slept, to hold the baby's tiny hands safe from the big bush rat who still patrolled for the atoms of wheat that occasionally sifted out of the grain shaft walls.

In the depths of one night I unravelled myself from sleep, disentangled myself from the embrace of one, changed the nappy of another, gave breast to the other. Then I seemed to hover over this panorama of four sleeping persons seeing man, woman, infant, babe, unsure into which of these selves to insert myself.

It was a cottage that gave us all the romance of the folk tale. At early cold winter morning I took my little hunter out across the tundra of the garden to gather the firewood of fallen twigs to stoke the furnace of our kitchen stove and bring the breath of hearthside warmth and milky porridge to maternalise our house. Over long evenings, the little people bosomed in their cushioned nests, we big people ate great dinners, talked world-making talk about new paintings, new coups of the art society, news of other friends in other places: a high theatre of excitement and comedy, each room a stage, each event a drama, each conversation a history. The little coach-house became enormous in its magnitude, an immensity of intimacy – families sprawling and teacupping in apply-dapply sunshine between daisy and geranium bushes, soup nights with bone and vegetable fumes embracing the wet overcoats inside the door and the wet paintings leant up against the walls. Art lovers took pity on the artist for having to put up with the updraft of family hullabaloo, when meditating great works from his innermost chamber, and got him a' quiet gladed studio beside the river. Artist took pity on himself for being exiled into cell of solitude where he had to leave his new-fledged works locked up all night.

> Each house relived in retrospect is both lens and
> magnifying glass on that organism, family life, whose
> growth in memory it graphs.

Just as we were outgrowing the coach-house like a chick
bursting through its shell, our life was flip-sided into a
new configuration. Brisbane beckoned us: a first suc-
cessful money-making exhibition, a legacy from the last
of my Patterson aunts, my mother now back in the
Indooroopilly house of my childhood, her arms out-
stretched for grandchildren, painter mates in the city
and our good philosopher and poet friends on their
mountain demonstrating the dignity of self-sustained
creative output. We bought our first young family house.
Highview Lucia — we called it by the children's name —
was a big old Queenslander, weatherboard on stilts, light
and airy like a mandolin, standing on tiptoe on the hill-
top to peer down on the night of a city turned into candy
lights. A visiting cat walking up the high front stairs
made the whole house quiver. The front door never had
a lock from the day we bought it until the day we sold it.
Ginger lily, francisia and gardenia marked the triangle of
path from the back steps, one arm leading to the outside
dunny, the other to the large deserted garage, a waiting
studio.

Our glistening chrysalis grew wings in that house of
many rooms, retracting at night into sleep like a snail into
its shell, so that I, listening to the other breathings through
airy doorways, felt we were a family whole. We hived there
for only six months: the Rubenstein Prize snatched us up
and catapulted us to London. We let the house to uni

students, left our beginnings of furniture and the recent Alice in Wonderland paintings all hanging on the walls, and took ship.

> A house is imagined as a vertical being. It rises upward.
> It differentiates itself in terms of its verticality. It is one
> of the appeals to our consciousness of verticality. A
> house is imagined as a concentrated being. It appeals to
> our consciousness of centrality.
>
> (Gaston Bachelard, *Poetics of Space*)

The large vertical maisonette in Jackson's Lane, Highgate was our first London home. It was a proper house, as read about in books, with solid walls, carpets and indoor lavatory — indeed two of them. It spiralled up through five levels to the attics, one a children's room to kneel upon window seats and look down to the road far below and ours where a bright alcove contained a dressing table easily converted to a writing desk, and a view on a clear day to the dome of St Paul's. Both had fireplaces. Half below was the sacrosanct visitor's or 'home help's' or lodger's room, and half below that the large sitting room and the dining room, one side partitioned off to make a wrap-around kitchen.

The next half below was the other unenterable, the linoleum-floored, tall-windowed studio, the painter there watchdog to whomsoever entered or departed. At the foot of the stairs was the little hall jostling jackets and raincoats, jumble of tricycles, pushers, shopping baskets and outdoor galoshes, below that the grand hall and the heavy front door. We owned keys. We had no grass, no earth of our own. Sometimes the promised excursion to the woods got no further than the downward journey from attic to entrance. By the time all the unsmocking and re-coating, unslippering and re-shoeing, face wiping and wee-weeing, bear finding and tongue wagging was done and the front door achieved, father had taken up his brush again, excursion cancelled.

We made ourselves English lives to go with this English house, like actors learning new lines, fitting new costumes, for the new play. Old friends were cast in the same play, the Arthur Boyds in a massive house just over the crest of the Hill, the Peter O'Shaughnesseys at the foot, attic to attic viewable, and the Percevals soon installed in the block beyond the haunted garden, all with small children. We chorused in a higher octave. Places and people, famous by name, now became known to us, and we to them. We, antipodeans, found ourselves strangers, exotics, discoveries, ex-patriots. Painter Blackman, critic Alvarez and poet Hughes became three musketeers. At theatres we saw plays from the page actualised, new ones break surface. Australian painters as a king tide broke upon the English art shore. The prestigious Bond Street gallery opened its hushed back room, hung with a single Degas in gold frame, to talk seriously about a show. The children went to nursery school with its stories 'sitting comfortably' and the nature table.

Blackman life got into gear, dinner party after party, publishers, editors, radio producers, comedians thrusting through the narrow door and springing up the staircase to swirl in wine and wit, Lotte Lenya singing *Mahagonny* songs and Brahms, sad Brahms in the wavering hours. We arrowed out to concerts, dinners, other people's parties. 'How many nights have you been out this week?' the lady doctor, called in to a child with fever temperature, asked. 'This child is suffering from Cuddle-me-Mummy disease.' I stayed home and enjoyed their upstairs party, pyjama dress-ups, 'Little Black Sambo' and 'Top of Old Smokey', corn flakes favourites, on the tiny gramophone, centre floor. Other little people came to our parties, swapped weekends.

> A house constitutes a body of images that give mankind
> proofs or illusions of stability. We are constantly
> re-imagining its reality: to distinguish all these images
> would be to describe the soul of the house; it would
> mean developing a veritable psychology of the house.
> (Gaston Bachelard, *Poetics of Space*)

We became more English and got a historic house at the top of the Hill, in the Village, a narrow one below, three above, original Georgian terrace. Two hundred years of wiped feet on doorstep, hands on stair rails, children's chasings, mothers' hushings. In our first year Coleridge's remains were removed from the outside graveyard of Highgate Chapel, opposite our door, to the interior. Yehudi Menuhin's Bath Ensemble rehearsed there. Margaret Rutherford waited at the bus stop. De Quincey had lived in the same terrace. Lamb, Wordsworth and Southey must have walked past our front door, not then painted red. We passed on the Jackson's Lane place to Barry and Rosalind Humphries, became visitors where we had been visited, leaving them the ghost that ran up the stairs, the friends addicted to the FITzroy telephone number and our garrulous friend Edith as lodger.

Read-about terms belonged in this house — the stair-foot door, coal cellar and larder, the reception room on ground floor, offices below, private chambers above. The children found the friendly corners, made cubbyhouses at each turn of stair, tribalised with neighbour children to the wild wood enclosure, haunt of witches and werewolves, for which we all held keys.

It was an archetypal house, the attics nested high in the tree of it, the cellar secret dark in the cave of it, the kitchen blood warm and nerve stirring, half subterranean about its ever-cooking never-cooling Aga stove.

The familiness of the old house re-enacted us. The clap-tap of its door knocker excited us to guests and out-ings: shopping in the village, theatres several times a week, daisy chain of mothers and children, picture-book dressed, holding hands at the crossing, off to the heath, parks, woods, cemetery. My mother came over to stay for a year, an icon in the low attic room next to the children, sewed, read stories, gently scolded. We gave another baby to the house, a celebration of it. Everyone took turns. The painter backed off to a safe distant studio amid bus stops and work-men. The passageways drowsed at night in clean cloth vapours of nappies laid over heaters. The sitting room from time to time transformed into a gallery hung with a fin-ished exhibition awaiting transportation. For the children, then, days, houses and playmates were all soluble.

I never saw this strange dwelling again. Indeed, as I see it now, the way it appeared to my child's eye, it is not a building, but is quite dissolved and distributed inside me: here one room, there another, and here a bit of

corridor which, however, does not connect the two
rooms, but is conserved in me in fragmentary form.
Thus the whole thing is scattered about inside me, the
rooms, the stairs that descended with such
ceremonious slowness, others, narrow cages that
mounted in a spiral movement, in the darkness of
which we advanced like the blood in our veins.

(Rainer Maria Rilke)

Many years later, on a trip to London from Paris, we crept
up to the front door and peered through the keyhole, and
were discovered. The house remembered was disquiet-
ingly changed, smartened up. The new owners had pulled
out cupboards, essential to the anatomy of our house, and
had discovered, which fortunately we had not, troves of
age-old dinner sets and God knows whats. My body memory, not visual, knows every measured space of that loved
house; can touch the night quiet columns of space sleep-
walked to turn the nappies over; can climb its three flights
of twisting stairs, as so often, carrying a safely quiet in bed
breakfast tray up to the tower king in his castle, while the
rabble below scurried and flurried off to school. The front
door, repainted whatever colour, is fixed at that epiphany
moment when I carried in the new baby to his adoration.

. . . a house that was final, one that stood in
symmetrical relation to the house we were born in,
would lead to thoughts – serious, sad thoughts – and
not to dreams. It is better to live in a state of
impermanence than in one of finality.

(Gaston Bachelard, *Poetics of Space*)

That Southwood Lane house was sold, my mother sailed home and our Highgate days ended. We went to live in Central London. It is always hard for a painter and family to find a place to rent that is large enough and bare enough. Twenty-five Hanover Gate Mansions, grand at the end of the last century when lifts came into being and now elegantly dilapidated, was a godsend. Squatters, migrants, gypsies, we made conspicuous arrival to set up camp in this larger-scale geometry of urban family life. The painter now had three studios: the grand reception room with balcony looking across to Regent's Park, the bow-windowed drawing room used precisely for that art – and sometimes with trestle tables crisp-clad in white cartridge paper, for banquets – and the large and lofty entrance hall as 'outpatients' ward for paintings still wet and likely to be called in for further treatment.

The playroom was vast. The children's stretcher beds were dwarfed by their castles of cardboard boxes and middens of drapes and dress-up garments, the theatre props of many games. Their scooters were left parked at the door for riding round the corridors to the kitchen. The baby had his own room, cot cage in the pen, and parents a state room of seclusion. My kitchen theatre was backstaged by the butler's pantry, ideal as a laundry for ever-ready obedient washing machine, and green-roomed by a maid's room, set up as cosy homework or television den. Walls were whitewashed, Kate Kelly checkered linoleum laid in the kitchens, old floorboards covered with nail face-down no-good hardboard paintings, cheapest Church Street market curtaining hung unhemmed at the auspicious windows and our scrap furniture redisposed. Shelves, pigeon holes

and desk were built in the kitchen for typewriter and reading machine amid the bubbling pots and babbling telephone, school homecomings and my mother's newspaper
clippings about art and other oddities in Australia pinned
up on a board.

'I wou'nt live 'ere,' said the Cockney who fixed the
wiring. 'A rambling farm house in the heart of London',
wrote a journalist. Itinerant Australians envied us. As other
flats were abandoned, we infiltrated first the Colin
Lanceleys and then Robert Hughes who, however,
refrained from having their names scrolled in gold letter-
ing in the entrance where those of Victor Gollancz, Sir
Henry Wood and Anna Freud were still valid.

In this parameter of dignity, authority of space, we
made ourselves at home, at rhythm with our poem. Out
to school by padded door and cautious lift, by big red bus,
the children went, elder son in galah pink and grey uniform of a theatre school, daughter in grey or checkered
tunic, red or green limbs in skivvy and hose. The baby
walked his day's march between cot clobber and kitchen
high chair where he conducted the miniature traffic in the
street below. The bigger better house gave rise to bigger
better paintings, bigger better parties. Door chimes sound
house alert to guests' arrival, odours of garlic and
hyacinths, polish and L'Air de Temps perfume.
Neighbours, noblesse oblige, took my grocery order
down to the local Sainsbury's. The rich children from the
block deserted their elaborate toyrooms to join in make-
up plays with make-shift sets. Our outdoor life expanded.
I could get us to Regent's Park, little hands holding on to
mine holding on to the pusher. There we had the lake, the

ducks, the swings, the cornet ice creams. On some
Saturday mornings early, elder son walked me down to
Selfridges to sample the give-away tasties from Irish Week
or fish food promotions. The master of the house went
'out' – to do the London galleries with painter mates, to
tread the macho strip with the 'musketeers', regularly en
famille to the local market, often to the grand parks and
little restaurants, once all for a weekend on the Isle of
Wight – and got appointed as cultural advisor to the local
St Pancreas Council. The lady of the house stayed home in
her parlour eating the bread and honey of rich hives of
words – from talking books from BBC radio, from
women friends whose gossip was nectar of diagnoses of
personalities, analyses of relationships, women's lore,
laced with juicy sops from their current reading – and
blackbirded out to theatres.

> . . . the houses that were lost forever continue to live
> on in us . . . insist in us in order to live again, as
> though they expected us to give them a supplement of
> living.
>
> (Gaston Bachelard, *Poetics of Space*)

One whole year, a second autumn and half a winter and
suddenly the curtain fell. It was time to go out to Australia,
transportation back home. 'Just for a visit', we said, as to
old people shunting into a rest home. We packed up,
ambivalent, sublet to yet another painter on travelling
scholarship. Coming home to Australia was a step-by-step
reclamation, one temporary home after another, dislocation for the children, a gradual disintegration of family. In

Perth we rediscovered the ocean and swimming, mangos and frangipani, were loaned a huge family house full of life-time's possessions and paraphernalia, travel acquisitions and indoor livestock of cats and axolotl fish. We kept our suitcases beside our beds. In Melbourne we were given the family suite in the sixty-roomed Tolarno Hotel, in which ship the Mora family now sailed. Old friends in new skins embraced us. We transplanted in shallows, painter to a graphics studio to make prints, boys to a dame school, daughter already run away back to Brisbane with grand-mother. Soon we too homed back to Highview Lucia to set up with our air of instant permanence, as though we could pick up where we had left off.

The older children climbed the zigzag hill to state school and the youngest still complete with dummy to kindergarten each day by yellow cab. I relived in them the smells and sounds, preoccupations and pleasures of my own Brisbane childhood.

We blackmanised the house. The man on the ladder latticed the verandah, painted the walls white. Man with mixer made cement paths and closed in the 'under-the-house' as additional studio. Every room in the house sang in its lightness of being, welcomed us for ever. But something in this lightness made us feel unreal after the solidity and substance of London. The painter took up brush, and addressed my longings of exile: 'Out here you have to make your own culture. Write a book!' — so, out on the verandah between ironing board and blackboard, I began to write about the little lives of certain chairs, a table or two and other inanimates of our acquaintance, our moving life.

> *The room is dying, honey and linden*
> *Where drawers opened in mourning*
> *The house blends with death*
> *In a mirror whose lustre is dimming.*

(Jean Bourdeillette)

After only six months old shark Sydney snatched us away
to sharpen us in its relentless teeth. We were in a homecoming spin that ended us up in painter's home town,
galleries and family disorder hanging on to the apron
strings of Old Mother Harbour. We yielded to impermanence, bought the Attunga Street house by default,
carelessly, as real estate, converting rent to purchase, to
be rented when we went back to London. We bought
store furniture.

It sat flat, with too little land, too little view, perched
doggedly on a sharp steep corner, where repaired cars
were brake tested on the turn, and proclaimed three
pencil pines in the front cement garden: 'fingers of night
and dark and death thrust up against the brightness of the
day' says D. H. Lawrence. There was a granny flat below,
immediate studio.

The house had enough solid rooms. All reeked of
Thirties glamour and a shady past. No matter what we did —
changing the rooms about, painting the house white, growing ivy, jutting an alcove out from the back bedroom to
dignify as dining room, sky-flooring the kitchen, rainbow
towelling the pink-and-black-tiled, grid-windowed, angular bathroom, man on the ladder ever present — its ugli-
ness defeated us. We planted jasmine over the fence,
flapping banana trees to distance the backyard. The

children liked it, chose their territories, braved new schools, did new homework and new best friends: learned to swim. Bondi Beach and Centennial Park became home paddocks. Local children funnelled in. Birthdays abounded. Saturday night, party night, grew out of our ears. 'Out here you make your own theatre.'

After a year and a summer, just we parents went back to Europe and London. We felt estranged. British art politics and galleries were unfriendly, friends there had decamped to country village retreats: two suicides, two halves of severed marriages (closest friends, Percevals and Humphries) settling for London. We were suntanned misfits. We gave up the mansion flat, arranged for goods to be sent out. 'Why did you so violently, viciously and vandalistically nail so many beautiful paintings down on the floor?' On eve of departure we telephoned our builder mate, told him to take the whole roof off the Sydney house and build a vast wooden studio on top.

> . . . for the poetry lover who reads with joy and
> imagination, it is a red-letter day when he can hear
> echoes of the lost house in two registers. The old house,
> for those who know how to listen, is a sort of geometry
> of echoes. The voices of the past do not sound the same
> in the big room as in the little bed chamber, and calls
> on the stairs have yet another sound.
>
> (Gaston Bachelard, *Poetics of Space*)

When it was all built, we saw what we had done, the pity of it, this clumsy reconstruction of our first coach-house, its lost innocence. We had even built a downstairs brick room with double stable door as entrance. Upstairs, elegant sloping stairs, the wooden studio had its loft doors also opening on to the side lane, and, an architectural disfigurement, a little square window at the end just like in the old coach-house loft. This muddled house had no raison d'être, no front door, no cohesion. An over-built suburban site, it asserted permanence.

Family life revved up and played on for two more years. Parties were centrifugal. Everybody came. Everybody was wearing psychedelic underwear at late-night dancing. Our Macarthur Park was melting in the dark. Someone Hopkins sang 'Those Were the Days'. We dressed psychedelic, danced disco, created fabulous, became famous, flower-power art on toe nails and bare breasts. Peter, Paul and Mary (not Paul) came to lunch.

The high tide of childhood rose upon this turbulent sea, their halcyon days in warm family nest bobbing on the ocean of it. Diaphanous little girls gave us ballets and opera up and down the stairs, in and out the doorways, papered the walls with drawings. The backyard lone tree castled kingdoms of climbers. Boys belting balls and a small solo rider in red plastic tank enlivened the concrete side passage. There were two cats, Pussy Willow so undistinguished that, when she went missing, nobody minded and the other, quite sinister, called Edgar Allan Poesy Cat. We shook ourselves free from that place by a leap of family embrace into family cabin on an ocean liner, family rooms in Italian hotels and most of a year in Paris. Before leaving Sydney we bought a broken-down Paddington terrace house on spec.

> We read a house or read a room, since both room and
> house are psychological diagrams that guide writers
> and poets in their analyses of intimacy.

159 Paddington Street mythologised us. We think of ourselves as the family that lived there. When we returned,
resident Australians, we entered this other house. Our
builder mate made it for us, setting his song to our music,
dreamed it up from the ruin – an originality of structure,
formal and flexible, hospitable and intimate, with a bold
front door and the voice of a loud clear knocker. This house
served the last seven years of the marriage, its secretive
rooms grew us all into separate lives. It gave form to my
feeling for family life. It had the spirit of the Highgate terrace, the airy flow of Lucia, the all living in one room of the
coach-house, the honest, brute and inviting Aussie ambience, and the fulfilment of a childish wish 'to have in my own
house as little furniture as possible and that as big as possible'. The more we brought our bits and pieces into it, went
round and round in it, as birds to make their nest, spiralled
up and down in it, growing in the enlargements of our lives
like snails in their shells, the more it firmed and sheltered us.

It was the flood time of teenagers, rock climbing
time for parents. I committed myself to tending its flame,
the beauty of it, the maternal well of it, to be there until
the children finished their high school. The painter travelled. He went out to work at his studio in the other house,
its downstairs rented to a Parisian family, tripped off to
Europe and Asia, sometimes to carefree beaches. Together
we made forays to exhibition openings in other cities; took
off on joyous excursions.

In 159 a short discreet hallway, one painting, bypassed a closed front room, standing apart like a hut, side-stepped at stairfoot into a large open living room bright in the alabaster air of a skylight roof and giving out to an intimate courtyard with its protruding old well, stone weeping wall, triple church stone archways, wash-house facade with stained-glass sheep windows from the old Wool Board. There were two bedrooms and bathroom above, a secret stairway to a double attic, and a long shed at the end of the bricked garden reincarnated from a remnant stone wall. Every room was separately romantic, making life in some way extraordinary.

The hut, or little sitting room, was the soft kernel of the house, its private place. Built like a wooden Saracen's tent, with free-laid parquetry floor and radiant sloped ceiling, it had a tiny fireplace, enough to make winter poetic. Its air was redolent with books and vibrant with music from speakers above the record stacks. The big room was heavy duty built, the long marble table made from gnarled slabs, out of a liquorice allsorts factory, mounted on solid hewn trestles, the large Welsh dresser vastly accommodating, the buttoned leather chesterfield large as a double bed, larger than the Chinese piano backing the stairs. The batterie de cuisine kitchen ran alongside, marked off by three brick archways, with a wine rack of sideways plumber's pipes above the herring-boned wooden benches, and an altar piece of solo worship at each end, toaster and telephone respectively.

I run down each morning and fling the front door open, letting in the sun, the passing footsteps, the leafhold of the great tree whose roots going down, down into the creek flowing beneath the house, disturb the asphalt; bring in the crate of milk bottles, put on some keyboard Bach to sweep the inner paths. For every evening's family dinner; as grace, candles, flowers and folded napkins are set upon the table, music chosen: Cleo Lane bridges the generation gap. Midafternoon, Sunday after Sunday, the large tray of hot garlic and rosemary baked lamb with all its accompaniments, the hot gravy, the clinked glasses, fill the plates of the many. The whole cleared table is laid out with slices of bread which, deft as the brush across the canvas, are buttered, crammed with savoury stuff, covered, cut, basketed off to a school function.

A sick child lies in our big brass bed. I sit at the desk at the other end of the room, typing. First after first sentence fails to lead anywhere. I roll it out, into the rubbish basket, begin again. A little voice says: 'I am wondering. When Daddy comes home tonight, should I tell him you have been sitting here all day wasting his paper?' A party is happening in the big room, people talking, drinking, squashed together on the chesterfield and along the pews at the table, leaning against the dresser, bumming the stove and sink, as many conversations as cockatoos in a single tree. Suddenly lights out, save for the two in clay bells over the middle stone archway. A poet stands there, Geoff Lehmann perhaps, or Les Murray, book in hand. Poetry is read, pervades the house, aerates the unsuspecting guests. The 'potting shed' up the back, with its own laneway doors, has a life of its own. Ping pong rages. The whole house is many mansions of music. Teenage throng in shed, youngest in attic, daughter and damsels in upstairs front and the clan in the kitchen can all play their own music, loud, and not cut into each other. They play out their separate lives.

> Sometimes the house grows and spreads so that, in order to live in it, greater elasticity of daydreaming, a daydream that is less clearly outlined, are needed . . . geometry is transcended.
>
> (Gaston Bachelard, *Poetics of Space*)

The house overflowed. One day, as we walked out the front door, the iron lace gate of the twin terrace hand in hand with ours was holding up a sign, For Sale. At the auction I bought it. 'By proxy, sight unseen' — the real estate man was dumbfounded. 'That's all right. I live that way.' The two houses married well. 157 was more feminine, more light. We pulled out the ground floor dividing wall, so that our front door opened now on a wide sitting room displaying twin upward flights of stairs, an ours and a theirs. We acquired serious furniture by swapping a tapestry with a Freudian analyst — the large confessorial sofa, a family of elegant ecclesiastic upright chairs, and some stern Scottish chests.

More than family members lived in the big house — young people like the girl in the Beatles song, leaving home, not understood; prophets without countries, friends from afar, people at turning points in their lives needing to pause. The house cherished, and questioned. More and more we lived our splendidly separate lives, and these others with us. This was the 'back home' where 'everyone' came, the hub where our ever widening circle wound up.

> . . . housewifely care weaves the ties that unite a very
> ancient past to the new epoch . . . A house that shines
> from the care it receives appears to have been rebuilt
> from the inside; it is as though it were new inside. In
> the intimate harmony of walls and furniture, it may be
> said that we become conscious of a house that is built
> by women . . .
>
> (Gaston Bachelard, *Poetics of Space*)

The new attic became the ping pong room, its kung fu walls
hung with Bruce Lee posters. The back shed was promoted to
an etching workshop, centre of a family business, Well House
Press, the kitchen of 157 its executive office. An intercom,
master and four servants, kept us all in touch, announced 'All
aboard. It's coffee time –' even out into the street.

My quiet time was spent in the cleaning and caress of
furniture, a soft cloth waxing and door knob shining, 'awakening old furniture from its sleep' and calming the confu-
sions of a life beset by changes and crises, a meditation of
devolution. I shared these household tasks with a Spanish
cleaner and, in bringing her into our midst, received intimations of that ravishing proud, savage Spanish core.

At first, when my mother came to stay, she would
clap the door knocker for re-entry, whereas younger son at
primary school had to lift the LETTERS flap and bellow. At
the end, that son was tall enough to reach the knocker and
she had shrunk, so used the slot to call yoohoo.

> I want to capture this landscape, the splendour, order
> and tranquillity of it.
>
> (Colin McCahon)

Verulan was country cousin, counterpoint, to 159 for these seven years. Named for 'Verulanium, three miles from St Albans in Roman times', it was on a branch of the Hawkesbury in a deep pastoral valley, our weekend and holidays outstation. A one-room cottage, coach-house size, intended as workers' and tool shed with conveniences, was put up below the cleared house site. Plans for the grand country home were dreamed up and drawn, and re-drawn, our final fixed abode, poem of life secure. While we carried out cauldrons of steaming potage, or boiled-up just-picked sweetcorn, to the outdoor table made of a single millstone, or sat around the big square moon-watching verandah I built on after our Japanese trip, we saw it so clearly, the house-to-be, its long verandahs, enclosed garden within its hollow square, a high stone house.

> Sometimes the house of the future is better built,
> lighter and larger than all the houses of the past . . .
> while it gives free play to the mind, the soul does not
> find in it its vital expression. Maybe it is a good thing
> for us to keep a few dreams of a house that we shall
> live in later, always later, so much later, in fact, that we
> shall not have time to achieve it.
>
> (Gaston Bachelard, *Poetics of Space*)

At each arrival and carrying in of boxes of provisions from the car, at every first inhaling of cow-pulsing, river-sodden high-skied air, our bodies vibrated with anticipation. Off with shoes and city skins. On deck the primus stove, outdoors the gathering of wood to light the combustion stove: some nights the sitting beside a smoky fire outside, story telling. 'Man on the moon?' a local old character had said on the pub steps. 'What moon? There's a new one every month. I've seen hundreds of them.'

One Easter by full moon, whose illumination seemed to make more miraculous the pulse of life in all things, something like a wake was held by the teenage throng, one of their gang having overdosed himself off the planet, 'died for our sins'. At Christmases they put up a tent and swarmed in it, slammed off down to the river and marinated in it. Elder son lashed a hammock. Daughter slid in a cow plop and said the country was embarrassing. Younger son became an authority on rods and lures. Sometimes they retreated there to study. For us elders it was the getaway place to which only closest and oldest friends would come. It was a place for reading long books, touching depths again. Indeed we parents went on going there in school holidays when the children no longer did.

An architect was engaged to schedule the building project. Meantime the builder mate made a simple large studio one step below the verandah.

Any talk of camping out and the painter felt Paris surged more hotly in his blood. He found he could not paint the landscape. He looked at the walls and painted the figures of his nightmare and, just once, a drawing out of landscape, a tree beneath which were mushrooms magic in moonlight. For one whole week, at my request, I was left alone up there with the bush to myself. A seed was sown, deep as music, deep as other seeds, unknown, that were already impulsing to split the rock for each of us.

We reached out to the landscape, dreamed that implanting ourselves in it would recapture the poem for ever. What we needed was the splendour, order and tranquillity of the inner landscape, the harmony that comes of these three together in right proportion. We all moved away. Rats infest an empty house. The builder mate bulldozed our clothes, all our personal effects, into the ground before the place was sold.

Our life with the bears

Beside the desk where I write there stands a Sepik chair god, one that was meant to be part of a circle, sitter facing inwards, while the masked figure faced outwards scaring off intruders. It used to scare my Portuguese cleaner dreadfully when we had it downstairs. She would hang wet tea-towels over it, tapering them downwards to perform the decency of a fig-leaf. But now it stands in my writing room, a Gog to the Magog of the tall polished wood teapoy with the uplifting lid that always reminds of the gentle ladies of Cranford and their fastidious making of tea.

Daddy Bear sits on the Sepik chair; or rather, Daddy Bear is somehow supported in mid-slump by the indentations of the Sepik devil scarer. Daddy Bear is very old. Daddy Bear is as old, save eighteen months, as my eldest son who is a grown-up person devoted to martial arts, pool-playing, pub-talking and other such manly pursuits. Allowing, however, for the multiplication factor of age as in the case of dogs, horses, elephants and mice, Daddy Bear is very old indeed. Besides, he has not had an easy life. It is not all the travelling that has worn him out, the thousands of miles in planes and trains and ships, that has made him so saggingly lacking in stuffing, so bald of arm and leg, so patched and scratched of ear, nose and throat; rather, it is the roles he has played in rooms, in parks and gardens and, especially on occasions of missing friends, inclemency of weather and other forms of boredom. D. B. never suffered ignominy in travel; sat whirling on a knee convivial as a ventriloquist's doll, sometimes with the airlines slogan 'Please do not wake me for meals' hung around his neck. At worst he was swung along, pouched in some outer coat pocket, protruding an arm of fur under the scrutinising eye of some customs officer eager to detect any drugged dachshund or comatose echidna.

Daddy Bear was six months old, older, larger, hairier and in some respects cleaner than his young keeper's sister when she was born. But his belly button yelp was never her equal. He shared her bonnets, bibs and bottles, and was frequently fed, nappied and bedded down beside her by his infant caretaker. Hence I was haunted in my motherings by the memory of an inauspicious photograph in Munn's psychology textbook that showed two four-year-old 'sisters', one chimp and one girl child who, having been treated from birth with identical care and affection, now stood side by side in identical Sunday bests, displaying a terrible disparity as to squint of soul and splay of fingers. My daughter, however, posed for her four-year-old photograph in a motherfold of bears, a godmothering Goldilocks who had provided for Daddy Bear a blue Mother and three Baby Bears, gold, pink and white in order of diminution, for all of whom she provided distinctly different clothes which she kept, quite rightly, in a porridge packet of appropriate brand name and pictorial identification.

When Daddy Bear was in full thrust of male accomplicement, he was belly-hugger for the game of avalanching down staircases, basketball flyer for aiming at the goal posts in Regent's Park, punching bag when hung from the ceiling until straight, and deadhead buried beneath the Saturday marketing of chops, plates and cauliflower in the carrier. Winston Churchill's funeral: we watched all day the slow cortège move along familiar streets strange with crowds of saddened people. The aeroplanes that flew across our telly screen flew simultaneously across our window panes. The cortège moved from street to river barge to private train. Next day our house was strangely quiet. The other children in the block had come to commiserate. All day Daddy Bear, draped in flags, laid upon a pillow, corseted in my black woollen skirt with drum alongside wearing the matching black sweater, was slow-marched up and down the passageways from room to room: then, loaded upon the plastic dish-drainer, he was slow-floated up and down the bath half-filled with water. Eventually, round about tea-time, he was shoved away into the linen cupboard wrapped, like our recent Christmas pudding, in a white tied cloth, while a squad of children stood rhythmically shunting him away. I think it was the following day that Daddy Bear was the Sunday roast, this time covered all over with silver foil before being laid out in the dish-drainer, laboriously surrounded with playdough potatoes, grass shreds of beans and glove-fingers of carrot, before being patriarchally slashed into slices by a rubber hunting knife.

Other bears played other roles at other times of our family joys and sorrows. Baby Bear slept cosily tucked up inside my daughter's nightdress when I was pregnant, but was properly abandoned under a park bush when the real baby was brought home. The colourful brother–sister bears were much given to thumping puppet-staged upon the kitchen table and there performing a little play in under-table voices, wherewith to catch the conscience of a parent so frequently attached to telephone and thus apparently unaware of the hunger needs of real-life children.

But Daddy Bear was tribal elder. He came everywhere with us; sat guard on the doorstep with the packed suitcases, the last to leave the old house, and, tossed triumphant through the doorway, first to enter the new. For years he sat up hospitably every Christmas Eve beside the tree with glass of sherry on one side and saucer of cake on the other, and was found slumped over in the morning with both empty. Later, he converted to dressing-up as Santa himself on the Day. For New Year he was tied up in a string bag of little bells and waked at midnight with all the sleepy people to ring in the New Year. Italian ships' stewards knew how to array him stately on the bunk and nurses in hospital how to ignore his stowaway huddle in the locker.

The later bears were of a different breed, of Bostonian descent, a modern mutation adapted to the whirlpools and eddies, swings and merry-go-rounds of the washing machine, unlike D. B. who was of an earlier age and showed the scars of the slings and arrows of misfortune. The youngest Bear for the youngest child was Honey Bear, chubby and sturdy, his limbs studded and rotatable, altogether the most athletic of the bears. He seemed to live the high life of a movie-star stunt man; a chandelier Batman, a clothes-line astronaut in wings and goggles. These bears were all each kindly disposed of, bestowed ceremoniously, while still warm with love, upon little friends who could not bear to be left altogether without us when we left London to come back to Australia.

There was, soon after arrival home, a crisis in the life of D. B. He was taken to visit a stranger, a woman with bears of all sizes, from mouse-sized bears carried in her handbag to a person-sized bear lying on her bed. She looked carefully at D. B. and said: 'You poor wounded thing. Look at your torn-up paws and hole in the head with the brain stuffing showing through, and only one eye. Let's take you to the Doll Hospital.' So he was taken and ruefully left, among all those dead dolls laid out in a row.

All week the children made hospital of themselves, bandaged and sticking-plastered one another all over, eye-dropped, pulsed and temperatured themselves; pin-jabbed injections, made up fearful medicines, held noses and forced them down; even prayed sing-song bedtime prayers for the success of Daddy Bear's big operation. A week later three children went to the front counter antechamber to bail him out. He was presented, all stitched-up, sham-pooed and straight-faced, so fur-fresh and strangely staring, hardly a friend any more. No speaking on the way home. Solemnity over the chocolate teddy-bear biscuit homecoming feast. Then tears. 'Daddy Bear's got blue eyes!' – when his eyes had always been brown. As with loved ones who come back after time, after illness, after disfiguring surgery, he was addressed but left much alone for a while, until we all grew new blue Australian eyes, healed our wounds of separation from old friends and old places. Then, once taken to the beach, planted king of the castle of sand, left out in a sun shower while kennelled in the letter box, head stuck out of the slot to wait for the postman, he was forgiven.

Thereafter he was jumbucked into the tucker-bag for picnics, bus-ried in the wash trolley out to the clothes lines, floated as green man of the garden clippings in the wheel-barrow up the path to the tip.

The fact is Daddy Bear is our house god, chief among the *lares et penates* of our family, for where he is, home is. So he deserves to be set straight to sit in state upon the Sepik chair.

$\mathcal{D}$AYS OF WINE AND ROSES

I first came across Barry Humphries in 1958 at a party at the Burstalls' out at Eltham – us tiptoeing along the verandah, Arthur Boyd shushing at the door – when he and Peter O'Shaughnessey were improvising a scenario about an analyst and client gradually changing roles. In February of the next year, on the night of the 20th to be exact, I was in the process of giving birth to my daughter but strenuously urged Charles and Hal Hattam, our gynaecologist friend, to put me on hold while they went to Barry's pre-departure performance.

It was not until our coming to London a year or so later that we Blackmans really came to be friends with the Humphries. They came to a party when we lived in that house in Jackson's Lane in Highgate that was graced by a ghost and in which they also subsequently lived. Rosalind, graceful, decorous, brimful of possibilities as a friend, presented a posy of tissue-wrapped wallflowers. Barry bolted up the stairs and spilt forward into the room and occupied one chair after another in eagerness to know and be known.

We saw much of one another after that in those five years in London when our lives seemed to flow close together, to intertwine and follow common currents. There seemed to be endless parties, most of them at our house. We were relentlessly meeting the English.

Quite early in the piece at one party Barry happened to collide with my glass and red wine was copiously spilt down his trousers. I hustled him off to the kitchen and liberally doused him down with dry salt and told him to pat it off. He returned to the party conspicuously, consolingly, rubbing his affected part, declaring that I had inflicted him with 'Cerebos of the thigh'. For this, however, red wine taken internally seemed to be the correct cure.

Blackman paintings had just started to sell before the public began to pay for its bum to sit upon a Humphries-watching seat. Charles bought Barry a disposals-shop duffel coat which he wore for some time, probably even on that ridiculous trip to Devon, whence he sent us a pretty postcard with a message reading something like: 'We are in Devonshire. Send money. Need tea.' On the strength of that tea – or the want of it – both he and Rosalind fell romantically head over heels over a cliff. The rescue by helicopter was the first real press Barry got in Britain.

At this time Barry was exploring his territory. Everywhere was stage and backstage for him. He knife-edged his way around London on people's tolerance and gullibility. Like us he rode in taxis after the midnight train curfew. These were hard to catch in the wee hours. When my white-sticked blindness was insufficient, Barry compounded the pathos by suddenly becoming an old old person pitiably limping on his right leg. On such occasions he would thank the compassionate driver, rewarding him in an old cracked Bible-rattling voice, with a garrulous account of difficulty of managing on small pension with numerous needy grandchildren, and then, on departure, proceed to limp away just as pitiably, but on the left leg.

One night we picked them up on our way to a theatre, Rosalind beautiful with a puff of thistledown blonde hair and wearing one of her fanciful Queen Mab dresses, Barry sartorial from a stint in the British Library Reading Room researching Victoriana. But instead of driving directly to the Salisbury pub with its Georgian glass windows to meet likeminded friends, we were peremptorily discharged by Barry and thrust into a crowded pub of most unlikeminded belligerent drinkers. Barry addressed the barman. 'A couple of drinks and one for yourself.' 'Thank you, sir,' came the customary obsequious reply with appreciative anticipatory smile. 'And what shall it be?' 'Straight waters,' replied Barry dead-pan. We drank our waters very quickly indeed and, when he thrust us hastily into the next pub, hung back lest he repeat the act. But this time we got our drinks – his favourite fancy at the time, Dairy Milk Guinness. This time he engaged the barman in a serious discussion about politics and raised the man to higher and higher expressions of disgust with the present government, hanging on his every word. But, just when the bar orator was reaching his peak of contention, Barry cut him off suddenly. 'Enough. I am not interested in your opinions, my man, just your accent.' Again our drinks were abandoned and our exit accelerated.

There was the time in the very early Everage days when he posed in Trafalgar Square with a London bobby asking directions while Rosalind, as a passing tourist, took the photograph. The Bobby gave this old Aussie chook a highly suspicious glance and he-as-she thought the game was up. But the bobby was prepared, after all, to treat kindly this outlandish woman who wore spectacles with no lenses in them. That encounter turned out to be a closer shave than when, dressed as E. E. and the call of Nature felt, retreat was made to a Ladies rather than a Gents public lavatory.

The Humphries were living on whatever small jobs either could get. I remember Rosalind asking me if I didn't think eight pounds a day was an excessive amount of pocket money for Barry to be getting around London with. Eight pounds would have kept us in humble tucker for a week, but I said I thought it was little enough and money well spent for the sort of research he was doing, and we laughed our way through another cup of tea.

Indeed the first time they made money with any glitter, it all came to grief on our doorstep. Barry had got the role of Fagin in *Oliver* in New York, having understudied it fruitlessly in London, and they had bought up big – an elegantly tailored suit for him, a billowy-sleeved tapestried gown for her, lots of books and records and a baby's layette for the oncoming 'little stranger'. With all this buoyancy and booty they drove down from the port of Liverpool in a hired car, carefully garaging it by night wherever they stopped. In London they drove straight to our house and from our door proceeded straight to the nearby Rose and Crown, which was by way of being our parlour for receiving guests out of the domestic pantomime. Home by myself guarding the sleeping bairns, I heard some men outside complaining of the difficulty of working in the dark, so I obligingly turned on the porch light from within. At closing time they came home to find their car doors forced open and their lovely loot all gone.

Moreover, when Barry telephoned the local police, they said it was their change of shift coming up and there would be an hour's delay before any arrival. We dined and drank a toast to Departed Friends – and Things – and in due course a couple of cops, distinctly unlike the 'Z Cars' heroes on Sunday arvo telly, arrived and bumbled about. Barry felt their dutiful incompetence deserved, nonetheless, a prize for endeavour, so he got out the remaining key and opened the glove box and presented them gallantly with what the thieves had missed – *The Naked Lunch* and *Kama Sutra*, a brand-new copy of each, then the two most notoriously banned books in the U.K., in the investigation of which they would no doubt have been much more assiduous. Some of the loot was later found on a rubbish tip on the outskirts of London. Barry retrieved his suit with one arm completely ripped out. He wore it at the Establishment Club for his first one-man stage appearance in London, walking tall, turning proud, showing off this suit bought from the best tailor's in New York and worn here and now for the very first time, with no reference to its missing member. He did not, however, find his professional scrapbook, his sheaf of scripts in progress, his photograph folio. Rosalind found her gorgeous dress intact, her baby's layette not at all.

From this time things picked up. Blackman and Humphries both began to make their names in London. Rosalind and I had our babies within a month of each other. My mother, then in her seventies, arrived from Australia for a stay of one year. By that time we were living further up the hill in Highgate Village and they had moved into the Jackson's Lane maisonette, known as the Littler-Bigger place because such were the names of the bumptious agent and wavering widow landlady respectively.

My mother's arrival was memorable. Her boat train had arrived early so she had got herself a taxi up to Highgate. We heard her outside remonstrating with the driver. 'Where I come from,' she announced, referring to Brisbane, 'people say what they mean and mean what they say. So don't ask for one amount then stand there holding your hand out for another.' On other occasions, in London buses where the euphonious conductor would intone the sacred sites along the route – 'Elephant and Castle' 'Green Man' 'Fiddlers' Arms' – my mother would clearly inform speaker and passengers alike, 'Where I come from,' meaning Brisbane, 'we have our bus stops numbered and people don't have to go on singing out all the time.' Given to speech-making of this kind, my mother became a favourite with both Spike Milligan and Barry – they being a current twosome by then, Spike living a bit further up the track at Muswell Hill.

Shortly after my mother's memorable arrival we went down to visit Barry and Rosalind for morning tea and the affront to the taxi-driver was dossiered. We ate Chelsea buns. We left cheerily and were not halfway up the hill home when Barry clattered and panted up after us. 'No,' he pleaded, 'I can't accept it. Your tip is far too big!' with which he handed my mother back her left-behind handbag.

When I had my third baby I was given a Council

Help, a 'daily', called Mrs Hoare. She was a gem and some of her sparkle shines still. She would knock at the door, then lift the letter slot and announce 'Hoare here'. Barry had just arrived before her one morning and leapt to this announcement, opened the portal and greeted her, 'What enterprising door-to-door service!' Her rejoinder was pert. 'You was on my bus,' she said, looking him straight in the eye – at this time he was wearing his hair very long – 'The others, they thought you was a Jehovah's Witness. But I knew you would turn out to be a friend of the Blackmans.'

Barry had made a splendid entry into the life of my newborn. These were our days of wine and roses. Barry had acquired his first car, he drove up the Hill bearing gifts – a beautiful long-stemmed rare blue rose held firmly between his teeth and a bottle of freshly juice-extracted carrot clutched between his knees.

I was holding court in the first-floor room with the high balcony; having been brought to bed of a boy, I spent much time in a state of milky togetherness therein and therewith. Greetings were gracious. I directed the beautifully perfumed rose to be enthroned in a befitting slender silver vase and placed altar-like on a corner shelf before seeking libation of the golden carrot. But when I picked it up from its resting place on the bed, behold, it had already done its anointing, Barry having neglected to warn that the bottle was corkless. Baby and robes and the lower limbs of me were all infused in a damp and sweet golden swamp. 'Very beneficial for the knees,' said Barry in decidedly Harley Street tones, as though this were the intention of the visit.

It was when driving this same car that Barry was arrested in Shaftesbury Avenue late one night by a constable on bicycle for driving with his feet up on the steering wheel. He explained then, and again early next morning from the dock, that he was simply putting on his woolly socks.

When I took the children to school past our old house in Jackson's Lane, I often called in for a cuppa and a chance to compare babies. Barry escorted me downstairs to the door one day. The two flights were not long enough to contain our conversation. We stood at the doorstep for some time talking on. My baby Barnaby flirted with his baby Tessa, squinted, pursed lips, spat out dummy. Barry picked up dummy mid-sentence, wiped it on his shirt sleeve, handed it to me to replace in the urging mouth. This procedure was repeated time and time again, our conversation never ending. Dummy spat out, retrieved, wiped, replaced. Finally Barry says, serious, puzzled: 'Why are we washing this dummy in this baby's mouth?'

It was our Highgate habit to gather on a Sunday evening at the local pub – Aussies passing through London and our circle of English friends would drink in the Rose and Crown and then repair to our house for a supper of soup and cheese. Indeed I calculated that when we stood on the doorstep of our house at 8 Southwood Lane, we were equidistant in footsteps from our bed on the fourth floor as we were from the portal of the said pub.

The Boyds – Arthurian and Davidian – the O'Shaughnesseys – Bryanian and Petrian – the Percevals, Kelloggs, all lived in the vicinity at one time. Brett Whiteley and entourage would flow out from their studios at 'one too many Ladbroke Grove' and there were always a journalist, itinerant painter or two, Buster big and burly back from a North Sea oil rig, ebullient Stoshac Halpern over from Paris. With this noisy contingent were the quieter but more incisive English intellectuals, critics, poets, producers – Alvarez, Duerden, Hughes and those exciting witty women who honeyed the gatherings.

Each of the Highgate pubs had its specialty – darts here, billiards there, cricketer celebrities at one, university characters at another. It came to our notice that at the Wellington – down the hill and some way along the Archway Road – there was a Sunday evening sing-song. It was an Old Timers habitat, with tablecloths and sherry from the wood, and a dais upon which a pianist called Denzil played old songs with his name in lights rotating above him like a halo.

This appealed to Barry immensely. He was intrigued with learning those old songs of the Twenties and Thirties that somehow never got to Australia, were pirated along the way by the American hits. But Barry was no passive learner. He was of the Learning by Doing methodology. We made the Wellington our weekly rendezvous and Barry took to the dais, rather crowding it out with his gestures and definitely cramping the flamboyant pianistic action of lights-on Denzil. For several weeks, the show went on; the patrons were pleased. Then came the night when the sherry was one too many and Barry lost his footing on the stage, tilted forwards, toppled backwards and back-dived into the harmonious arms of Denzil. That was the end. Soloist and his happy band of choristers, we all were exiled and retreated back home to the Rose and Crown.

From a trip over to Paris we brought him back a copy of the magazine *Bizarre*, on the cover of which was a man with zip fly pulled down, its toggle poking out like a tongue. Barry devised the idea of an anthology of bizarre moments in photograph, anecdote and verse. There was for instance the woman behind the counter at our local railway café who wore a starched uniform with apparent caterer's logo stitched on to the pocket which, however, on close inspection declared 'I Lipread' causing Barry politely to ask her, 'Miss Lipread, another coffee please.' We fell to discussing lips and I to extending my comic children's verses into the scenarios and sensations of lips, whereupon Barry commanded me to prepare a lipscape or lips suite for his *Bizarre* anthology. Some weeks later he came around to pick up my contribution. Never tell a comedian that you have not taken him seriously. I said they would be ready the morrow eve. Next day Charles implanted me in the Amalfi coffee shop in Soho and bribed me to make good my promise by providing an ever-more delectable cake for every quatrain clinched.

I felt that some aspects of Barry's private comedy were getting out of hand, or rather out of context. My mother had found Barry a very gentlemanly well-spoken young man and took him too much at face value. I beseeched him not to let his *Bizarre*, in which I was the only living writer, fall into her hands. It was banned by every respectable British bookseller. I also asked him to watch his tongue in her presence. She had, after all, lived a long hard life and deserved to be spared from some of its rougher edges. Barry accordingly curbed his utterances but carried the curbing rather too far. He would turn quite coy and say he really could not go on with the story unless he was sure that Mrs Patterson had already retired to bed. This became a fixed phrase of his – '— less — Patterson . . .' He used it on stage at Ronnie Scott's Night Club. It was the origin of a name that sprang later from his lips, the baptism of Les Patterson.

When we moved from Highgate into Hanover Gate Mansions we were even more available for sudden short visits from friends. Barry sprang upon us one Sunday with John Bluthal and Spike Milligan on short delay for a recording session at St John's Wood EMI studios. Soup and speculations on the way of the world were partaken of, conviviality extending into bowls of apple crumble when, at sight of the clock, alarm bells sounded. All three leapt to the lift, spooning fast, promising to leave empty bowls in an upcoming return. A moment later, a whistle from the street. Two storeys below Spike was catching hold of a passing taxi by the wing of its open door, John pointing over his shoulder to the lift, Barry mouthing and miming 'No money!' Charles fished a fiver out of his pocket, thrust open the window and threw it down. It wavered in the breeze, descended indirectly, lodged in the branch of a tree halfway to the ground. Taxi driver impatient, Spike now within, John holding door, Barry shinned up the tree, which brought him suddenly like an apparition over the window-sill of the mansion flat below where the retired Naval Commander and his wife sat all starched and silvered spooning at their Sunday roast. Barry plucked the note like a bird in hand and, looking them straight in the face, felt obliged to explain: 'Money grows on trees.'

Barry picked up all sorts of characters in London and

shoved them in his tuckerbag for later, some that he found
in his researches and some that were thrust upon him. We
had one, a loutish youth from Melbourne media society,
whose name I have gladly forgotten. He drifted into our
lives, was apprehended as a baby-sitter and then became
inextricable. He was always broke and, once over the
threshold, showed every sign of staying for ever. In return
for which hospitality he forever assured both Blackman and
Humphries that his father/uncle/brother who owned the
biggest television station in Australia would make them a
star as soon as they set foot back home.

When our extravagant expressions of grateful gratitude for his promises ran out of extremes of irony, it was
necessary to keep him out of their range. Barry would see
him coming first and pass out of the letter slot in the door
either a sandwich, a beer-soaked sponge or a torn ten-bob
note.

In time, and at about much the same time, we did,
both families, come back to Australia. It was the late summer of 1966. Barry was riding high. He had a one-man
show at the Comedy Theatre in Melbourne. We went the
night after we arrived back. He gave us comps to centre
seats four rows back – and we didn't recognise the plant.

He was trying out a new skit using a character called
Neskafka. Neskafka was a trendy Fitzroy restored-terrace
owner hanging his walls with names now becoming
sought-after – including Blackman. He was forever going
in a hostly flutter to answer the front door bell. Time and
again he addressed characters from our mutual London
past that were unknown to the Melbourne audience. I
alone tittered. The audience was meantime held in

prolonged suspense. Finally, when I could hold myself in no longer, he confronted at the door this door-slot-fed excruciatingly boring character. I gave way. Alone in that whole crowded theatre I roared with uncontrollable laughter. Barry intervened. Coming confidentially to the footlights he explained sotto voce to the audience that one sometimes had a weird character in the audience who laughed at nothing and it was, on the whole, better to humour them for a while and let them get it out of their system and 'then' he promised 'we shall have no more trouble from that quarter'.

There was however one small quarter of homecoming Melbourne that threw Barry into unpremeditated disarray at each recurrence. Many and oft a time as he ran late, juggling new lines of script before him, chatterings of children beside him, coats, keys, reminders and corroborations of appointments from behind him, he would with his other hand dial 015 for Time on the telephone and be rewarded with the sepulchral admonishing tones, just those Godly tones that had been engaged to read the Book of Genesis on the BBC, the all-too-well remembered tones of his old collaborator and overseer Peter O'Shaughnessey, spitting out the pips, announcing the overstepping of the hour, his debt to doom precisely in minutes and seconds.

A new life took shape for us all then in an Australia whose attitude to its painters and comedians had changed very much. Fame and fortune descended upon us, robbing and restricting us from much of our fun, committing us to sentences of life in the public eye. New territories, new stresses, new associations, new geographies, all carried our frail crafts on farther streams.

$\mathcal{A}$ YEAR IN PARIS

I

OUR PART OF PARIS

Winding up to our third-floor apartment there are always odours on the stairs – odours of cat, coffee and cooking. But, because this is Paris, the odour most often is of coffee. The café-bar Le Paris occupies the ground floor, shuts only from three to five in the morning, and makes maybe the best coffee in Paris.

Between the first and second floors there is much running to and fro and snatches of song as the work girls from REA Models – indeed the little seamstresses of Paris – pass from workroom to showroom. Bourgeois families have decent four-piece apartments on the next couple of floors – us with piano-tinkling daughter, newlyweds with telly set and baby, a teenage girl who bounds up stairs attached to a large Alsatian dog, the black family who go out so dressed up on Sundays . . . The fifth floor is a plimsoll line of domestic status in Paris where these old buildings have no lifts. Above the fifth floor the light grows dimmer, the stairs narrow as they lead up to the ram-shackle rooms where an assortment of numerous solitary persons shuffle, mutter and cough.

Our windows overlook the small, grimy, cobble-stoned square around the old city gate of St Martin, and the grand boulevard along which a torrent of traffic rushes towards the Etoile, heart of Paris, a mile further on. Nevertheless the owner, who has our apartment up for sale, instructs that it be declared an apartment with 'grand standing' and a 'vue principale'. It is also demonstrated, to viewers, then, that its carpet is 'tapis fuzzy-felt', its ceiling too low and its price 'trop cher', too high.

Apart from a glance at the gates – Porte St Denis a block away is bigger, more magnificent – there is not much to attract the tourist to this part of Paris. Unfashionable, unbeautiful, St Martin is a dense, busy, working quarter of the city, between the historic broken-down Marais and the sordid approaches to the Gare du Nord and Gare de l'Est, a sordidness which seems to infest the precincts of any long-distance railway terminus in all big cities. The nearby metro station Chateau d'Eau is not, as translation might suggest, a water castle but actually a city sewage reservoir.

However, St Martin has its scene and its savour. For centuries the area round these gates has been the centre for the rag trade and the brothels. Hotels de passage inter-sperse with the wholesale garment stores. Commercial travellers from the provinces come here. Awaiting them are the live theatres – six in the boulevard – the many small blue-movie houses, the Breton fish restaurants, the Normand bakery and the girls of the Rue St Denis.

At St Martin all night the sound of traffic surges like the sea, broken only by the seagull shriek of police or pompier swooping down on crime or fire. By morning there is added the tomboy whistle of the gendarme on traffic duty and the underground rumble of the metro. Down in Le Paris it is time for morning grand crème – milk coffee – and croissant. 'House of the Rising Sun' plays on the jukebox. Lazlo, the great dog chained to the till, is having a chunk of raw meat. A wire basket of hard-boiled eggs stands on the counter, beside it the long buttered crusts, tartines. A few devotees punch away at pinball machines. The regulars are there. The lady with lap dog sips her hot chocolate. Two old cronies – he with bandaged legs, she with torn-in-half scar down her face – are on something like their fifth red wine for the day. 'Bonjour M'sier 'dame!' – catch-cry of French cordiality – as the door opens and shuts.

Outside winter prevails – a buttoning down of maxi-coat, knotting up of scarf, off along the boulevard . . . The shops are open now – fashion shoes, watchmakers, bridal gowns, stationers. Prisunic is already astride the shoppers with its ding-a-ding-dong dime-store chimes. Every hundred metres or so the glassed-in terrace of a coffee bar juts out on to the wide pavement. Theatres and cinemas are closed and still. Posters for *Hair* are up outside the Théâtre de la Porte St Martin, stills of *Les Aventures Amoreuses de Robin Hood* outside the cinema Le Far West, and a giant portrait of the cabaret singer Charles Aznevour up outside the Théâtre de la Renaissance.

The eccentric shops are open early. The little man, whose shop has the air of 1910, is polishing up his lenses, brasses and hydrometers. The proprietors of Vêtements Tropicals have pushed their glass show-cases out onto the pavement to make room for customers to penetrate within to the jungle of pith helmets, sleeping bags, mosquito nets, rustproof tin trunks and garments for the good-tempered missionary wife. Mops sluice out from doorways across pavements the citron-scented floor-wash. Boutiques of the exotic open later. The Sex Supermarket has books of pornography of encyclopedic pretension alongside hygien-ically sealed paperbacks, instruments of pseudo-surgical import alongside interlocking male and female plastic dolls. The windows of the trick and magic shops show an unseemly array – masks of fractured skull, bloodstained bandage, Poe-ish cat fiend, gouged-off thumbs, clusters of lifelike maggots, jack-in-the-box mustard pots, boxes of cotton-filled chocolates and onion-flavoured chewing gum. A soon-to-open sweets shop and the building site of proposed new offices are both receiving deliveries. Taxis slide along their rank. The newspaper man in his corner kiosk has saved our American paper. The billboard man is sticking up advertisements for concerts and a new circus on one of those cylindrical street stands in which are kept the twig brooms of the street sweeper.

Off the boulevard on either side are the narrow streets, odorous with their old life, ungainly with modern traffic. Busily from the entrances to laundromat and super-market come the bearers of loaded carry bags. The play-ground noise of schoolchildren and asphalt echo of their chase stops short at the clanging of a bell. A postman pings in and out of the furrier's door pursued by the rich, warm, balmy animal odour of new pelts. A sour, crumpled heap of humanity, a clochard, still lies huddled for warmth over the grid in the pavement, through which comes up the rancid hot air exhalation of the metro. La Cuisine is cooking its chickens and sprouts, stews and sauces for the day, its windows already a splendour of salads, pâtés, coquilles St Jacques on their shells and meats in aspic.

At the post office a new stamp is on issue, a square one commemorating the seven hundredth anniversary of Roi St Louis, king of kings. Businesslike philatelists stand and inscribe stacks of special First Day Covers. The chairs are all occupied by the more presentable clochards, dead to the world, their snores rhythmical. A glazier, bundle of panes under his arm, cries to the cliffs of buildings orbed with windows, an ancient sing-song 'Any windows to mend?' In a shop no bigger than a telephone booth, a little old bespectacled man carefully examines and prognosticates upon a coat brought in for re-lining, 'Silk or sheepskin?'

Through the Porte and a few streets further on there is a market, a covered market, a hall, not noisy with spruikers like an English market, nor a jostle of foods, pots and clothes, bartered over, like an Italian. Close to a dirty curb a stall piled high with dairy-fresh creams, butters and some of the three hundred and forty-seven different cheeses of France, has laid out glass pots of warm, sweet-breathed, new-made custard crème caramel. Next to it is a gallows array of rabbit, duck, goose and hare, mercilessly complete to eyebrow, toe and tiny tongue. Empty boxes on the stalls are re-stacked, mounds of scrubbed carrots, pale smooth endive, snow apples, spinach, horny pink pomegranate, soft ripe furry figs, Martinique bananas, clementines from

Spain, pale Israeli grapes . . . A blood and entrails stall specialises in giblets. Beside it are pots of tulips, sheaves of mimosa, posies of cornflowers and the close cauliflower-shaped bouquets patterned of small flowers.

On the fishmonger's slabs are great whole salmon and tuna, tiny sardines and silver sprats, the red dorarde of Matisse and golden carp as from a moat, tanks of live glistening trout, pink crabs, long eels and the escargots vivants – snails alive-oh. A woman buys a live lobster; as it is being weighed, it nips her finger. The butcher for lamb and the butcher for pork – the legs adorned with paper rosettes bleu-blanc-rouge at the ankle – flank the vendor of wooden tubs full of rice, olives, dates, nuts and prunes. Guarding the entrance to a glass cave walled with bottles – waters mineral or gaseous, wines red or white, natural fruit juices, all labelled with legends – stands a pram-sized basket of miniature toy-like bottles of liqueurs.

Choosing the food: that is the heart of the matter for every French housewife. For the French their country is farm, orchard and kitchen garden. At the market they touch, taste, discuss and decide with care on the provisions for the day, those whom the deep freeze and bulk packages of 'Le Shopping Supermarket' have not disinherited of their fine feeling for food. Lust of the stomach, adoration of the table, the glamour of hunger – it is the core of French life.

At half-past noon the market is closing for a few hours. So also are many shops in the side streets – cobbler and corner grocer, homely hardware and family chemist. It is lunch time. A whole aroma of hot foods stalks. The streets are filthy. The air is cold. The windows of baker and charcuterie are marvellous with the pungency of fresh-made foods. Knots of people at their doorways overlap the metre-wide footpaths of the narrow streets. Some, clutching savoury packages, cluster at the entrance of the PNU (TAB). Women emerge from the hot sweet embracing interior of the bakery carrying long thin unwrapped loaves or balancing on palms the twist-top tissue-wrapped fruit tarts, fragile cakes or the round shortbreads called almondines. Workmen come out from the Cuisine to lean against post or car or sit down happily on the curb with their bowls of steaming hot meats, garlic-rich casseroles, vegetables in sauces of cream or cheese.

At the restaurants and brasseries tables are filling, waiters running. More ground-floor space per city block, more conversation per man-hour is taken up with eating and drinking in Paris than in any other city. Le Paris is buzzing, reeking with the hot cheese and ham aroma of the toasted sandwich called 'croque monsieur', the national snack. Lazlo is dozing. 'Let It Be' plays on the jukebox. Algerians jostle at the pinball machines. Outside another squad of young backpacking Swedes relentlessly arrives, turns the corner, heading towards the cheap hotels at République. The woman across the road, literally in her box office, a wardrobe-sized container, shuffles her theatre box plans as requested, sells tickets, noon to nine.

At evening when the bars bristle with the change of life from day to night, Jewish clothier after shut of shop and prostitute fresh from the hairdresser sit drinking side by side. The legends of Parisian haute couture and female elegance are brought to earth here. All day the clothing stores sprawl out on to the pavements with racks of coats, shirts, blouses, skirts, pyjamas, roped together in dozens,

Part Three

grosses, thousands, nothing for the individual, no personal fitting. All night the prostitutes stand in the doorways and on the corners right the way down Rue St Denis, in Rue Blondel, and other dark side streets; are regarded by the locals as just another branch of the working class. They are often surprisingly pretty, and come in a wide range from petite blonde to buxom negress, schoolmarmish to motherly. Their professional dress is distinctive: high boots, tight bright sweaters over tight slacks or leather miniskirts, seen through their maxi-coat worn open. Their make-up is spectacular, not garish – silver or gold eye-shadow, two-tone lipstick, and a most particular coiffure.

The hair-do is elaborate, immaculate and inviolate. From five in the afternoon the girls are to be seen arriving for their appointments at the hairdresser, and departing adorned with their night's insignia. On the other side of the Porte St Denis – that triumphal arch through which have passed the grand armies of France in victory or defeat – there is a network of alleys and arcades going off towards the railway stations. They are made up of little boutiques for blouses, lingerie or kiddiwear. They bear scrolled names – Sylvie, Lorette, Jacqueline, Giselle. Each is kept by an aging madam who stands at her doorway soliciting customers in a most familiar pose.

The beggars also stand and wait. By evening there are many of them down in the metro subways, a threadbare woman with baby unnaturally quiet, a man who sits head in hand with shoes off revealing toeless feet, a blind man rasping a violin, a student making wire jewellery. Clerks from the office, children from school, hurry home across their path.

After dark, pavement booths come alive selling potato frites, syrupy crêpes, sugared almonds and hot chestnuts. Fortune tellers with names like Varvara or Zena turn their dark mysterious eyes, heave ponderous bosoms and for a five-franc piece their mechanisms emit a confidential card of your future fate. Night students at the nearby Poly-Teque, who have been buying art materials and pop records, thrust out of Gilbert Jeun when it shuts at seven o'clock.

Now the restaurants are in full bloom – foods Provençale (much thyme and garlic); foods Vietnamese (delicate crab and asparagus); foods Alsatian (peppery pork and sauerkraut choucroute); foods à la Grandma (leek and potato potage, and rabbit pies); from dirt cheap to a princely price. Chez Julian's in the Fauberg St Denis through its revolving doors is huge and full to the brim twice a day. The art nouveau ceiling hangs rich with grease. Crockery is cracked. The waiters are rude. They wear long white tablecloths tied around their waists and rush down between the tables with a basket doling out bread to left and right. The squid, the mackerel, the beef casseroles are superb to hungry stomachs. A three-course meal, including a glassful of wine, costs barely a dollar.

Special to this area are the restaurants in the style of Marseilles. Indeed the boulevard a little further along changes its name to Boulevard des Poissonniers. The good fish restaurants keep a fishmonger set up on the pavement outside. The splendid sea drench and salt stench of his oysters, clams, mussels and lobsters baptise the hunger of those who enter. A diner orders. The waiter goes outside and buys. Only then is the shell prised open. The Louis XIV is a grand restaurant between the two gates, built in the time of that king. Rolls Royces and Cadillacs park imperiously astride its pavement. Within, vistas of waiters bear down on tables with ice-bed platters of fruits de mer: sheen of oysters, brine of mussels, fragrance of the spiky sea urchin with flesh sweet as nectar of the deep, and trays of hot crustaceans, bouillabaisse soups, fish with their sauces, and quenelles delicate as mermaids' bosoms. Outside riot police on motorbikes ride past. A spruiker collects a crowd for his Man eating fire and Man escaping from chains. Two cars swerve, thump, dent. Their drivers curse, police whistle. But inside the feast holds court, huge and sumptuous. Night after night, street after street, these restaurants are full. The diners are not the rich, the expense accounters, tourists or celebrators who eat out once in a blue moon. They are the people – friends, whole families, lovers who kiss between courses – who live here among the crumbling courtyards and dark winding stairs. Cave dwellers of the city – their hunger is magnificent, course after course, midnight and after. Then they go home – happy. Bon appetit.

II

OUR LIFE IN PARIS

It was our rich time. It was our family time for opening the door on another people's way of life and squatting in it. The mining boom made fortunes, paintings sold like hot pies. The art dealers came to Paris. They brought me big bottles of perfume, took us out to famous restaurants, left with a roll of canvasses. We bought a Mercedes 250SL. The children went off across Paris to the bilingual Sacré Coeur school at Neuilly near the Bois de Boulogne, Charles to his studio in the Cité des Arts at the other end of the Marais. Locked up in the St Martin apartment, I read for eight hours a day, the largest talking books on long-play records from the American Library – Joyce, Proust, Dostoevsky, James – and took to writing.

We wanted to live somewhere in Paris not already staked out by Hemingway, Orwell or Sartre, not in constant line of tourists' camera fire, not coca-colonised by American converts. We found it by way of a newspaper ad and my blundering French.

We read the ad at six o'clock. We inspected at eight. At ten we sat around an agent's table. We gave the runner a large wad of notes. He peeled some off, handed the wad to the agent, who peeled some off and handed the lesser wad to the owner, who gave him the keys which he gave to the runner which he gave to us. Documents were signed all round, hands shaken; practical people the French. By midday we were in a year's possession of this five-room apartment amid jungle traffic and gale force odours.

We were on the third floor, which would have been the second floor of the original 'hôtel' but, by a process of horizontally doubling the space by putting in false low ceilings, were cooped into Parisian urban density. What would have been one grand room originally was celled with cardboard cut-out walls into five. All were light, with heavy full-length double-door windows that turned the street noise down low, warded off the chill air. In the kitchen, stove, bench, sink were hip-high – oh the petite femme. In the glassy dining room, shoulder-high potted plants seemed to be already seated at table. The single sofa in the sitting room became older son's bed, the stretcher folded

up behind the armchair was for younger son. We parents
slept in a corner quadrant room that was cartographically
at the intersection of the second, third and tenth arondisse-
ments. Our daughter's cupboard of a room looked down
into the side street. It had horse heads erupting from the
wardrobe, which we subdued by the stabling of a hired
piano alongside. By holding a champagne glass to the
cardboard-plus wall she could hear the television in the
room next door.

Within an hour of entry we made two interesting
discoveries. The huge enticing altarpiece washing machine
in the bathroom 'ne marche pas' — a phrase to haunt us in
Paris, meaning 'out of order' alias 'gone bung' — and a billboard hanging out of the daughter's window announced 'A
vendre — Inspection vendredi' — meaning it was for sale and
visitors could come on Fridays. Despite the greatest elo-
quence my French could muster, there was no reduction in
rent for these non-disclosures. Our cat retaliated, tree
climbed the pot plants, ring-barked the leather chairs. I
spent Friday mornings cleaning hard and Friday afternoons
in conversation with the owner, Madame Passarini, while
we waited for buyers who seldom came. But there were
'avantages francaises' — a telephone with cord so long it
reached to stove and bath and every bed; two lavatories
that saved argument; furnace heaters everywhere.

With French in our ears we slipped into it for our little talk — what to eat, to buy, where and when, and pillow
talk. Elder son, who had failed his first-year high-school
French, walked the streets, saw that the people had French
faces, made himself a French face, thus spoke with a French
accent and, having got the music of the language, easily

slipped the French words into place as he played pinball day and night with the Algerians in the bar below. He spoke the lingo as well as any other non-reading-and-writing Parisian. Eleven-year-old daughter learned to speak with the pure vowels and aspirates of the classic education. The children went by underground to school – an understatement. On the map our apartment was exactly opposite a metro station that, with just one change, would take them to Neuilly. In fact it was four winding flights of stairs to street level, a hazardous crossing diagonally across the square, a moving maze of cars, then a descent of six flights of stairs or escalators (frequently 'ne marche pas') to their platform. When winter came and passengers doubled in size with overcoats, we saw our young son fit only seventy-five per cent of himself on the train as the doors slid shut and the monster sprang into pace. After that they travelled premiere classe.

Eating at home was almost a luxury when the cost of eating out was generally the same, cheaper, at the self-service buffet-type restaurants. If we went en famille to the Grandma-style little place across the rue, the lady would immediately set aside a serve of floating island dessert for our youngest. If we ate there à deux, she would inform us if a waving handkerchief from daughter's window indicated a war between brothers.

One day our daughter came home from school, burst through the door and straight into my arms in shaking sobs. 'Raped in the metro?' Sniggers in the sobs. 'Socrates' last words were not to forget to pay the grocer for the cock.' Deep education. Her history classes were often taken on the hoof, the teacher stopping outside Conciergerie or Notre-Dame to recite its story before they entered. Younger son brought his history home in the form of endless ack-ack-ack spurting monologues, leaping from arm to arm of furniture, French mowing down Germans. On Saturday, elder son haunted the flea market on the outskirts, mainly lured by the anticipation of the aromatic spitted kebabs, and one day came home wearing a World War I gas helmet which he wore to school for some time. Younger son, desiring also to be head-pieced, grabbed up the postman's cap off a mail bag one day when its owner had apparently nipped in for a quickie.

Charles went off each day to the other extreme of the Marais adjacent to the Jewish quarter of St Paul to slot himself into his studio at the Cité des Arts, this long modern block, enterprise of the Cité of Paris. Madame Brunau had midwifed it and now nurtured it, stocking its tiers of studios with artists, composers, sculptors from all parts of France and of the world. She fulfilled the gesture of national generosity that addicted the sojourner to Parisian galleries, museums, art materials and cultural innovations. But she did not see any need for conviviality, congregation or a cross-pollination diluting the Parisian influence. The foyer was unenticing in its bare efficiency, public telephones all overheard. The corridors were long and clean as any institution. Only by the exotic names on doors, smells issuing through keyholes, was there a sense of microcosm of the wide world's macrocosm. The artists were not distracted. Families, who wished to live in the discomfort of frugal space, were permitted: babies, no pets.

For the first half of the year Charles had an Australian studio overlooking the car park and children's playground which he preferred to the superior view over bridges and river. After that Madame procured a makeshift studio, a Salon de Réunion – billiard room – in a derelict building nearby, earmarked for future demolition and land acquisition. With memories of the old coach-house, we again whitewashed walls, dragged in cheapest and least furniture, electric wired for lighting and heating and the painting was on again. C. B. dreamed to paint the mulatto lover of Baudelaire, Jeanne Duval, but came close to being knifed up in his attempt to procure a negress from the street. Georges Mora, making timely appearance in Paris, managed it more elegantly. The painting emerged much later, the black figure floating over the cityscape, captioned at its first Australian showing as 'Aboriginal in Paris'.

The apartment was our depot, family life its moveable feast. We took to the streets, as our children to the language, became habitués not only of restaurants and museums but also of paint suppliers, toy shops, repair shops, hardware and the lost property venue; signed our name Blaquemann at the dry cleaner to assure a right return. On Saturdays we went to the shows, on Sundays out to parks on the outskirts, on some weekends to tapestries at Angers or the castles of the Loire. We left a brandnew pair of shoes under the bed at Mens and Daddy Bear in a wardrobe at Blois, both retrieved. The penumbra of family life infested every château and cathedral. At Christmas we went over to London, to friends and familiarity of childhood festivities of the Sixties.

Other Australians crossed our tracks. John Coburn was making his Opera House curtains at Aubusson and the family lived in a quintessential French white farm house just outside Paris, an absolute opposite to our apartment.

Our same-age offspring floated between the two. Clif Pugh came to do an eight-week etching course with Charles Hayter, but hated Paris so uncompromisingly that he did it in four weeks of two shifts. Matcham Skipper from Montsalvat was so bushed in Paris, so unable to bluff his way through, that he cowered in his Cité cell talking to himself on a tape recorder; challenged Charles to a duel, bagettes at one metre, rather than hear a word from him in French favour. Joslyn, gentle wife of Carl Plate, another inmate at Cité, coached our youngest in keeping up his Eng...h reading. Cassie Plate, insistently doing her H.S.C. study at the kitchen table, false-hoped our daughter into one day doing the same.

Younger son had his seventh birthday in this upside-down Podean place, in the back-to-front midyear summer. In this great city of gastronomic splendours he demanded sausages and baked beans, toast with peanut butter. Poor little boy, victim of unexotic upbringing, he must be feted on his birthday. Ingenious parents, we ran the 'legumes haricot' to earth in a tall tin in the supermarket, bought 'saucissons' at the butcher, very red ones, then found they were made of horse meat. We got frankfurters instead. The 'pain mit' sliced bread dried like blotting paper at opening, and after vast research the 'pâté d'arricide' paste of peanuts was located at last at the Moroccan grocery, 'made in Canada'. Birthday cake was much easier to find but much harder to choose. He allowed us to substitute little breadsticks dipped in sugar for the candles on condition he could shoot them down with his surviving Australian pop gun.

At the Champs Élysées 'round point', roundabout

crossing to Avenue Montaigne, coming home from school they changed over from bus to metro. Unenchanted by the historic resonances of these illustrious names, they dragged along, the boys in those high-waisted French clothes that shaped the bum so cuddlesome, and carrying chain-store replicas of elegant French portmanteau. This change-over point incurred a ritual. It was always absolutely agonisingly necessary to make pee-pee at this point. Public lavatories are in the basements of café-bars, approached by dropping a coin at the counter and descending stairs beyond. The mission obvious thus accomplished involved transit through overwhelming culinary odours, and thereby incurred the absolutely agonisingly necessary ritual, the taking of hot chocolate and croque monsieur.

We parents believed the metro hoarding promises of ever better health by drinking a litre of Evian water each morning before rising from the horizontal. It replaced the several customary cups of tea that had been the Australian pre-conditioning for morning coffee. Supine, we succumbed to the percolations of the personal plumbing, then took our grand crème coffees in the bar below reading the morning's mail, ferreted from our streetside box as new-laid eggs from a tree-fork nest. We became locals, the proprietor patient about our lapses due to excitement or brawl, leaving our gloves behind or forgetting to pay. He entrusted the children with rainy-day coffee to take upstairs to mummy-in-bed, but would not serve me another coffee after five o'clock, however, would make me 'trop nerveuse', but agreed to my adding a rhum to a petit crème, thereby adding 'Café Queensland' to his menu.

Inability to speak French in no way muted C. B.

Cheerfully he read me *Figaro* in a crowded metro, pronouncing each word as though English and inserting a kind
of hiccough for each apostrophe. 'Ce n'est pas grave' said
the policeman on the telephone as he informed us that
M. Blackman was in hospital without loss of 'conscience'
after having been knocked down by a car in the Champs
Élysées. He had been packaged and padded in thicknesses
of winter clothes. We found him sitting up telling his life
story. 'Woman driver,' he said.

We didn't make French friends. That would have
involved upgrading our language and giving up the time we
had fully occupied with trips to galleries, concerts and cinemas. Besides, the French schoolchildren observed, as in
ancient Rome, Thursday (jeudi) as games day and did
sport; had school Saturday, church and family on Sunday.
My daughter and I went each Saturday morning to a ten
o'clock symphony concert, then to a library. The boys preferred the Cinemateque, a famous old movie every two
hours for about thirty cents, waited for the Russian
Macbeth to come round again. We hadn't expected *Jane Eyre*
to be all in French, were shocked when it began: 'Je suis
Jane Eyre, sans mère, ni père, sans soeur, ni frère.' No sister, no brother, the pathos got them in at once. We bought
the book from a supermarket. We also bought the English
classics in simple language for beginners, saved them having to read long books later.

On a trip to London we met Edna O'Brien and
briefly we fell in love. I speak poetry not sex. We sprang to
each other's company, yearned to walk and talk together
endlessly. It was my blindness she loved. She wanted to tell
me all the streets and faces, all the skies and the leaves on

the trees. She would come to Paris and get a little apartment nearby at the République, where she would carry me
off each day from the lock-up apartment and we would
write together and she would read my writing and read
hers to me. At Easter she did come. We went to the
Louvre, her first visit. She got only as far as the Cezanne
still life of oranges. She gazed: 'All the oranges have souls':
she gasped. But after that she turned her attention fully on
to a young man sitting on a centre couch reading a letter.
'It's a love letter', she said, and described nuance by
nuance the feelings that passed across his face and then by
inference of invention the very lines of the letter that must
be conjuring these changes. She said he didn't speak
English and I hoped it was so. Men broke up our incipient
liaison. She would get carried away unpropitiously by some
unpremeditated man met over dinner at La Cupole or
nightcap at Deux Magots, and my husband, there and then,
decided we should do a moonlight flit, hoisting children
out of their happy school, beelining for the *Galileo*, bound
for Sydney, about to dock at Genova. The little family of
snowmen we had made from the window-sill harvest after
the late March snowfall were unhoused from the kitchen
freezer and put back on the sill to weep for our departure.

$\mathscr{P}$LEASURES OF SOLITUDE

I have never understood why it is said that an Only Child is a Lonely Child. For me the world was wonderful, people were kind, my solitary childhood was a happy one. I spent much of it by myself. I did not feel deprived of family life. The privacy and independence of solitude seemed to me to be the natural human state, making it difficult to understand how so many people find being left alone itself a deprivation, a source of loneliness and boredom. Enjoying oneself, enjoying working alone, enjoying the things of one's surroundings – these simple pleasures of life are perhaps the province of those with an aptitude for solitude, a quiet addiction to it.

As a child left quite alone I liked to do forbidden things. I liked to lick the gravy from my plate, or lie flat on the floor and eat from my bowl like the dog. On pocket money of a penny a week I saved up to buy a fourpenny pound of soft brown lumpy sugar which I hid behind the books on the shelf for the joy of clandestine sweet-eating. I would do my homework sitting in the nude for the fun of imagining the teacher's shocked expression if only she could see me while correcting it.

Daydreams, and the acting out of fantasies: I have enjoyed some quite childish pleasures when wholly by myself. With the world's worst voice I like to sing out loud in various accents, to dance with the abandonment I had at ten years old in red shimmering satin and tap-shoes on a suburban stage, or as a teenage floor-show jitterbugger. Fortunately, when my own children were in their teens, the terrace house was the right shape for the young son to be up in his attic kicking magnificent goals to the action-replay tape, or, risen up from his page in the *Angler's Guide*, to be hauling in a prize catch over the banister, while my daughter behind her closed door, draped in a length of butterfly silk, was staring, swaying, turning in front of a mirror in the vision of a dozen different gowns, while I was downstairs secretly dancing myself silly in an exotic Greek night club in the closed-off music room, and my elder son, in an attic lined with Bruce Lee posters, was perfecting a high kick to flick off the light switch, unlatch the window.

My solitude is most complete when I have the house to myself. It is the exquisite pleasure of a self-made still life to sit alone in an immaculately clean room full of cherished things beside a bouquet of flowers with a cup of fresh hot coffee, chamber music coming from the speakers, a cat lying somewhere near, enfolded in the moment. There is pleasure in the intimacy with things that share one's solitude. In the still moment of contemplation, or the colloquy of use, there is time to understand the timelessness of these inanimates. Then the particular shape of a door, the familiarity of a teapot, the intricate enamelling of a bowl, the iconography of a painting, the remembered poem, become personal. It is pleasant to have a word or two to say to the pot one is cooking with, or the chair one is dragging off to another sitting place. 'Scientific tests prove' that plants are sensitive to the thoughts and caresses of those who attend them. But the indoor inanimates have their mysteries also. Living not in earth but in affection, they outgrow the indiscriminate present to inhabit our memories of time and place, to appear without warning in our involuntary dreams.

I am always drawn to a room which has grown up tenderly around its owner like a still life portrait of his affection, where the things, carefully chosen or haphazardly come by, have been transfigured through the medium of solitude into a texture of tranquillity. I remember a man we knew in Brisbane a long time ago, a shop assistant, shy, intent. To enter his modest one-room flat at the end of a cement pathway between two buildings was to be received into a kingdom of private adoration. Six large Australian contemporary paintings, hanging frame to frame, splendoured the wall-space of that quite ordinary room. Long-play records were new at that time. He proudly sat us down to the rare experience of a half-hour of unbroken music, Delius' 'Songs of Sunset', as night came on, while in his kitchen booth he prepared a practised recipe-book meal. It was such privilege to have him share with us his bliss of solitude.

I think of another man, Johnny the timber-cutter who lives alone for weeks at a time in thousands of acres of mountain scrub. He couldn't wait to leave school to get into the trees like his father. He sleeps his night in a hut here or a derelict Combi there, manoeuvres his mighty bulldozer deftly as a delicate instrument to fall the tree exact to place, and cooks his meals over an open fire. His manor hall is sky and earth. The murals on its walls the details and distances of a bush he intimately understands. He reads by firelight – the books of Blackmore, Hardy, Lawson, because they tally with his own daily readings of season, stone and creature. His visits to the nearest one-pub-store-post-office village have a larrikin air while he spends time with a mate on a farm or building work. But within a week he has had enough, has loaded up his sup-plies and driven off in his dusty Landrover for the solitary scrub where, he says himself, he is a really happy man. 'Suppose you won a Pacific Ocean luxury holiday cruise?' 'I'd be hanging over the side looking out for an island with a few logs where they could drop me off.'

The fantasies of If and Should! If I were not blind, I think I should have gone off on long journeys and walking tours on my own. Instead, I have had a different pleasure. When, in my twenties, I was given a talking book machine, two of the first two books I chose were Dostoevsky's *House of the Dead* and Apsley Cherry Garard's *The World Journey in the World* – two strange solitudes of Siberian prison camp and Antarctic exploration, two great thrillers to the under-standing of the supremacy of the human spirit over physi-cal circumstance. I noted that, about two-thirds of the way through, a second reader took over the *Worst Journey*. Later, in London, I heard a familiar voice on BBC radio interview. It was Duncan Cass, the first reader. The story had over-taken him. He had broken off and taken himself for a year of Antarctic solitude and now was telling his own story.

Over the years I have had hundreds of books read out to me, wonderful books and wonderful readers, so that the trivia of domestic work in kitchen, in laundry, have had their narrow dimensions demolished by the greater presence of other places, other lives. A good reader gives a Turgenev love scene the tangible fragility of a blossom sprig of jasmine, gives the recitative of a genealogy in an Icelandic edda the elegance of a passage from a well-tempered clavier. I love especially the company of the diarists, the autobiographers, those who have spent their solitude with words, and of these especially those who have ventured into strange territory alone – Laurens van der Post into the forest, Antoine de Saint-Exupéry into the sky, Norbert Casteret into the caverns of the earth – and have brought us back their stories luminous as poems. In such company I have taken pleasure in the excesses of superogatory housework, cleaning out cupboards and polishing furniture, to prolong my sojourn in their vision. With such company I have been well provisioned for those unbidden solitudes when I find myself islanded by family absences from home, or marooned by illness or injury.

There are those others, the unheard, unseen accomplices of solitude, persons not present. These are not just those people, known or imagined, who are brought to mind in the reveries of idleness, seen as on a stage through the eyes of a director taking their roles in the play of life. What was or might have been, but rather of those whose presence is implicit in the activities of solitude. There was our neighbour, the careful gardener, up and about digging the beds and delving the buds at dew-sweet hour of morning, and trimming, culling, hosing at moon-late night. He had with him already the passers-by who would stop in brief silence to gasp at his slope of flowering hillside in a glimpse of joy, the hand into which he would sometimes give a bunch of perfumed stock or lavender, basket of marigolds and zinnia, just as surely as there was, always at his elbow, the mother or school teacher or whoever it was who cultivated in him, as a boy, a love of gardening. His solitude was his salutation to them all.

In the same way I saluted also, but sometimes with a pang of impatience, those who would sit at evening around my dinner table as once again I peeled the vegetables, interviewed sniff by sniff my shelf of herbs and spices. The impatience was because, an insatiable letter-writer, I yearned to sit in the embrace of far-flung friends, more delightful than a diary, their arms open wide to me in the words, the cadences of their letters that slap to the floor through the letter-slot. On the days, sequences of days, when the slap from the letter-slot endowed us only with bills, catalogues, answers to business correspondences, invitations to openings, I humbled to think of the sad sustained fortitude of Charlotte Bronte who, having conceived love for the Belgian sea captain and having received one tender moment in return, waited with a daily evocation of expectation for eighteen long months before his one indifferent letter arrived, while all the time the image of Rochester grew relentlessly more marvellous in her mind.

Letter-writing is an exchange of intimacy. The telephone is for talk; as such, is anywhere between the tension weapon of a public phone with a queue of change-jingling callers and the comforting puppet, with which, clutched in his hand, the aviator poet Antoine de Saint-Exupéry would often fall asleep, line open to South America. But a letter is the gift of a spontaneous soliloquy to the person in whose presumed presence it is made.

For thirty years my mother and I talked to each other on paper two or three times a week and from whatever part of the world we happened to be in. Indeed, my mother was not truly my friend until we took to paper, its reciprocal monologues, its agreed familiar territory. With my friend Judith Wright, through decades of word-woof woven intimacy, so often over the years our letters, however intermittently written, have crossed in mid-air — between the thought and the realisation . . . From time to time we meet in one city or another, shout at and steer about each other. But we really feel more comfortable page to page.

Cats are the deities of a writer's solitude. Called or not called they offer their company. There was the comedian cat, Boyng, who presaged my taking to the typewriter by construing himself in the carriage bed before I arrived, then insinuating himself into a comfortable coil in the wastepaper basket, coyly beseeching to be leafed over with forthcoming sheets of paper. For other people, it is their dog or horse or lizard.

We visited Ian Fairweather, the old painter on Bribie Island, only once when he was living listlessly, disconsolately, in the concrete shed of a house the local council had built to keep him decent. He sat in a previous patch of sun on the narrow unswept verandah, girdled in a dressing-gown, a stack of magazines on one side and carton of beer cans on the other, within thirty metres of his bark and sapling shack where he kept his dreams alive.

He spoke quietly, pausefully, with the indifference of the recluse as to whether he was heard or answered. All that he had to give he had given in visual imagery. He was disappointed, somewhat, that we did not want to play chess, that most unloquacious form of friendly intercourse. When we departed, he waved. Then at once he turned his attention confidentially to the low end of the verandah where his familiar, an arched yellow goanna, materialised from a dapple of shadow into which he had been transformed by our presence.

Another time we sat amid the casual gregariousness of a throng of horse-folk in a country pub, discussing 'the ride'. More room was made on the table for yet another onset of hamburgers, crisps, whiskies, shandies. Last midnight sixty of them had set forth on horseback on an endurance ride, going down from a mountain top at half-minute intervals to ride down the steep mountain side, to follow fire trails and river tracks, to brace the dawn and bitumen roads. All afternoon they had arrived at the village arena one by one, or bunched together, weary and exultant. Every one who completed the hundred miles with a fit horse would be awarded next day his Quilty silver buckle.

But the real prize was something more private. For months past there had been the long solo night rides to train the horse. Always there was the rising before dawn to go out from friend or family to exercise the horse. Why? They looked in on themselves for answers: 'the challenge', 'to find out something about me and my horse'. Then a young woman, crippled of body and troubled of family, epitomised: 'When I'm alone with my horse, I'm at peace.'

These words contrast curiously with those of a most cherished friend, Edith Tighe, who is given to declare, 'I *enjoy* myself.' One of the most genial, curious and garrulous of people, she was nevertheless happy to go off in all directions by herself. Off she went to concerts, church, Chinatown, race meetings and foreign cities. 'I don't need to have a whole lot of people tugging at my elbow or hanging on my every word.' Her inner monologue of observation and reflection, funny things and forums, fountains forth later in wonderful spurts of wordflow in letters, talk, reminiscences, all delivered with her own rococo ornamentation of verbiage.

She is the very person for whom museums are accumulated, paintings painted, gravestones inscribed, gardens laid out, the whom it does concern. With a singular disregard for dress or prospect of meeting the right people, she sallies forth to view a movie, consume a delicate morsel at a corner table, deliver several ill-assorted little bits of nonsense to some little folk (for she was the perennial aunty), making her own discoveries of people and places and their waywithal. She held forth to us, as though home from the seven seas, about 'the poor benighted creatures' or the journey 'way to hell and gone' consequent on misdirection. Nothing she did was without its spice of interest, because 'I enjoy myself!'

I telephoned an Irish friend and asked him what he's doing. 'I'm at home by myself,' he says, 'which is better than nothing.' Some are born to solitude, others have it thrust upon them. Relieved at last of the burden of the future, the fullness of the present becomes precious. My mother in her eighties was one of those who, having

outlived her contemporaries and immediate family, chose
to live alone. She lived on in the house that her long-ago
husband had built for their marriage; roamed from room
to room warmed by the presence of past events; kept her
garden flowering in soil whose seasons she knew by heart:
planned the nearest morrow, watched from her verandah
the many little dramas being performed on the children's
playground opposite, and the backs of houses laid out on
the hillside. Round her were a clutter of things trivial or
treasurable, 'items' or 'possessions', and some of quite
temporary kind – tomatoes ripening on a windowsill,
books with markers protruding, knitted squares for a knee
rug. Paintings on the walls heralded her mornings, sen-
tinelled her nights. She was lonely only sometimes when
the departure of a house guest disturbed for a while the
decorum of her solitude. 'When I'm alone, I know where
I am.'

THE CAT THAT GOT AWAY

Boyng lived with us for a couple of years, the most beautiful cat we ever had the honour to have in our household. Actually Boyng was not beautiful at all. He was the stock-type silver-grey mackerel-striped tabby of any catalogue of cats. But he was so intelligent, so witty, so comical a creature, with whiskers too long — a personality rather than a cat — that I really expected that one day he would unzipper himself right down the middle and someone would step out and say, 'Ha ha — it was me inside there all the time.'

Boyng in the city was a lounge-lizard cat with certain eccentricities. He liked to lie about in provocative places — concave within a shopping basket, tucker-boxed on top of the telephone books, snailed up in the cradle of the typewriter, hibernated in the sun-scented lavender bush. He was not afraid of heights — would bask upon the beach-warm ironing board when the shirts had all been done; would lie vigilant spread along a bookshelf row, or pigeon in a hole among the books, communing with book worms; would ornament himself like a leering Toby jug among the vases and decanters of a kitchen dresser top shelf, and would paw down and pull the string of the terracotta pottery bell if unnoticed. He especially liked to lie doggo behind my stack of recipe books above the stove where he could peer one eye over to see who was entering, what cooking.

Perhaps this acrophilia was the result of his living an island life as a kitten on the top of our long marble table. There he would mirror-gaze into the face of every flower of a new bouquet; would tap gently and lower a listening ear on to each unwrapped parcel; sidle about between the monumental salt and pepper grinders like a tourist at the Horse Guards, aware that he, Boyng, was as picturesque as any other deposit upon that table, as worthy to be drawn into our family album of intimacy. Later, as a life-size cat, he could climb up and walk about among the groceries as soon as they were delivered and unpacked from the grocer's box, cursory as a dealer at a jumble sale, until he found his tin of cat food. This he would manoeuvre to the edge of the table, propel it over and roll it to the place on the floor between the brick pillars where he liked to be fed; then, if no one noticed and came to open his tin, he would appeal by getting up on to the high stool and rocking it to and fro by pushing a paw against the pillar, knocking out the rhythm of his need.

His paws were agile. He would reach up and rattle the door knob of a room where we were gathered; would flap away at the letter-slot of the front door to be re-admitted after an evening stroll. Poor Boyng had no voice. Only the smallest pin-prick of sound inhabited his purry furry throat.

This explains his interest in mime. Perhaps by some shrew of spells he had been transformed into this cat-time of life; explains why he paid particular attention to each new thing that came into the house, attentive and intimate as though by clairvoyance enquiring into their previous existence. He bestowed upon these things the blessing of his presence – would lie symmetric on a visitor's coat, collapse head on between paws on the open pages of a book, or endow his perfect curve of sleep upon a record left still upon the record player. A poster was brought home, left rolled up lying on the table. He became a ferret and insinuated himself into its mysterious tunnel, then, gently widening himself from side to side, got it spread out so that he could pace about upon its pictured surface.

Thus he teased out the limits of his indoor life to feats of meaning. He would hide among the collars and sleeves of coats upon the hall stand, flip out a paw on to passers-by; would skulk goanna-like around the unseen side of the pillar as we moved about the house; liked to be worn as a hat, or to be paper-bagged and dumped in the kitchen bin; or jailed up inside the slatted doors of the saucepan cupboard.

But, like all comics, he liked to be taken seriously. Our daughter confided in him. She habituated him to breakfasts tête-à-tête. They sat down together to their simple fare, Vegemite toast and milk. She did him the courtesy of cutting his toast into tiny squares and serving his warm milk in a shallow cup. And once he did her a fine favour in return. She, coming home from the beach, had de-escalated herself peremptorily from the car in a cascade of towel and costumes, and her watch had leapt away down a grid in the gutter. Just as the rubber-gloved wooden-spooned searchers were giving up, Boyng suddenly appeared, strolled over authoritatively and pointed incisively to the exact murk of muck where it lay.

In the country Boyng was a tiger. He bided his travelling time in the car disconsolate in a basket, protesting with the emission of all the foul city-fed odours he could muster. He would emerge reborn, stretch his animal length and whiskers to the country air that prickled with momentous smells and minutiae of movement. He would crouch, stalk, pounce, leap in the air to catch an insect, creep home in step with a half-killed rabbit; flash through the grass or up a tree, tail twitching. He would follow along with us on walks for miles, then complain with his little squeak of noise at sandy patches, lie prostrate in front of us when he was tired out. We would carry him like a baby until he unpitied himself and suddenly sprang off to a flicker of passing prey.

He would stay out all the icy-cold moon-shining prey-stirring night and lie tea-cosy warm and still all day beside the fireplace embers, digesting. There was a possum who liked to come inside that country cottage at this time. Possum liked to go dashing about the tops of windows and high shelves, knocking down bottles, skipping about the rafters, swinging his tail down over our heads and charmingly reaching down to take the crunches of stale bread and crisps of apple we gingerly handed up to him. All this fascinated Boyng immensely. He could not resist the chance to play this game himself, and so would follow around behind the possum, mimicking his actions like a cheeky child behind the village idiot. But he was always able to dissolve into shadow if the possum turned his way.

It was when we returned to town after a particularly long spell in the country that Boyng decided to leave us. It was one of those periods in our household when there was an excessive amount of rushingly going out and boisterously bringing in people, when shirts pile up unwashed, letters unopened, cat unsung. He might well have tried to make a dignified farewell. Instead he left with unseemly notice of departure. He cat-walked the length of my shelf above the stove, kicking down and smashing all my little bottles of herbs and spices, felling flat the stack of recipe books that had been his fragrant and favourite lurking place. He was never seen again, not even hitch-hiking back to the country.

$\mathcal{T}$ELL YOUR MOTHER LOVELY

We had been living in our terrace house for just over two years, about as long as our three children had ever lived in any one place, as our lives moved on from city to city, house to house. Towards the end of the year the pattern seemed to stir pangs of change in us all. Young son came home from school each day with ever more desirable reasons for becoming a weekly boarder, in increase of worthiness from pillow fights and meat-pie lunches to extra muscle-building sport practice and better homework done under supervising prefect's eye. My objections proportionately subsided from gasping at the vastly greater number of shirts, pyjamas and socks seemingly needed by one boarding body as compared to same home body, down to muttered trivia of a merely motherly kind. Elder son, on the strength of his second pay packet, left home to join a 'pad' nicely situated within spitting distance of his old school. He fitted all his worldly goods into one taxi boot and drove off waving our farewell gift, a beautiful blue enamel teapot, into the fleeting world of instant caf and

tea-bags. Husband embarked on elaborate plans for a
sojourn back to Paris to work on a postponed lithography
project. Daughter thereupon resigned from school in
anticipation of accompanying us.

There was a nice familiar air of disturbance in our
lives, a happiness of expectation. Suitcases appeared more
habitable than furniture. Remarks flew about as to what
tenants would find right or wrong with our house. But
somehow our New Year resolution never quite got off the
doorstep. There were no boarder vacancies. Elder son
came home for Christmas and stayed. Pad life had its problems, the who-does-what discontents over sloppy
kitchens, missing records, overcrowded beds. Husband's
exhibition commitments loomed date lines ahead. Paris
sank below the horizon of possibility. Just then my garden
started to flower in a quite endearing way and it seemed
the house had won the day over all our plans.

Not for our daughter. She had made her decisions
and, maybe because of the prevailing conjunctions of her
planets, she took off on her new course, regardless of our
parental back-sliding. She leapt at one single bound clear
out of her childhood. She abandoned her attic, leaving
behind the whole clutter of her girlhood, and made herself
a new home in the back shed of the house which her
brother had deserted. The blue carpet men came, the
white paint men, the pine shelving men, and rendered the
transformation.

Her fever was contagious. If we weren't going to
change houses, then we could all change about our places
in the house – young son to attic, one; front first-floor
parental bedroom to back rear, two: a chess game in which

it was only necessary for every piece of furniture in the house to become a pawn for everyone to be happy. There were advantages all round: returning Christmas guest son, couched in the downstairs music room, formerly sitting room, would have the run of the record player; daughter in back shed would have a life of her own; young son in attic would have a bed for a friend; parents in upper rear would have a quieter place to sleep, and an upstairs sitting room out of the mainstream of teenage traffic.

Now the sensible thing to do would have been to hire a pantechnicon and load every household thing into it, let it drive around the block a few times while meantime exorcising the house of every outgrown school book, unpartnered shoe, broken toy, covey of cockroach and other pests, and then drive the pantechnicon up to the front door like newlyweds and re-occupy the dwelling. But we suffer from a sense of detail. So the more the Christmas cards came clapping through the letter-slot and the relatives to dinner, the more chests got halted halfway through doorways, half-cleared shelves filled up again with instant bundles of yesterday, until there was a situation reminiscent of a Roman traffic jam. Meantime elder son went punctually to work, young son catapulted out the door to beach or cricket clinic, daughter stocked up with new ideas and friends. They muralised the newness of her abode, filled the ashtrays and discussed Life. Husband sensibly shot off to the bush with cat and painting gear.

I was left drowning in domestic disorder. Occasionally my daughter and friends would emerge from her chrysalis process to shake free her sewing machine from its waterfall of half-made garments, patch-pinned jeans, op-shop cast-offs in metamorphosed, bright bouquets of braids and fretted frills. It took several of them some time to wrest the desk free from its pack-horse burden of text books, art folders and folios of notes, dribbling bottles of inks and glues, scrabble of buckled stationery. On the way down the narrow stairs, the poster proclaiming BLESS THIS MESS was torn asunder.

It was clearly no good insisting that she decently clear out her attic for the incoming brother. She could only escape from her previous life by dispossessing herself of all its memories and attachments, without regard for the reality that these were left behind her in the form of so many real things – the possessions of her past crafts and crazes, dolls that had slept on tearful arms, ribbons of bygone plaits, rolls of 'gorilla-colour' paintings and folds of fraying tie-dyed cloths, the papier mâché masks and lop-sided puppets, that had been such treasures at their first bringing home from those Saturday morning classes serious little girls go to, safe in the belief that the boys are all away doing stupid boy-only things.

It was not that young son's clearing-out could never get beyond the re-reading of *Five Little Firemen*. The clearing of the sisterly Augean stable was too much to ask. Daughter took headlong flight into the crises and heartaches of adolescence, by taking only the clothes, books and records of her choice. She looked over her shoulder to announce that she had worked out a new course of study, and flashed off to a Proficiency Reading course to upgrade her bookability.

Only I cared for the old things. With a flotilla of cardboard cartons, I plunged in and salvaged whatever was

passable of un-scribbled-on exercise books, four-limbed
dolls, unchipped china animals and untorn dresses. Three
days, fifteen cartons and umpteen vacuum-cleaner bags
later, I had cleared away into past tense even the caves of
old dead scrapbooks, pop posters and decomposing panti-
hose, the costume dolls of many lands long locked in conference under the bed, and unclogged the corners of
cupboards from their crushes of unthreaded beads, toeless
slippers and little squashed boxes of spilling out sticky gold
stars. One whole childhood painlessly removed!

As Brett Whitely used to say when everything turned
out all right, 'Tell your mother lovely!'

On First Looking into Blackmans' Home Life

In Melbourne in May 1993 the Charles Blackman retrospective exhibition 'Schoolgirls and Angels', paintings and drawings with guided tours, annotated catalogue and biographic video, opened its Australian tour. Four decades of the artist's work were represented. For three of those decades we were wed. I visited the exhibition in its second week.

I approach through the Botanical Gardens, gold russet leaves thick on paths, people in overcoats and scarves, distant perspectives through bared boughs, voices brisk on chill air, 'Charles Blackman' bannered on the National Gallery facade, Alice in the Boat flies skywards.

There is a 1960 photograph of Charles and Barbara with two infants outside the Gardens kiosk. We are leaving Melbourne after a decade to go to live in Brisbane. I wish, I promise myself, always to be in Melbourne in May, always to be out of it by June. All through the Fifties the pleasures of autumn, the comforting in cosy knitted jumpers and scarves to shuffle through fallen leaves in Hawthorn streets, are followed by miserable winter bronchitis. We read Verlaine beside the lake beneath the trees in these Gardens, and Rimbaud's *Illuminations* with the pink-legged Cape Barron geese listening like flamingos on a croquet lawn.

City kids both of us, the Botanical Gardens are a comfortable familiarity, a public privacy, from childhood birthday parties, parental tea-house treats; in Sydney, first kiss close under an umbrella on a wet deserted path, last legal kiss in the great greenhouse, a Rousseau world of difference secreting us.

Exit gardens of memory. Cross singing tram lines. Enter galleries of present. 'When entering the exhibition it is advisable to commence viewing from the Murdoch Court to gain the full effect of the artist's development.' Walk through a life. Stills from an autobiography.

> Art is the means by which the essence of humanness is given form, by which it becomes transcendent, or the means by which elements of a personal experience are transformed into universal truths . . . Art makes chance into history, the mundane into mythology. Mythology deprives the object of which it speaks of all history. In it history evaporates. It is a kind of ideal servant. It prepares all things, brings them, lays them out. The master arrives, it silently disappears. All that is left for one to do is to enjoy this beautiful object without wondering where it comes from; or, even better, it can only come from eternity.
>
> (Roland Barthes, *A Barthes Notebook*)

*My Bush Trip: at Windmill camp
outside Broome, 1979.*

*Insert: with Melissa
(Becky Brown),
at Derby, 1979.*

With Judith Wright: her sixtieth birthday, 1975.
(Photo by Axel Poignant.)

Christmas Day 1978: on Swanborne nude beach.

With Marcel Veldhoven: at friends' wedding, 1983.

At 'Indooroopilly': sitting in my father's chair.

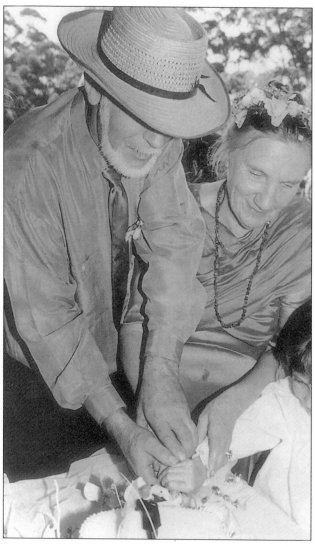

The Wedding: Marcel and me with granddaughter Clementine, 1992.

With Ross Mellick: at The Wedding, 1992.

With Betty Churcher: 'Friends from Schooldays', 1994.

With Barrie Reid: outside Heide, 1993.

*Generations: with Christabel and granddaughter Pepa
and baby Miguelito in Spain, 1992.*

With Marcel at 'Indooroopilly': 'Love is the Wine'.

At 'Indooroopilly': reflection.

Making friends: cockhorsing with Orlando, 1994.

This is a balancing trick, how to fit so many angels on the head of a pin, so many memories into the present moment. Angels, I ask for invisibility. I do not wish to have 'the look of roses that are looked at'. I am an old tree now, knotted and gnarled; their gaze carves into me to release the maiden Daphne, early photographs to go by.

In the moment of death all one's past life rushes before the inner eye in a flash: 'and the moment of death is here and always'.

My first visit to Melbourne, May 1950, from Brisbane which knows no such autumn; utter shock to see through a train window the whole sun, a golden ball on the horizon, painting by Paul Klee; bareness of fences and brick walls, nudity of tree trunks with gilded garment leaves fallen about their feet, an earth bowed down before advancing sky; on doorsteps, pots of daphne with their icy breath of Heaven.

Barrie Reid has brought me to Melbourne with him on his annual leave from the Public Library. He is giving me the chance to improve my knowledge of current Australian culture and meet important people. He is uplifting me from my bed of suffering where I am beset by a nervous breakdown, brought on by the loss of beliefs, eyesight and past year's lover, a paintingless painter from the south.

On the way down in the train he briefs me on the coffee shops – Gibby's, The Blue Room, Cinderella's – where I shall meet the Langley family and people from Montsalvat; the Murrumbeena potteries where I shall meet the Boyds, and most of all, Heide, the farmhouse behind the low lavender hedge at Heidelberg where, if I am good, I shall go to meet John and Sunday Reed.

Actually it is all well planned. He is taking me to people and places where I shall hear of the scandal of Charles Blackman who passed through early in the year leaving a trail of heresies, misdemeanours, stolen neck ties, pawned books, arrogant remarks, irreverent questions. Among them I meet again one who speaks my language, the independent nonconformist antimythologiser, John Yule, a reliable narrator who sees the running out of town of the 'scruffy evasive little fruit-picking person whom I am well rid of' as pure comedy; gives me his mother's address in Sydney, to which I send a telegram announcing my date of train return.

By the next May, Charles, John and I have moved out of the tin shed in East Melbourne where we have been living, three peas in a pod, with our rolled-up mattresses, row of chairs painted along the wall and enamel eating bowl. John moves into a gardener's cottage in Alphington, we into our Hawthorn coach-house. Our Melbourne lives take shape. In mid-June John is best man at our Registry Office wedding. By walking all the way home to Hawthorn we have just enough money to buy a tin of sausages in Wellington Parade.

This is Melbourne forty-two years later. This is all about schoolgirls and angels. 'Begin the promenade of the work on show, chronologically, passing the juvenilia, moving into the 1951 *sequentes* Schoolgirl series.' Where memories begin is childhood, is schooldays. Lovers learn each other by exchanging tales of childhood, grafting together by this attenuation, making of their separate pasts the twin soul inhabiting two bodies, the mutual dreaming.

Brother of three sisters, he wears girl's underpants, girl's shirts to school. Brother without a key, he sits on the doorstep waiting for schoolgirls to come home. I start

High School during wartime austerities; have to make do with a left-over mis-make school hat, its brim outlandishly large, and school shirts made by my dressmaker aunt, their collars outlandishly wide – 'Bubbles' photographed in school uniform, complete with black stockings, pleated skirt and lace-up shoes. History is made of the years before and after the 1953 first showing of Schoolgirl paintings. Video pronounces. Guides explain. Viewers look through the windowpanes of the picture frames. For me the paintings, the walls, the visitors, the video screen are all the same, invisible in my invisible world of blindness. My world visible is a virtual reality of recollection.

I visit Barrett Reid, retired Public Librarian, retired editor of *Overland* magazine, living at Heide, the house behind the low lavender hedge. We sit and talk in the old library, now carpeted, but still with a wood fire. Virtually, it is a night in May 195–. Sunday Reed, in powder blue corduroy slacks and cashmere sweater, is sitting beside the fire on the hearthside stool hunched over a book talking about the reproductions in it with a little dry laugh. John is sitting on the big soft sofa with pale canvas covers, legs thrust forward, hands linked behind head, intermittently, sceptically, taking part in a conversation. Seven or eight of us in the room, little tray of coffee cups on the low table, anecdotes and speculations stirred and consumed.

Outside the circle of talk I muse to myself. Forty years ago when this house was young, other people whom we do not know – except in a way for smelly Mrs Brown whose ghost goes up and down the passageway – sat around this room, arguing, planning, joking. Now in forty years time, who will sit here, whom of us will still be talking here . . . our elders gone before, our contemporaries scattered, just two of us left, an old moth Barrie and an old moth Barbara smiling together over memories, cross-wiring present projects, correcting each other's forgetfulness, redolent as autumn fires, fuelled by all that we have known and have been known by. So it transpires: 'An Emperor dreams he is a Blue Bird singing in his garden. Or, a Blue Bird singing in a garden dreams he is an Emperor.' And all the time the White King writes it down lest it all unhappen. I turn to Sunday and I say, 'Sun, how about that Superveille book about stolen children you promised us?' Outside it is chill, damp, musky, a very old earth communes with a very ancient sky, so clear tonight.

A television documentary, 'Dreams and Shadows', is made about the artist's life, by a filmmaker, one of the enquirers, voyeurs, gazers into our fish bowl, a generation away from the Blackmans of Chrystobel Crescent. To make a scene more delicate, a make-up world is made up. On cue Ryton schoolgirls swarm on and spill off a much arriving tram. They will have copies of faded videos to show their grandchildren — 'That's me, third from the left. What funny old uniforms!'

Only a few of those captured schoolgirls are here on the gallery walls, so few. They jostled for space night after night in the cubbyhouse sitting room in our coach-house home. It is midnight, coffee time on radio 3UZ, 'My Little friends it's coffee time'. Our milky coffee heats up in a saucepan balanced on top of the kerosene heater. Charles and I stare at them, sitting side by side on an improvised sofa made by roping a soft old kapok mattress covered with green burlap over a couple of boxes.

My damp coat and cap hang outside in the brick-floored stable. I still wear my many winter layers. I am not long home from doing a life class for the Vic. Arts, journeying home by change of empty trams and resounding footsteps in silent winter streets, past Martin the picture framer in his loft over the road still tapping away, the prince in the tower condemned to frame a thousand paintings before he can sleep with the princess. Charles is clowned in paint-smeared ragged jeans and unravelling jumper, tea-cosy cap and paint-daubed shoes; has been painting since I set out this morning, as the quarter to eight news began, for my first Tech life class of the day.

We drink out of big Swedish mugs, yellow or dark blue, and dig into a paper bag of fresh crisp biscuits, a pound packet of loose assorted. All around us are wet shining panels of painted schoolgirls. He has just carried them one by one down the vertical wall ladder from the studio loft trapdoor, one at a time so as not to rub against the wet paint.

The jonquil yellow bought on Monday is doing well, but the larch green won't last out the week. 'The third that lies in our embrace' is a great devourer. I insist that one personal thing must be acquired each week – a shirt, a towel, a blanket – before the studio monster is fed with ever more boards, brushes, paints. Wash the brushes thin. Decide which pictures to paint over, or at least paint on the reverse side. The schoolgirls watch us until all the biscuits are eaten and we have got to know them. Then it is 'Bedtime for Bonzo' for all of us, schoolgirls passed carefully upstairs to lean against studio walls, us to our single bed under the low-barred laneway window in the coachman's closet. More paintings tomorrow, schoolgirls fresh daily.

Melbourne, Olympics 1956: the city hardly knows itself. Such excitement. So many changes. News lines buzzing. Traffic pulsing, the air cheering, the radio informing. The new television awakening us to new experiences – and here to stay.

I am pregnant. Such excitement and changes all over. I hardly know myself. Charles is a short-order cook in the kitchen of the Eastbourne Café. Tables and extra tables, overcrowded. So many dinners all at once. The French radio and television personnel are eating there. The kitchen hardly knows itself. Plates fly through the air.

I have had my first talking book machine for just a few months, a turntable with heavy 24 r.p.m. discs. Robin Holmes with BBC aplomb reads Lewis Carroll. 'All on a summer's day . . .' 'You're nothing but a pack of cards.' Alice, girl woman, appears on the easel. Curiouser and curiouser. Her body changes size. The flowers are growing, colours changing every board. 'Eat me' to the growing babe. 'Drink me' to the world, that changing place. The city, the Blackmans, the paintings will never be the same again.

On Monday 17 May 1993 the exhibition opens in Melbourne. So many old friends there, not me. Suppose in fact this exhibition were happening not here but in, say, Helsinki – exhibition of a wholly unknown painter, catalogue without any biographical notes, no mention at all of a blind wife. What magnet, what homer, what keyhole, what catalyst would the viewers see, the critics cite on this first looking? I am at home. My Spanish granddaughter, five years old and speaking no English, sits beside me reading a story book picture by picture, talking it through to herself.

My blindness is my secret, a locked chamber because nobody has the key. Nobody asks the right questions. They key in their imagination of blindness, the fear, the exotic, the dark into which we all go. But my blindness is luminance. For me they all went into the luminance, as my world grew indiscriminately lighter. Now the schoolgirls, the Alices, the family icons, the beach and park and disco people – they all fade in memory, invaded by light. Remembrance too becomes lighter, takes leave. But the angels are within. 'You are all my angels!' cries Dostoevsky down the alleys of the blood, cries it to the convicts, to the child set free to be set upon by wolves, to the dying priest, to the gentle prostitute. For how else is the Divine to be known, if not seen daily in the faces, hands, napes of neck, the flower on its stalk as well as in the 'dear little unloved child of tears'?

> I travelled through a land of men,
> A land of men and women too,
> And heard and saw such dreadful things
> As cold earth-wanderers never knew.
>
> (William Blake, 'The Mental Traveller')

The schoolgirls are, after all, in transit between the home where they eat and sleep, and the school where they work and play. Transition is perilous. Falls the shadow.

The day of the opening is also the day of the funeral of John Maxwell Nicholson. I speak with Charles in the afternoon. He says, 'We, who knew Max and had our lives so marvellously touched by him, were fortunate.' Max, in reflective mood some years ago, said to me, 'I seem to have had more effect on other people's lives than ever I've had on my own.' I write in my diary, 'He demonstrated to us the humble, civilised, dignified, illuminated life.' My children, and some of their friends in teenage years, had the privilege of going to the Melbourne Gallery with Max, standing back with him to give full attention to this work and that, listening to what he spoke out of his wide experience of looking at paintings, knowing life. I loved to walk in the Botanical Gardens with him where he would behave in the same way to an avenue of trees – the stopping, standing back, giving attention, describing to me form and detail, then stepping forwards, our hands held, carefully reading the arboreal title. To have life, and have it more abundantly; to see paintings and see them more attentively.

In Sydney in May 1977 Max is living with us at 159 Paddington Street. A large man, he is sitting arrayed before his breakfast, an affirming aroma of toast and a panoply of gentleman's relish, jams, marmalade, honey, set out before him, coffee poured. Charles is snatching up his cut lunch, an apple, a clutch of paint rags, about to leap out the door to go to his studio a mile away. 'That's bravery,' soliloquises Max in theatrical mode, 'to go into an empty studio and face a blank canvas . . . to stand before it and confront the depths . . . to bring up something and put it there. What a heroic task.' His morning salutation was always some version of this. This day Charles turns on him. 'One more speech like that, Max, and you'll be out on your ear. It's bloody hard enough without you singing a song about it.' Then he slams out the door.

Teacher to student on how he paints:
'First I sits m'self down. Then I works m'self up.
Then I puts down me blacks. Then I pulls out me lights.'
The teacher is Fuseli, the student William Blake.

After the first brush stroke it is work, skill, stamina. But, between the blank space and the image, the empty canvas and the finished painting, falls the shadow. 'The form comes from Heaven,' says Blake, 'the energy from Hell'. The Shadow is the no-man's land that must be traversed between the two. It happens again for the painter between the finishing of the work and the public exposure. Between the hanging of the exhibition and its opening, falls the shadow. The painter who has plunged naked into the Unconditioned, must clothe again his social self. This is the difference between the Sunday painter who enjoys himself and the painter of other kind who must lose himself, the one who has the itch and must scratch it, the Fisher King who must salve his ever-agonising wound with the fingers that have touched the fish in the waters of the Unconscious. For Jung the Unconscious is metaphored as water. The fish spawns, grows, circles, eludes, is glimpsed, caught. Ultimately the question must be asked: 'Whom does the Grail serve?'

I make a third, last visit to the exhibition. Barnaby, the younger son, comes to Melbourne for a day between overnight trains. This is a rite of passage for him to see his father as art. For him also it is a reflection of a life of which he is a part. He seeks his point of entry – the 1962 'Family' paintings done at the time of his gestation, the hard-edge Interiors, when he first trotted about the London mansion flat, a natural part of his world; finds himself in the 1968 drawing of his five-year-old self with hammer; 'the hammer,' he recalls, 'with chocks of wood handed to me in the studio to keep me quiet for a while'; remembers his playmate Lee Ann who stole a grape (a companion drawing), who died soon afterwards in a car accident; then Red Leaf pool and Centennial Park, family outings became paintings on the walls after school not much noticed. It is an inner struggle to extrapolate image on the wall from moment in the heart, aggravated by captions that seem to him to go beyond annotation into interpretation. 'Interpretation is the revenge of the intellect upon art, the revenge of the intellect upon the world.' (Susan Sontag)

John Yule, friend of the Fifties, joins us. We regress to those early Schoolgirl paintings. This a Blackman lifetime beyond Barnaby's reach, a heritage of parental anecdote. 'These paintings speak a language I understand,' John says, 'whereas those after Alice come to me in translation, so to speak.'

Translations and resonances. Reflections on reflections. For me everyone's description repaints the picture. Anyone who has shared the Blackman life out of which the paintings have come, anyone part of the parturition process, will make contact, a live-wire shock of recognition.

Much stirs in this son, seeing in this other place paintings long lived with, familiar, close to his bone, and others that call his attention to a part of his life that had escaped him. Some have grown unbelievably larger or smaller in transplantation. Some that hung on stair or stood behind a door are found as poster, print or postcard in the Gallery bookshop. 'East, west, north, south,' went the popular pie jingle of the Fifties, 'They're in everybody's mouth.'

For us this is holy ground and we have now to render it to Caesar. These viewers all around us are entitled to this territory. We give it with grace, recognising that what seeds in them may be some essence already intoned in our lives.

'The mountain gives birth to the mouse,' is an old proverb of Horace restated by Barthes. 'The mountain is not any too big to make a mouse.' The father unknown, the father behind the one who came to junior football matches, cooked dinners, got drunk at times, went off to Paris or Surfers, was not a conjurer's hat, but a mountain. An enormous process takes place before the mouse of a painting takes shape, signifies, gives local habitation and a place to persons and things close around him, translating subject into object.

The biography may be subtext, but it is of another order. Family members, we grapple in the green room. The young Parsifal, after all, on first looking on the Grail, could not ask the question, 'Whom does it serve?': only much later. We sit for a coffee in the cafeteria area and are not ashamed of tears.

'Remember Richard?' – a mate of Barnaby's from Perth who lived for a while at 159, one of the many young people who entered the all-life living room of that not large house and said, 'I didn't know that people could live like this.' 'Like this' was piano and dresser face to face ('Look at the haloes on the knuckles of the Girl playing Mozart!' just overheard.) – long marble slab trestle table with church pews, stone archways into kitchen, double-bed-size buttoned leather chesterfield with the triptych

Blue Alice above it taking up the whole wall.

Richard now lives back in Perth, works with his good Sicilian family in their bistro and has opened his own gallery upstairs. When the going gets rough, he takes himself off to the Art Gallery of Western Australia and sits himself down in front of the *Blue Alice* there in its new home, restored to minted freshness, the years of cigarette and coffee fumes quite absolved.

Remember Paris, a visit there in May 1968 just before the revolution: in a bistro in Rue de Fosse we chance to sit face en face to a converse couple, he blind, she a painter. Egyptians, Australians, in fractured French we muse upon the mirrored paths. Strangers familiar, sharing a sly joke, we embrace a radiant moment, smile of the dark angel.

A decade later, a Chinese restaurant in Perth, in May 1978. My Blackman life ends here. After the configured torment of Scott and Zelda, Colette and Willy, before the Nightmare after Fusole, and the incarceration of The Room of Edgar Allan Poe, falls the shadow. 'I will be your eyes,' he said at the beginning. Now the blinds must be pulled down on those windows to the world. We had wrestled long and well with that dark angel and are not ashamed.

The shadow of the dark angel is absolute. 'The blind and the not-blind are no longer useful to each other.' I write a letter of resignation from marriage to take effect on our twenty-seventh wedding anniversary in mid-June. No renewal of copyright. Finito la musica. On with the dance. A painful switching-off of the support system. Flames are not quenched. Our paths diverge towards separate bright horizons.

On the other side of St Kilda Road, towards the river, the Flame of Remembrance burns for ever in the inner shrine.

When we were young we thought that love was proof against that dark angel, and we did not think that in our lifetime these paintings, that were our hearts' treasure, would turn to gold at a collector's touch. Paint rags to paper riches.

> *And if the Babe is born a Boy,*
> *He's given to a Woman Old*
> *Who nails him down upon a rock,*
> *Catches his shrieks in cups of gold.*
>
> (William Blake, 'The Mental Traveller')

Angels, the head of a pin is a hard place to do battle or to dance.

Schoolgirls and Angels, Alice and White Cat, Faces and Flowers, and all the images on gallery walls are configured in my personal iconography, with a patina of looking before and after. Again and again, they will be looked at for a first time, looked at and referred to as the Blackman chronology. 'The map is not the country.' This exhibition is my own Rosetta Stone.

PART FOUR

$\mathcal{N}$ATURE'S POEMS

It is the first Christmas Day of my strange new solo life. A quartet of transients, we picnic on Swanborne nude beach in Perth, wearing only hats, accompanied by a heyday bouquet of daisies planted ceremonious as a flagstaff beside us in the sand under their own umbrella. We consume only jelly and champagne. Glass after glass we down another jelly baby. We toast our unscheduled lives and the sunset diving headfirst into the Indian Ocean before us. I have been bewitched to start a new life here in this Western Australia that I hardly knew a year ago. How has the West won me? It was the Spring. Briefly, magnificently, the wildflowers were with us. We had them on our tables by request from the florist, in a grand exhibition in Kings Park, rough-set in terraces of rock with recorded bush noises and bird song, and spread out across miles of inland spaces.

Driving back along the fevered hundred-mile road between Coolgardie and Southern Cross, nuggeted with goldfield anecdotes, we had stopped and set foot on the desert in its wildflower sudden splendour. Clump by clump the low-flowered bushes fielded out to the flat horizon. The surprise is that no single clump is like its neighbour, and its like cannot be found again among the muster of individual originalities. Here was a tall scarlet pipe-cleaner topped with three furry green fingers, here a soot-velvet stalk flagging a ten-finger baby's hand, here an airborne sea urchin hammocked in a web of wire leaves, here a celluloid shirt button feathered in lolly-pink paper, here a forethought of follicled insect leg with unflown gossamer wing, a spindle in grey-thread foliage, here a splatter of star in a well of dark frond, here bushfire ember spirals, and studio-sculptured waxwork mobiles in miniature. It was as though the Almighty had chosen this barest hessian of earth's surface on which to make notes, to embroider His essays on petals, stalk and leaf, and had set down in flower form a myriad little poems, philosophies and fragments of prayer, to be annually remembered. And then He doused it all away with a handful of dust into the blank of summer drought.

I witnessed this Western Spring, this mysterious garden estranged from water, these allusions to antique biology, and felt a great upsurge of spirit. If God can make such statements of natural imagination in flower form from such a drift of things, then I could start another life with whatever was there around me, a nuova vita, right here in Perth.

My grandfather, and therefore also I myself, became Australian by baptism of earth. Swede and seaman, at seventeen he made his first acquaintance with the ocean, suffered the misery of its disturbance across a world until he reached land where he lay down long and grateful, let the ship sail away, went inland, changed his name, became a landscape gardener, lived on another fifty years, never visited the sea again, kept his hands upon the earth and grew flowers everywhere. His daughter, weathering two widowhoods and fifty years of office work with books and figures, kept herself green with gardens, digging them and loving them; would walk me through the Botanic Gardens looking into the faces of flowers and naming them; would meander me over paddocks seeking everlastings and sarsparillas; would scramble me deep into sandfly-biting bush to gather wildflowers that no one would ever miss; went in her old age on country tours to visit gardens pictured in the newspapers.

Mole, that personable creature of the Wild Wood, remarked that he was kept busy 'writing poems and other little jobs about the house'. So my mother, coming home, would attend to the flowers first, stroking the lower leaves away from the stalks, setting them safe in water, weighing them in her hands and kneading the heads to shape the bouquet properly, then putting it in its place, before she got around to taking off her hat, opening her letters or answering my questions.

My children, brought up in houses where the walls were constantly disappearing behind a welter of paintings and, moreover, where the paintings were re-arranged more often than the furniture, sometimes as often as between one mealtime and the next, used to find it 'creepy' to be in a place where there were no paintings. Places like seaside holiday flats with calendar fig-leafed on the nude blank wall and plastic flowers all idle in a plastic vase upon a plastic table; the homes of schoolmates thick with carpets, drapes and configured wallpapers, suites in motels, airports, doctors' waiting rooms, were all 'creepy' — somehow embarrassing.

Daughter of a mother who was always with flowers, growing gardens when we lived in places with earth of our own, being given bunches of flowers large or small by friends, and even people of slight acquaintance, when we lived in upstairs rooms, I too have a sense of unease at having to spend time in rooms where there are no flowers. The poem is missing. The poem or gift or soul's divine breath, or whatever one calls the living essence born within us that cannot die, needs constant confirmation. Life is fugitive. Confined within the presence of things of lasting and material value, which cannot die being already dead, it feels threatened. Flowers are fragile. Flowers in a room, like music in its span of time, speak in a language beyond their moment of being; are, Nature's Poems.

Flowers promise. 'Every slip or seedling I plant,' my mother would say, 'is like a child to be brought up.' Flowers are voluble. 'Can flowers talk?' asked Alice. 'If there is someone worth talking to,' replied the Tiger-lily. My mother made me friends with her home-grown garden flowers — the casual perfection of apple blossom, the formal configuration of delphinium and hydrangea, those with abundance of florets on one stem, or, conversely, a single brilliant nasturtium that has struggled, contorting its spine stalk, pricking its petal ears, through obstacles of leaf and shade to reach the necessary sun. This is to read the words of the poem.

So I tend to remember people in our moments

shared with flowers. A very small child grasps a given flower and will not give it up — *my* flower like *my* shoes and *my* hat, as though it too were a grown part of his body, part of himself. Aunties of my childhood, on Sundays, well-done from church and cookery, cull from their garden beds stocks, sweet-peas, pansies and poppies, sappy and sweating pure scents, for the guests departing after the afternoon's high tea. In my late teens, a pen-friend, sailor, first lover, homes on my doorstep, barricading his shyness among strangers, bearing a huge floral arrangement tall as a dancing partner. The longest lover has a particular articulation of intimacy with flowers. He would place a single flower beside a tea cup or scatter several, splendid among the wraps of breads and cheeses and coffee pot, making a small repast into a celebration.

Our children, having witnessed this father grab up the flowers from the table in one hand and a certain jug or biscuit barrel from the wash-up tray in the other, and rush out with them to his studio, the way another father might whistle up a dog to jump into the car beside him as he drives off to work, and having watched their mother purposefully carry a bowl of flowers upstairs, the way another mother might carry off a mop or tea tray, to sit beside telephone and typewriter as company to the morning's occupation, have made their separate peace with flowers. The eldest, come of age of driving licence, took on the weekly bulk marketing, enjoyed the budgeting and bargaining, brought home always festoons of the most profuse flowers along with his scoop of cheap capsicum or boiling fowls. The daughter spent her young pocket money on boutonnieres of rosebuds or the cauliflower-shaped posies

beloved of the French, to sit squarely before them prognos-
ticating with her watercolours. The youngest, geared on his
way to football, greeted one birthday by appearing on the
doorstep antlered with a half-dozen wand-long daffodils.

Flowers sentinel memory. I am in an after-care hospital, joyous with a new-born babe. A painter friend comes
lumbering down the twelve-bed ward towards me, portly
and staggering under the strain of a recently sprained ankle
and an enormous armful of zinnia which he throws down
upon me so that I am quilted in a garden bed of stiff petals,
gaudy and hurrahing in purple, puce and orange. He says,
when I am overwhelmed by such abundance and wonder if
there is any garden left at home, that his mother will not
mind, he doesn't think, for after all, he mutters later over
his shoulder, she was a mother once herself. He is sitting
with his back to me gazing out upon the panorama of
motherhood. Fred is then a young man intent on painting
and paternity.

Years later, we are going overseas en famille. We are
gathered at the airport knee-deep in baggage, much both-
ering about passports and over weights, time schedules and
cameras. Our friend Max, the scholar gypsy, who has lived
through many countries, many airports, but with little
luggage ever, comes to see us off, lovely with a sense of
ceremony that we have overlooked. From his proffered
embrace I receive, delicate as a new-born babe, a sheaf in
mauve tissue paper and discover, long-stemmed and elegant within, a dozen bud-opening tulips. They are more
beautiful than all of us, King-Solomoned in our new shirts
and shining travel bags. Thenceforward, in the aircraft
where they are placed in the ice box along with the beer

and the tonic water, in a northern hemisphere hotel where they are awarded at once a tall silver vase, I am identified not as the blind woman, or mother of three, but demonstrably as 'the lady with the tulips'.

Flowers, seen or remembered, seen again in the inner eye, evoke in their stillness, in their silence, the reverence for life that must perish. Flowers, pondered in their formation, perfection and transience, speak of life that passes. At that time in the West when I was thrust into another phase of my life, I met thousands of wildflowers, invented flower forms that seemed unreal. It was as though God had grabbed up handfuls of pins and needles and puffs of smoke, husks and cobs and hanks of hair, lubbered corals and sealess shells, unbeknown wings and fins and claws, half-thought-of tails and lobes and tendrils, wisps of stick and straw and any wayside thing, and made them all into flowers. It was as though the Maker, browsing at the end of his day of Creation of the vegetation of earth and sea, had let His mind wander on towards the creation of birds and beasts and fishes and the complexities of human kind, idling twilight thoughts before the creation of night and day, after which He would turn to the business of devising creatures, of which gladly I am uniquely one. Perth and its people flowered for me. Their confidence, spontaneity, initiative, acceptance of all comers of all kinds, humanised that spirit of place. I felt at home.

$\mathcal{I}$NTO MY LOOKING-GLASS LAND

There comes a time in the middle years, at the passing of the half century, to look at oneself in the mirror and see, as my poet friend likes to put it, that now the shadows begin to fall on the other side of the mountain. It is time to pass through the mirror, to reverse the images of one's life, and enter into the Looking-glass Land. It is time to set about doing those things long dreamed of.

So it happened that I decided to give up indoor and city life, family and friends, to take long-service leave from telephone and typewriter, door bell and date book, in order to get out and lie upon the landscape of my country, to give way to an inner longing for earth and distance, stillness and stars.

Right when I needed them, a couple of new people appeared on my scene to travel with me – good patient people who understood the land, were not given to wearing watches or reading newspapers, were practical with cars, curious about nature, its creatures and changes, able to hunt and live light, careful in their observance of the lore of the land. Together we went on a five-month journey around the western half of Australia.

We, like many explorers before us, set out from Adelaide; not with camels and saddle bags, but with the steed of our day and the accoutrements of our time. The blue Range Rover, our gallant four-wheel drive, was armoured and ignobled with the impediments of Top End travel – bull bar and windscreen protector, roof rack and ladder. Into the back we stowed all that we needed for our season of living out – furled tent, folding table and chairs, swags, saucepans, sheepskin, and sleeping bags, spears, guns, knives, fishing net and tomahawks, camera, woomera and underwater gear, radio-cassette player, tucker-box, tool-box, primus stove, pillows, tarpaulin and violin. On the top we weight-balanced and battened down petrol tank and water tank, spare tyres and wheel, jerry cans and suit-cases, and, surmounting all, a fibre-glass boat with motor, oars and anchor. Finally we crammed in two large cartons of supermarket groceries and a huge red plastic garbage bin and lid for innumerable future uses. This was the first of over a hundred packings-up in desert, bush, beach and caravan park.

We set forth, just four of us, into the misty dusk of an early June evening. The planning was over; we were on the road, waved off not with flags and cheering, but by a sister with sprigs of jasmine on the doorstep of a stone cottage. Norman, driving, glad to be heading out again towards the shirtless, shoeless country, put on a cassette of country road music. Linda, shy at having been the only black person in a white township for the last week, began to speak of her people back home at Aurukun on the Gulf side of

Cape York. Joyously, the big black cooking pot wedged between their two front seats jiggled its contents of enamel plates and mugs, cutlery great and small. Melissa and I were jammed into the back seat between Esky and case of neighbourly apples. I shuffled to find foothold on the floor amongst the sliding sponge bags, loose tools, medical kit, spare shoes and tins of home-made cake. My little three-year-old mate wriggled herself a nesthold, alternatively clutching and dropping her treasure, a small plastic basket handbag, intent on stock-taking its contents – hairbrush, toothbrush, tiny torch and baby doll, her private get-away gear.

We sang. We drove out by houses and town lights, farm fences and darkening hills. The road received us. By midnight and headlight we put up tents, caved ourselves in snug against the cold, slept sheep-fleeced upon the dry bed of a river. I lay down upon the earth to sleep for the first time, limbs spread, and felt, like the coming-in of a tide, a great peace engulfing me, an all-pervading happiness. At sunrise I awoke in my new land, dew on ground and tent cloth. The child and I stumbled about over dry rocks. We picked a twig of nuts and laid it, secretly smelling of warm winds, beside the jasmine in the car. I was in the dream, through the glass and into the garden. 'Every day a flower,' the child promised, our days to be measured by flowers.

Our days were lived whole between daybreak and sundown. After the first day, a day made long by driving sunwards, westwards, we made our first proper camp, getting the tents up and gathering wood before the fall of night. We were somewhere out beyond Ceduna. Norman turned his blanket into a toga over his shorts. Linda, shivering in the first winter of her life, hectically flung together dry grass and scrap wood to start a fire. Lit by its flame, the child's arms grew giant shadows on the rocks. In that silence we were one with trees and stones and sky. The stars were very close. Afterwards, satisfied, we sat around the embers, Linda's story-telling purring on. Then the fire woman reached up and took down a star and put it in her cooking pot.

Next day we crossed the vacant spaces of the Nullarbor Plain. All day cars, less loaded than we, sped forwards past us. Lumbering semis, haulers and road-trains middled the road, labouring eastwards. But the horizon was unmoving. The faster we proceeded, the more it stayed the same. Dry earth, gibber stone, salt bush, spinifex. It was no good trying to arrive anywhere too soon. 'A slow kind of country': so said the Queen to Alice in the Looking-glass Land, when she complained that the faster they ran the more they got nowhere. We are figures in the landscape, like Alice, not far from those cities of desire where 'land is worth a thousand pounds an inch', those factories of industry where 'smoke is worth a thousand pounds of puff', and are here where 'language is worth a thousand pounds a word'.

We rush onwards. Our wheels devour the miles, the tripmeter digesting them by the hundred. Emus in the distance. Flicker of an occasional wombat, head out of a hole, into a too-bright sunlight. Once, that new weird creature in the landscape, ratbag cyclist pedalling eastwards, pack on back, waving, cheerful. 'A strange kind of country' too. On the high plain of the 'nul arbor' there is always a tree somewhere in sight. Where the land is too fuel-less for bush fires, sunsets blaze. When the land stops sudden — DANGER says the sign post — precipitous all the way to right and left, the wild Bight sea, far below, gnashes violent against the insoluble land.

Melissa makes it more strange for us. Good with words for a three-year-old in both her black and white languages, she uses colour emotively the way other children use paints. For her, what is new is 'green', what is known and loved is 'red', what belongs to her is 'pink'. So all our desert day we travel through green, with red kangaroos about to leap upon us, and, at moon time, have a pink fire and pink tents to sleep in. Perth, towards which we hasten and where we shall know people, is 'purple'.

At Yalata Mission we stop. There are artefacts on show. Linda, coming from a people diametrically distanced, looks at them disparagingly. Norman, tribally initiated, a 'white Aboriginal', who hunts like an Aboriginal and makes his own spears, handles the weapons discriminatingly, feels each boomerang for balance, weight and angle of thrust. Melissa craves a snake undulating in the strata wood of dark and light, and I a splayed kangaroo that jumped over the moon. At Eucla, first roadhouse over the border, the shower water sticks to us, soap stays wooden — salt water. We have enough fresh water left to boil our billy for tea. We drink sprawled high on a windy sandhill, impeccably white, implacable sand. Long ago rabbits devoured the network of plants that corseted the land in shape. Sand devoured the town. Its houses have all gone under the hill, all except one.

Driving by night, headlights conjuring a road. Kangaroo sudden, dazzled, indecisive, thumps the bull bar, dead on. Brake of car, out with the sack, put him in the tucker-bag. Morning awakens us beside a pool, clear, shallow, icy cold. We females strip, leap, squeal, emerge fresh, clean from dust. Norman has the fire made, the leg already cooking in the ashes. We share it out in notches, pulling back the skin like a banana, eating the sweet hot flesh. Linda says he's better cooked whitefeller way, skinned and put in the pot with water.

Kangaroos on the road by night, museums in the towns by day. A night and a day and a night, and we arrive in purple town Perth. Dear Queen, we travel too fast: we know. This is the timeless land. We have seen the man wrapped in white paper beside the road and shall take the advice he gave to Alice; we shall buy a return ticket whenever the last train stops, meaning we shall come again to these places too swiftly passed.

From Perth we go north and eastward, as the coast goes. Oh Queen, we are hastening, urgent as rabbits, to keep an appointment for the midwinter weekend up in the Kimberleys. We go leaping through the rough landscape and across great dried-up rivers as though they were your fields and brooks. 'It is', as Alice remarked, 'something like learning geography.' At this rate we are turning over several pages of the school-room atlas at once – Greenough, Carnarvon, Pilbara. There is such immensity of sandland held together by tufts of spinifex, so much sparse grassland chaperoned by low scrub, so much horizon undistinguished among low hills between the small undefined towns that we pluck at for showers at the roadhouse, refills for the Thermos, petrol for the car. Alice, remarkable Alice, we too can upturn judgements and say: 'We have seen mountains compared with which we would call this a valley. We have seen gardens compared with which we would call this a wilderness.'

There is much repetition of distance between a detail that marks the memory. Once, at dawn, at false cock crow, morning star bright in the sky, a ploughman steers his paddock by lanterned tractor. A bottlebrush, picked for our flower of the day, smells pasture-sweet of cow breath and saddle leather. White trees, before Geraldton, bow down to kiss the ground, wind-blown, horizontal. Thick seaweed on the seashore at Dongara, treads like icy eiderdowns.

Halfway along the mapline, we heave off the highway and spur westerly towards Exmouth. We break free from speeding and spending to camp for five days – antithesis – an isolation somewhere beyond Coral Bay. Norman has brought us here to show us one of his most favourite places in all Australia. Linda is sick of 'shit-sitting in cars' and wants to 'get bush'. Melissa just wants to go fishing, fishing. I want to stop and think.

We put up our tents on a grassy foreshore, a Paradise place in its simplicity of white sand, blue sea and cloudless sky. Daylong we browse at the sea's edge amongst claws of rocks cloven with crushed coral; swim about in the wave-kick and weed-kiss of saltwater shallows; sift handfuls of necklaces, small sea shells, pink, mauve and pale; arrange the drifts of sea leaves, plastic, tactile. In late afternoon we prise off clusters of periwinkles, clumps of oysters on the rocks. At evening our fire smoke stings. Reek of our stew, cabbage and potato, stains the air, enflames the hunger. Oysters cook on their chunks of rock, opening themselves for us.

Now I start to survey this Looking-glass Land in which I find myself. I have come from east to west, from whitefeller to blackfeller way, from sound to silence, from the question 'Who am I?' to the answer 'I am this.' The sea laps upon the shore as it has done before my life and shall do after. Its eternity laps in me. The earth, that served us with its fire and fish, nourishes all creatures, human and other, welding together the devouring and devoured. As a child, I searched the mirror's mystery to see that I had shape and movement, mine and none other's. An adolescent, I gazed at the image in the glass to look in upon myself, turned about to see my parents as separate people, in order to discover my separate self. Now, through this looking-glass, I know my other parents, Mother Earth and Father Time; no separation. I have learned the time of clocks and history. Here I am part of the old slow time of rock, the quick leap time of fish. I lie upon the landscape and let it be my eyes, my ears, and every sense; feel sunrise and sunset as a receding and return, as inspiration and expiration of my breath.

At night we put in the boat, go out with the spotlight and gidgy, the short spear. We explore the sea's creatures: turtles in shallow water, crays in rock shadows, schools of catfish in a circle around a master. Sea slugs and baby octopus are forked into the boat for me to feel. We midnight-feast on crayfish, wordlessly.

We further our journey northwards. White man has landmarked this landscape. This is so much power in this ancient land against the pittance of man-made markings, town, house and dam; and so much patience. We are struck with the primitive force of it when our ark goes clunk in the middle of uttermost nowhere, somewhere over the dried-up Fortesque. We wait in the silence of centuries for another car to come our way.

We are towed over a hundred miles by a man in a ute. He has driven some seven hundred miles up from Bunbury on a hunch to track down an old mate in at Dampier while the strike's on. Tinny by tinny he tells his tale. Clue by clue in the 'company town', merry with enough birthdays to go around, U-turn by U-turn with the tow rope snapping and shortening with each knot, we pursue the mythical mate. He is found. He is numerous. We are tugged and trundled by a group of advisers, car diagnosticians all, and manoeuvred into position on the beach front, tethered to a tap. 'Tomorrow' they say (sober). 'No worries. We'll fix her, for sure.'

We bed down in our bags and swags upon the beach amid the slapping of water on moored boats, the frolic of late-night after-party Saturday people, and the safety of stars. Here, derelict at the town's edge, car has become corpse, belongings become flotsam. Out there, a little way to sea, a buoy marks the hulk of a ship wrecked; back there, on the land, silence marks habitation become ghost town. Desert and ocean consume them, as sleep consumes us and our worries. The screech of seagulls discovers us to the day, and an empty beach.

Just as Alice, like the Queen foretold, was led out of the forest by a knight in white armour, so our car is got back on the road by the mates. Dear Queen, we jump your brook into the next square – 'The Fifth is mostly water' – and arrive in Kununurra, 'place of big waters'.

We keep our appointment. The town is hosting a

celebration of past being made present, a piece of bygone way of life resurrected – the opening of Argyle Homestead Museum. It is all water now, the old Argyle station, part of an inland sea of dam water, that was a million square acres of beef cattle country, home of the 'kings in grass castles'.

Here the landscape is magnificent and man's marking of it marvellous. These East Kimberleys are dramatic. These flat-topped, sharp-shouldered, red-rock, purple-shadowed mountains have shaped the skyline into a familiarity of homeland for the ancient people of the land, for the century of white men on horses who explored, settled, mustered in its vast plains and deep gorges, and for the decade of newcomers who have engineered modern man's re-shaping of the landscape to tame the flood waters. The mountains are splendid in all the pink, orange, rouge of sharp-sided rock, flushed at sunset to all the shades of rose, gold and violet. Man's reciprocation is dam lake shoring into gorges, roads folding into landfall. Earth responds with renewed fecundity of tropical growth, foreshores of water fowl. Coming into Kununurra now is like arriving in the Promised Land – but arriving too soon.

The town is turned on its head with contradictions, gutted with enigmas. Cattle country, but not a butcher's shop in town; a lake full of fresh water, but only bore water to drink; oasis in a desert, but no gardens; native trees – wattle, bauhinias, flowering gum – mark out and name the town streets, while the countryside blazes with sunflowers for an oil harvest, and the impertinent, pernicious, pretty, purple-petalled camelbush squats all over the abandoned pastures. The sugar crop grows and is burnt. Trees in full heat are snow-laden, with corellas, the small white cockatoos. Last week a boss cocky lost patience with his blackfeller workers, dumped them out of the back of his truck and threw a bag of flour over them. Drinkers at the long cool marble bar say that all this man-made country balances precariously on the back of a big white elephant. The story behind the beautiful picture unfolds.

I skip camp for the day and night of formal celebrations, borrow a typewriter and become reporter, companion to my good old Perth friend, Dame Mary Durack, historian and family elder of the Argyle station: lunch on the river cruiser, dinner sixty miles away at the Lake Argyle hotel. Such a gathering – government ministers' speeches, old timers' stories, family reunions. Four tables are ceremonially arrayed at the dinner – three in parallel for whities, place-marked for the Duracks, the Kununurrarians, the visiting officials, and one, on Dame Mary's insistence, horizontal but at a certain distance, for the tribal people. At the late hour of disarray, Dame Mary and I take off to the horizontal, the table with no alcoholic drinks but most merriment. Singing begins, hilarity because someone has poured hot water into the didgeridoo.

We two defectors return to our guest status, luxury rooms at the whitefeller hotel. My mates creep in and join me. They make landscape of the room, turn on hot showers and waterfalls of laughter, make jellies in the arctic zone refrigerator. Melissa makes a tent out of sheets.

Next day we make the other pilgrimage out to the Homestead – just us and Dame Mary, a school bus and as many Aborigines as can clamber aboard. An unruly departure; 'lations' of old Argylians sit on bonnet and roof of our R. R. All stop at the hospital where Elsie flushes out all those due for 'jections'; and another fluster at the school house where the young are whooped like chooks into the hen-coop. Only those with memories come on this voyage. The oldest of them, a couple reverent in their muttered recapitulations of landscape now so swift, travel in style in our chariot. Melissa has melted into the bus mob.

The Homestead was retrieved, the kernel of it, saved stone by stone from drowning and re-erected. The four rooms are vignettes now, caverns of memorabilia, honouring respectively the cattle kings, the queens of home life, the stockmen and the native people: grooved desk, diaries, thonged leather chair; flat iron and camp oven; cow-hide rope and saddle bag; pandanus dish and copwood coola-mon carrier. I linger in the front rooms, their evocation of childhoods, firesides, musters, hospitality, long times spent in waiting. The Aborigines crowd into the back ones, shy-ness dissolving in recognitions. 'That one R. M. saddle – my daddy help make it.' 'That my Mum, that photo, she born this place.' They duck under the barrier ropes across doorways to touch and point.

Mary is out on the verandah – 'All our living was done on the verandahs' – pouring keg of lemon cordial into paper cups, emptying out packets of biscuits. Memories roost in a cross-beam of chatter. 'All gone.'

We return not to camp or hotel but to riverside cara-van park. Old lady Range Rover is sick. We take her to the garage each day like grandma to the hospital. We fish. We swim. Eyes of crocodiles burn red in the night. We slide the boat in under the large dark tree full of flying-foxes slung upside down. These creatures so delicately made, so delectable to eat, their sepulchral smell and mad-house screaming stifles us. Melissa insists on keeping a dead one as a doll, wraps it up to sleep beside her.

Alone, at first light, I creep out from my tent to catch that breathtaking moment at break of day, when the whole world is so freshly beautiful that my heart stops in a pang of love, in which I know that I am not witness only but part of this beauty that moves in me, brings tears into my eyes. One morning a stranger joins me. In a whisper, no louder than a rustle of reeds, she sees for me, tells me the movements of the birds, their colours, their names, giving me the passion of her knowledge.

There was a blue bird once singing in a garden, dreaming he was an emperor. For Alice on her marvellous journey there was a Red King who was asleep and dreaming, dreaming her, and, sitting on the ground in a cleared space, a White King awake with his memorandum book, writing everything down to make it real. She knew them for the poles of the enigma, the paradox within which she had her being. She too found herself with tears in her eyes. 'You won't make yourself a bit realer by crying,' said Tweedledee. 'There's nothing to cry about.' But she knew that tears really were proof of her reality. As each sunrise stirs our camp to life, I know I wear the Alician crown, an inner infinite joy.

$\mathcal{U}$NLIKELY GIFTS

A little person came to visit me. A two-year-old child, accompanying parents, carrying importantly its little suitcase; sat down on the quietest corner of the carpet and proceeded to unpack, solemnly, ceremoniously, bringing out 'my cup', 'my car', 'my book' and then, pointing a dogmatic finger up at the female of the two adults at my side, 'my Mummy'. After that, the little visitor seemed to feel at home enough to get to know me and my house. I too carry about with me a swag of treasures to be brought out on occasions of need. The swag is that quiet place within me, its contents 'my memory', 'my story', 'my picture'. Being now of an age when my ship of life is in full sail, great with cargo, sailing unaccompanied, I am able in moments of waiting or repose to sort out my stock, a strand at a time. I am off on a country journey, comfortably cushioned in the back of a van, safely out of earshot of the conversation up front. I choose a theme to browse upon – this year's happiness from unlikely gifts.

In summer my young son came to live back home for

a while. He arrived with his familiar trappings – bed, bike, mini-fridge, maxi-desk, trunk of clothes and box of books – and, as well, something dark, fluid and whiskered. Whereas the aforementioned accoutrements were pre-fixed 'my', this latter was significantly called 'the' cat that came with Barnaby. We fed it, photographed it, felt it tip-toe on to the bed and found it to be, of all the cats that bestowed themselves upon this house, the most dignified and companionable of creatures. At first we called her 'Cat-came' for short. Then, on a night of jazz and jollity, we declared her a permanent resident and gave her singu-lar personage the name of Ella.

It was on a quick trip to the shops, to buy milk for the cat and the crème caramel, that my daughter Christabel came upon them – a row of teddy bears, in a second-hand shop window, sitting straight and spruce as though for a photograph before the picnic began. As our friend, Pixie O'Harris, had recently published her Teddy Bears Picnic book, with salient family member portrayed there in inno-cent guise of a bear, we decided she should have one of these bears. We interviewed them, one by one, as to glaze of eye, firmness of fur, quixoticism of expression, and chose a singularly chubby creature with hard bulging bingy and bowing limbs, cuddle-shaped back, balding shoulders, smile bursting its stitching under insouciant leather snout and his growler all gone. He resisted wrapping and had to be presented like a bouquet, pink neck ribbon and brown button eyes cheerily protruding. Seated in the best arm-chair, our bear was given greater welcome than we had anticipated, for, many a grandchild as Pixie has, many a bear as she has borrowed as sitter, this was the first teddy bear she had ever been given in her life. How many owners he has had, how many years he may be old of, is of little importance to a bear. Sitting comfortably, he lives again.

A present worn and furry, with a life of its own, but of a definitely different kind, was given to me in my turn by quite a different kind of artist. I had last seen John Wolseley on a July evening with his two sons out on holiday from their English prep schools, about to set out for the Centre, that landscape that he documents so idiosyncratically in his art, to meet up with an Aboriginal friend and his two sons, to walkabout together for a few months. Now he reappeared in my Paddington sitting room, tall and sartorial in his canary-yellow corduroy suit, wide-brimmed suede hat and shoulder bag, to present me with a souvenir: 'something only you will appreciate'.

It was a hat. It was an old and mouldering, stained and holey, squashed and sun-seared hat, anonymous, unclean, but, when approached by the nose, resplendent with secrets nostalgic to me of my bush travels. It sang a song of dust and distance, of the cockatoo-call, crow-fall, rain-waiting land and its people, their fire smoke and stories. Pinned up on my wall, it was a private incense of the long roads, the horse sweat, diesel fumes and honey-scented melaleuca paper-barks, of ancient red rocks and still starry nights.

More shareable was the perfumed birthday present from a gardening cousin, a box of hulled lavender. Set in my desk drawer, it spills at every rummage for stamps or sticky tape. Measured out in less than coffee spoons, the flour of lavender, a pinch in every letter, payment of bill or filled-out form, even the annual one to the Deputy Com., ekes out the year.

I like those gifts that make me a link in the chain of giving. Very late at a party I was already drowsy, deep on a divan, waiting for the scrag end of guests to ebb away so that I could claim it for my bed. I was aroused by the enthusiasm of the talker at my feet. David McCreedy. Earlier in the evening he had introduced himself as the jeweller who had made the beloved silver retrousse bird bracelet I was wearing. He was now in high rapture about his new love, geodesic domes, a jewellery of architecture. I was captivated. In our talk over the next hour, there was that rare conjunction in the transit of two minds, a transfer of insight and imagination. In wordless celebration, he took from his own neck a delicate gold chain and put it about mine: something to be given again someday.

On a somnolent autumn afternoon beside a lapping river in another city, I in turn sat talking for an hour with a woman of slight acquaintance and much sorrow. She spoke to me of her son killed by his own hand and of her husband killed by the cold hand of cancer. She just wanted to share with me the silence of her sadness. How could I say that I could feel the hurt? I fastened the warm chain about her neck to embrace that trembling throat.

My mother, hale and hearty herself, now at an advanced age, suffers the deaths of her life-long friends, more each year. After one such death at Easter, the relatives presented her with a precious emerald brooch as souvenir. She pointed out that she would rather have the everyday cup and saucer that her friend had used, feeling that in the daily ceremony of drinking from it, washing and wiping it, setting it in place on her shelf, she was still keeping company with her old crony.

At ninety she lives alone in an abundant garden of her own making, presided over by a giving tree. This presents itself as a grapefruit tree, enormous, prodigious, its yellow fruit like the golden apples of the Hesperides. Actually, what this tree bears is butter cakes, bed socks, pots of honey, magazines, mignon lettuce, concert tickets and nursery plants, and all the other things brought to her by the neighbours, tradesmen, playground parents, who receive from its prodigality buckets of grapefruit, jars of marmalade.

This year the tree is taking its sabbatical. It sulks, shrouded in a black fungus, dormant and fruitless in nature's rest time. One day my mother arrives home to find on her doorstep four huge grapefruit, enough to fill her waiting jars. No donor has confessed. It seems they found their own way there, magi of the grapefruit kingdom, coming from afar, rolling inexorably towards her doorstep.

Once this year giant fruit found upon doorsteps arrived by method more mundane. Midyear, I spent some weeks in Far North Queensland at a study centre, a farmhouse frocked with flowering shrubs amid cane-fields. On the last day we climbed up Devil's Thumb to photograph the waterfall, swam in green tropical shallow sea to pick up coral, caught butterflies, pressed flowers, saved shells – all the attempts to take home with us some evidence of the poem we had experienced. Those of us, West Australian by home or heart, marvelled at the distance and difference of these sandy shallow shores, from that jagged coast of the other ocean of deepest blue. We gathered the most preposterous coconuts that lay grounded under their palms and queued at the Mossman Post Office to send back to persons in Perth these hygienically sealed, self-wrapped, box-type packages, with love and milk, stamps adhering, addresses inscribed on the hairy surface, message on reverse side like any postcard: to people without coconuts from people without overcoats.

WHITEFELLERS WALK ALL AROUND

I

On Arnhem Beach
September 1979

Dear Christabel,

You had your fourth birthday in winter in a London
house, woke to frost flowers on your window, looked
down from your third floor to a no-tree street. Your
Australian godmother, poet, sent you her latest
collection, a book of poems about birds, Australian
birds. Your father and his two English poet mates went
to mourn the death of the wife of one, burst free from
her bell jar. Here we are half a world and half a
generation away from all that.

It is dawn, not quite dawn. It is beautiful. We are
sleeping in our bags, six of us, between two fires on this
northern beach. Linda and I sleep at each end to keep
up the fires. I have just blazed mine up. The moon is still
in the sky, and the morning star too. The sea pounds
away a little below us. The sand is white, brightly white,

soft and fluid on the sand hills, but coarser here near the sea. I reach out from my bag and sift gravel of small shells through my fingers.

Now the birds begin. My fire smokes. Daybreak is near. The young Aboriginal boy lying next to me has called my name twice, softly. He is watching. He has moved the little girl, his half-sister, close under his blanket. He is watching his familiar world waken around him.

We shall have crabs for breakfast. The big black pot near Linda's fire has eighteen small crabs cooked in it. Norman caught them last night here at the sea edge. He had a scaring tussle with a sea snake in the process. The poisonous thing wrapped itself halfway up his spear and, when he shook it off, struck at him again and again, leaping from side to side across a small channel.

Yesterday was Melissa's birthday. The night before we drove out from Nhulunbuy to Oyster Beach, a bit south of here on Cape Arnhem. We slept on gentle earth, a down of pine needles on the soft sand of a high dune. We awoke to find things from other people's camps scattered around us — a thick rope loop hung from a tree for a swing, two billy cans bigger than those we carried, and an iron grid for the fire. So we made much porridge with honey in it and lots of toast, several pieces at a time. 'Melissa, it's your birthday. You're four today.'

Birthdays don't mean much to Aboriginal people who, in their own way of life, would not record or remember a date of birth that way. Linda tells me she

once told an old tribeswoman on Groote that it was
her birthday and then found it hard to explain to her
what 'birthday' meant. Why celebrate a personal
birthday when the tribe does not separate out
individuals in that way? Birth belongs to the whole
tribe. When a baby sees his first bird or a child catches
his first fish, then everyone celebrates, puts on a feast
and dance to make the event more splendid, more
memorable for him.

We celebrated Melissa's birthday anyway. Patrick
gave her a life belt – which she calls her 'life boat' –
because we are teaching her to swim. Norman, her
father, gave her pearl earrings and a pendant shaped
like a chrysanthemum, bought at Broome, and she
wore her long red party dress all day. I gave her
Matchbox toys of vehicles we had seen along the roads –
caravan, horse float, tip-truck, Jeep. Linda gave her a
book, *Kanga's Shop*, and baked her a special damper
with apricots and coconut in it.

But we didn't have any candles. Trevor, her full-
blood half-brother, made some from twigs with twists
of paper tissue on top. We sang 'Happy Birthday' and
took photographs. Melissa thought it was the damper's
birthday and that the damper was being sung for her.

Among Aboriginal people things get 'sung' – a kind
of magic. Norman wears his headband of red wool
given him by the elders of the tribe where he was
initiated. The red wool is a modern version of the old
traditional hair-twist stained with blood. The oldest
man of the tribe sang it for him, to help him catch
himself a good woman. Linda says she was caught by it

when he wore it in the pub in Cairns where they met. When she is angry with him, she tries to get his headband and burn it.

So Melissa said she would eat all the damper herself. But she was told that if she did not share it she would be turned into a thieving sea eagle — like the one that stole our bread and then our damper out at Bard Creek and left us hungry.

We ran down to the sea for a swim. It is winter, just a little cold. Then we packed up the car, piled in and drove north over soft sandy tracks, scratching through scrub, sometimes through patches of mangrove, once through a place called Apple Garden full of wild apple trees and other fruits.

The whitefellers up here in the North have two seasons, the Wet and the Dry, but the blackfeller people have about twelve seasons of differing lengths depending on what foods are available. We saw many blackfruit and the little golden berries called boyen. But they will not be ripe until the next season, about six weeks away. Meantime there is the short but happy kingfish season. All the people will come down here, sit, watch the sea, wait. Then, when the big big fish come close into the shore, they will all run down with their spears. A great feast time will follow.

There were lots of agile wallaby about in the scrub, and plenty of goanna, called bilka. We whities are not permitted to hunt on this land.

Trevor is ten and sees everything first. He was watching for turtle tracks as we drove over coast dunes. Suddenly he leapt straight out of the car

window. He had seen the soft ruffled sand patch where
they have dug in their eggs. Some tracks are four foot
wide from footprint to footprint, big turtles. But
turtles are cunning. They make false tracks leaving an
overlarge churned up surface as decoy. Bilka, in front
of us, was also looking for eggs.

Spears, like divining rods, were probed down through
soft sand. At a find, we prostrated ourselves. We lay on
our bellies and scraped out the sand, as fast as we could,
down beyond an arm's length — cries of joy when eggs
were seized. Then a scurry to get them out against the
wall of falling sand — forty, fifty, sixty . . . The most we
got was ninety-six in one hole. What a variation on the
birthday party peanut hunt!

The eggs are the size of ping-pong balls, some twice
the size. The skins are leathery, not brittle. We ate some
raw, biting a hole and squirting the briny whites and
thick yolks into our mouths. We stuffed them into a
pillowslip to take back as a treat to the old women at
Gove, Yirrkala. When we stopped to boil a billy for tea
and damper time, we boiled some eggs and I liked
them better cooked. The whites stay fluid but the yolks
thicken to a dusty richness.

Two men drove by in their Suzuki, both white, both
nude. They had been out fishing. We swapped them
eggs for a large fish, a turrum which I carried wrapped
in my wrap-around cotton skirt. The turrum fish was
as big as my thigh.

We went on driving north, very slowly. 'Floating
Island' was in view all the time, just off shore. It is a
sacred place. No one dares go there. Boatmen make

long detours. The great serpent lives under it making
bad magic. It does not hold its place with gravity,
moving strangely behind and before us.

After midday it was hot, balls of fire hot. We walked
down a fiery sand slope burning our bare feet and got
to Policeman's Camp, a place suddenly cool under
pandanus palms. There was a slung hammock, a little
inlet for bathing and a fireplace for cooking our big fish
in ashes. We ate with our bare hands, joyously scooping
up great juicy warm chunks. We dozed.

We went on in the cool of evening to another soft
camp under whistling pines. We curried up the rest of
the fish in our billy can, adding garlic, ginger and
chillies. Linda and I gathered wood. The men went off
with their spears. The little hunters ran hand in hand
down tumbling sandhills and came back laughing with
lots of baby crabs, playthings, in our plastic jug.

We brewed up hot chocolate, told stories, asked
riddles. The men would stay out until after the midnight
tide for crabbing. So we lit up our night fires on the
beach and got into our bags. We remembered it was
Sunday so we sang Sunday School songs, first in English,
then in pidgin. Then Linda sang them in 'language'
which is Wik Munkin. Then Trevor sang in his Goometz.
'You in your small corner, and I in mine.' Melissa was
the first to fall asleep under the stars.

So now, my darling daughter, sleep well between
your sheets, have sweet dreams in your bedroom
within its safe walls and ceiling.

Mother

II
At Aurukun, November 1983

Dear J. W.,

You would have enjoyed all this. Marcel and I did get
ourselves out to Aurukun after all, just for a week, to
pay a visit to Linda, meet her Mum, see her place, just
as we talked about on our bush trip. No one much
comes out to Aurukun for a visit. We came out on the
Bushy, a D.C. 3, landed into the old familiar heat, dust
and flies. Out with us came the quota of regularly
visiting Government men, cartoon characters in their
open shirts, shorts, high socks, clutching their despatch
cases, some locals back home to family embrace from
spells of hospital or shopping over in Cairns, and a few
others, black and white, back from trips out, clutching
lengths of pipe, swags of vegies, packets of spare parts.
We staggered out with our welcome cargo, boxes of
fruits and vegies, freight twice the cost of contents. No
Linda to meet us. A wiry European claimed us. 'Linda's
over in the hospital, check-up. I'm Jacky.' French
accent, Marcel quite delighted. Naughty Linda,
springing this on me. That's why she laughed and
laughed on the telephone. She has a French lover too!

Jacky took us down the dust road, up a high flight of
steps into their house, none too tidy. 'Every day she go
to the hospital. Not sick, just hot.' The air-conditioned
hospital waiting room is the most popular place. Most
days the women manage a headache or belly pain to sit
and chat for hours in the cool. The Frenchmen were
straight into French talk — the state of the nation and
how to put it right, the variables of the language and

how they arose. Linda bounds up the stairs, kids behind
her, fruit from the fridge plundered. Hello, kettle on.
Embrace, questions all over.

We are lodged over in the dongars, about as
primitive as accommodation can get. But then people
don't come here for their holidays. Two parallel rows of
step-up mobile tin sheds, each with one bed, one chair,
one nail on wall, one fly-wired window, women's and
men's bath-house blocks at the end and one laundry
tub. The first tin shed is a kitchen — chipped Laminex
table, sink, stove, tinny toaster, battered pans, teapot
and cups, spoons and forks, no knives. It is all locked
up at night, no locals admitted.

We buy a chicken for twelve dollars, a cabbage for
eight, feel like the rich relations. M. cooks up a great
meal and children appear from everywhere. He saves
us a few bones and potatoes. No beer. Aurukun is dry.

A hot slow place. We browse about. Linda has a
'government job', she says, shows me the tape
recorder she's been given, money to be paid for her
oral history and tribal myth recordings. Gradually I
meet her relatives. We sit all afternoon with Aunty
Jean. She does one side of tape in long looping streams
of family memory, then the other side all in 'language'
about the black crow totem. Next day we take it over
to hand it in to the administrator, not that he knows we
are coming. We sit on the old black stump outside and
wait. When he doesn't show up, Linda chucks the
rotten tape into the fire. At evening she arranges us,
and chairs. She is bringing her mother. We wait. Her
mother is frail. She carries her up the stairs, sits her in

a corner. A reverence takes shape around her shyness,
stillness. We have no language. We smile, hold hands,
her dry tired hands. Husband and most beautiful
daughter both died by pay-back. We had promised our
mothers to each other all through our bush trip. Linda
had addressed 21 Essex Street on all my letters and
when they got to Brisbane – I had dropped out by then –
they headed straight there and landed in on my mother
for a fine high tea.

Then it's pension day, party time. All sit round
playing cards, betting and winning, a way of tribalising
the money. We sit it out drinking tea, the Frenchmen
talking about Africa. Before this Jacky was in Senegal.
White women don't turn him on. Linda comes
bounding in with fistful of money, laughing, dancing,
teasing Jacky, then rushes out again when his back is
turned. 'What people,' he says. 'Used to hunt tucker,
now just hunt dollar.' Linda returns, sulks. Money all
gone. Lenore won. She get washing machine, get it out
on Bushy. They will all wash their clothes until it dies.
Sooner or later someone else will win another. Let's go
fishing.

I fall back into Aboriginal life way, just sitting around
listening to stories, never knowing when or if
something is going to happen, ready when it does,
wandering off at night to where the sticks clap, singing
is. There's going to be a house opening soon. The men
are practising for it, over there. Old woman died. The
hundred days is about up. Soon the first rainfalls will
drink up the footprints. Janette with her tiny baby joins
us. She is shy, slight, a swift shadow, almost a slip of a

girl. 'My cousin. Up from Edward River. Thirteen kids. New man here.' She is leaving Maisie here. Maisie's about seven, same age as Jelma who was on the trip with us. 'Edward River mob wild ones.' We are going fishing. Jacky is tracking down a boat.

The government men slap on their breakfast steaks, eat with penknife. They give up on trying to find the people on their list, no sense in it. On with the itinerary. I have cottoned on to another cousin, Alison Wooller, first chairman of Aurukun. I think she's great — one of the great women of Australia, really. She knows how it works. She has seven kids, all from white fathers. She goes out to get her babies. 'Not this mob but their children will be the ones in universities and big jobs. For sure.' She hops about, cooking, singing, scolding, cuddling, gets them all to bed. 'My peace of mind time now,' she says and we talk. 'Whitefeller,' she muses 'he walk all around. Blackfeller he stay still.' It touches my heart. I have travelled to Europe and back, time and again, and all the while this land of hers, this moon, have stayed right along here. She belongs. I don't feel I belong to the land in Paddington Street. Nevertheless I tell her to come and sit down at my place sometime, when she is doing conference down south.

One night a commotion. One of the men is drunk, violent. He runs round and round the place screaming. 'Who's taken my mummy, my daddy?' It freezes my heart. No child here is more than an arm's length from love. Dirty nose is wiped, hungry belly fed, cut knee salved, a loving hand always near, the big family. You'll

understand how his screams of loss made me weep and
weep, the mother earth of it all that we whities just
don't have.

Linda and I wander over to the air strip at landing
time. A surprise. Another aunty, from the Weipa mob.
Here she is, Aboriginal lady in Paris attire beaming all
over. It's Thancoupie the potter, on home ground after
eight years away in the big world. She's the shape you
don't know whether to go round or jump over, bouncy
ball of warmth and energy. I catch her at the dongars
sitting at the Laminex table under the rattling fan
cracking crab and drinking tea with her sister Murtle
just back from taking the grade eights on a walkabout.
'Come on, take a chair.' She's straightaway got herself a
wrap-around skirt from the craft shop with black
crows block print, same as mine, and has on her
Australie 1983 T-shirt, souvenir of the Aboriginal
display now on at the Musée de l'Art Moderne in
Paris. She's come for a month to give pottery
workshops. She's telling about the crowds in Brazil's
capital, the Maori tapestries made from root fibres, the
feast in Fiji where the old man touched her face and
hair believing Aboriginals the same people floated too
far west; the variety of food in New York, the cost of
perfumes in Paris, chuckles, checks herself from
sounding like a white woman, talking money; wonders
if she's still a bush woman able to catch him fish, dig
him yam, get him sugar bag.

She's at home alright, feet slipped into thongs,
speech into that dialect so rhythmic, so redolent of
snapped twig, water ripple, clapstick cadence of

blackfeller talk. Our walk over to Linda's house in the
cool of the evening is like royal progress. She waves by
name to old men on doorsteps, calls out to children to
be careful with their sticks, silly boys knocking down
the green mangoes, can't wait for them to be ripe.
'Lations run out to greet her. 'Granny Gloria.' 'Hey,
world travel lady.' 'Aye, come back this place.' The boat
is ready and she'll come fishing with us.

We get away on the tide just after sunrise. Several
sacks of cement rock hard at the landing station.
Swarming kids try to get aboard. We take just Maisie,
Jelma and Paddy. 'No more room. Next time.' We go
down to the mouth of the Archer. With a line we get
catfish, throw back baby shark. The children catch the
big ones, queen fish and grunter. Gloria cheers them
on, enchants them with stories about Hong Kong where
thousands of children live on house boats, go to school
on school boats, go to shop at shop boats. We pull in.
Maisie walks into the water and catches fish in her
hands. The beach is under almond and coconut trees.
'First missionary planted them. Girls camp.' Maisie is
straight up the tree getting us coconuts. Amazing
Maisie, she'll feed us all. Linda, as usual, has got her fire
going, throws tea leaf and sugar in the billy to boil. I, as
usual, say, 'Backward race of people. Forty thousand
years and never found out how to make a cup of tea.
Now another forty thousand to find out how to make a
good one.'

The fish are on the ashes before the tea is down.
Gloria has hung her beautiful French leather handbag
over the branch of a tree, made her beautiful silk scarf

into a skirt for Maisie while her dress dries out. She
has clumped up some wet sand and Paddy moulds a
man, with five limbs, all vigorous. Her bagful of stories
bubble out. She did a mural at Edmonton, Alberta and
they want her back to teach. But could she stand the
snow? 'Snow makes ice cream,' says Jelma. She raises a
split coconut to her lips and laughs to see herself
raising her glass of champagne just like this at the
reception put on for them in Paris. 'They were showing
our traditional art like contemporary art, like
performance art. The old men – they brought them
over from the Centre and Top End – had to make their
ritual sacred ground sand drawing behind closed doors
then allow it to stay there for the duration of the
Bienniale. You know, it should be wiped away at once.
That's how we are, not keeping things.' Paddy had
turned his man into a canoe with oars. 'At this cocktail
party after the opening, the elders squatted down in a
circle. Big handsome men, wise men. In the set of their
heads, furrows on their faces, you could tell what sort
of land they came out of. Well, some of the young
women with glasses in their hands went over and sat
down with them. That is an awful thing to do, women
to sit down with elders. But of course these girls didn't
know and, as I say, they were wise men. But I
shuddered.'

We fall silent. 'If I had to choose between Paris and
the bush, it would have to be this.' The fire heat has
cooled from the sand. Fire colours are alive in the
sunset sky. 'I loved Paris. I love dressing up in all the
lovely clothes, the smocks, necklaces and scarves, and

all that bistro food, but this' – the ancient bush darkens, the Gulf sea laps – 'When comes near time to die, when I'm old, gone flour-bag, got the pension – this beautiful life, like my childhood, that's what I'll want.' Then she jumps up, takes a penknife out of the smart leather handbag hung up in the tree, 'But now, I can have both.'

I tell you all this. I lie in the night conjecturing what images you would paint or collage out of all this. It is a constant amazement to me how so many of my friends get on so well with their lives without my telling them how to do it!

B. B.

$\mathcal{T}$RANSPARENCIES

Transparence means experiencing the luminousness of
the thing in itself, of things being what they are.

(Susan Sontag, *Against Interpretation*)

'You're nothing but a pack of cards!' said Alice — or, modernised, might have said 'stack of transparencies' — to
those who, taking themselves for real, sat in judgement
upon her. 'Let's consider,' said Alice, '. . . a serious question . . .' — this was at the end of her Looking-glass Land
journey — 'Who was it that dreamed it all? . . . It *must*
have been either me or the Red King. He was part of my
dream, of course — but then I was part of his dream, too!'

I
WATER
My schoolgirl daughter sits opposite me at Doyle's
harbourside restaurant eating fish. It is the Seventies. I
wear a long purple and green kaftan over bare legs with
orange sandals, dangles of silver necklaces and a pair of

wraparound mirror sunglasses. Her favourite childhood poem used to be *To an ant I'm a giant. / To a giant I'm an ant.* Now she looks into my eyes and says: 'When I look at you, I see what you would see if you could see. I see me.' What is the serious question asked of the mirror? 'Who am I?' The I sees, as it will, what it wants to see – the I seeking me.

The bush trip into my Looking-glass Land made in the year after I turned fifty was the outcome of a self gaze, exactly that made by Alice when, turning her back on her familiar room, familiar tasks, familiar phrases, she looked so deeply into the pool of the mirror, the reflection, that she passed through and beyond it to a perspective where truths were contradictions. The more one drank, the more the glass was full.

In the days of sea travel it was traditional for first crossers of the Equator to be the guests of King Neptune (perhaps even the captain himself) who threw them into the ship's pool and reclaimed them as they emerged. That bush trip was also an equator over which I passed. Neptune – the King of the Deep, the planet who rules over Pisces – tossed the coin of me, plunged me naked into deep water for a breathless moment, set me down in my other hemisphere. I returned changed 'bronzed as from a myth'.

> If you bring out that which is within you, it will create you. If you do not bring out that which is within you, it will destroy you.
>
> (Gospel of St Thomas)

One's Hindu horoscope charts the life-line as a path-finding from south to north node. The south node is the tail of the

dragon where one comes from, the place of natural inclina-
tion, the familiar, habitual, known way. One travels forward
towards the north node, the dragon's head, an extreme
opposite, the uneasy, unfamiliar self, where, if one dares,
one shall discover the other that lies within. I needed time
to get my bearings out of the old Blackman life into this
nuova vita: time to understand the wisdom of opposites.

My father's cousin Olive, a precise petite figure in the
suit 'tailleur' which she has worn since the Twenties, comes
to stay with us at 159 in the Seventies, when just widowed
at eighty-four, and is shocked. When at last we find a quiet
moment, she takes me to task. 'Your life is so busy, all
action and excitement, always arranging, arguing, plans
and crises. Intuition seems altogether stifled. Don't you
know the Tao saying *Don't just do something: stand there?*' Of
course I knew only the opposite, a command at high pitch.
She explains what 'standing there' means. Instead of rushing about doing things one stays still and contemplates: a
process of Wanting, Willing and Waiting.

Now, in my new days, I lived in a certain stillness. I lay
myself upon the face of the waters, let myself float at ease on
deep water, waited to be taken on the current. The halcyon
nest of my ocean was Perth. I used to letterhead my address
as PEace.on.eaRTH. I waited. I said Yes to everything to see
where it might lead: jazz club, Jung Society, Writers'
Fellowship, Oral History Association, public broadcasters,
jaunts to islands and country places, visits to two seers. One
tells me I shall write many books – she can see shelves of
them, histories and biographies. The other sees a tall handsome man with foreign accent, our going forward together.

The new skin grew, the new strength of swimmer. It

was time to strike out to dry land, to return to Sydney, to house and family, and take direction. Solo now, I replaced the wall and returned the double house to single. 'All my life, changing houses,' I say to Olive. She too had been an only child, a painter father, a pianist mother, lived in hotels, moved house easily. She is my sternest counsellor, staunchest friend. 'You are a child of Neptune, here in your life's map, the horoscope. Here is Neptune, ruler of Pisces, all the fluid, elusive, dreamy, poetic, spirit (spiritual and spiritous) things, all that flows like water. Here it is in your mundane House of Home. Look at the shape, a trident. You have the grand trine all in earth signs and then this, its line shooting straight up from your base to your mid-Heaven point in Pisces, your worldly side, your face in the world. It shows you will change, move from house to house, no fixed address, no solid structure of family. But you will take your spirit and fortune into each home with you. See, you are an invalid, housebound. And doesn't the writer write at home? But, within your different homes, and your symbolic house of self, you are unlimited, boundless. Other people will move through your house, bringing their dreams, inspirations, some as creative spirits in good fortune, some at the basest dream fantasy level of drugs and alcohol. Your own will must choose.' I understood then how I had leapt forward and crossed my equator.

'You see, dear, you cannot lead a conventional life. You haven't got it in you.' That's clear. It seems to me that so many people stagger through life reeling under the shock of finding that they are alive, and dead-set on defensive action – getting status and security, flattery and furniture, fame and fortune – to fortress themselves against its being taken away from them, instead of ranging out from that rejoicing centre of knowing one is alive, to see how vastly much there is of it.

What I wanted, when I got back to Sydney, was to go to the Sydney Piano Competition, having looked forward to it for four years. At the first sessions I coughed incessantly, needs be shut out. Another door: my Jungian analyst friend from Perth was giving a ten-day lecture course in Far North Queensland, at Diane Cilento's school, an annual winter community at Karnak, a farm house among the cane-fields. Somehow I would get there. A friend gave mention in her newspaper column 'Enjoy', my telephone number given. Several people called. When Julius, a tall handsome man with Hungarian accent, came to the door, I said, 'Actually I am blind.' 'This I know,' he said. 'Patrick has told me, and tells me not to go with you.' From a public telephone in Cairns he telephoned the novelist, with whom he took tea most days, a voyeur's voyeur. 'I am here — with the Blackman.' Julius was never explainable, always courteous, never intimate, generally adventurous.

I stood beside him there in plaster and bandages. I had travelled north with this unknown man. He would stop at a deserted place along the road and announce, 'Time for a tree' and lead me to a tree for me and then, some distance further away, a tree for himself. Then we would put hands on each other's shoulders and 'exercise from too much car' in the schoolyard manner of 'Shake up the Sugarpot'. Half a day's drive north of Rockhampton he stopped the car and got out without a word. I woke from a drowse and, without waiting for any stage directions, got out of the car and on to the side of the road to do sugarpot. Sudden plunge — down, down. Water and sharp log – immersion for a breathless moment – more sudden springing up to clasp the edge of a bridge and into the car and change into dry clothes. Then the shock, the embarrassment. My first blind-man's accident. Poor Julius, thinking I was asleep, had gone forward to see the source of a long line of cars' hold-up. He heard a plunge as of stone hurled into river and realised I had fallen over. Town by town, shock by radiating shock, hospital by hospital, I got my wrist in plaster, whole leg in bandage. Only a few weeks earlier I had attended a convention of blind people where someone had told me of his falling off the platform at Prince's Bridge station and how quickly he leapt up more than his own height to regain the platform in escape from an oncoming train. In my instant of fall I remembered Peter and leapt like him back up on the platform and into my motherly dictum of always carrying a spare set of clothes in case you fall in the water.

Thus we arrived at Karnak late but warmly welcomed. Dinner had been served but a student, Marcel, brings us plates of chicken and potato. In that pulsing tropic creekside, wide verandahs have been built around the house, edged with flowering shrubs, and a shed paved with river stones, walled and windowed with bamboo, for student quarters. Some forty persons assortimenti for ten solid days explored Jungian thought, asked questions, gained his deep perspective, were steered towards that farther shore. Julius did not come to the lectures. He roamed about, ever helpful in kitchen duties: 'I want to examine people who come to places like this.' Marcel, the Frenchman, worked mostly in the garden. One day the two turkeys got in and ate his spinach. He screwed their necks. Within the week he served roast turkey in an encirclature of spinach. On departure, an unexpected tenderness in his adieu.

Life moves in us; we move nothing: an easier way to 'fare forward, voyager'. A year, a threshold, later, Marcel and I meet again. We come back from Rydal in the Blue Mountains where he is building stone walls at a monastery become a goat farm. Ruark is with us. We find Fabian on our doorstep, and in the letter box an invitation to the launching by Dame Joan Sutherland of Charles Blackman's *Alice in Wonderland* book happening just down the road right now. We shall go. I leap into a blue Alice dress of voluminous Indian cotton — Charles himself bought it for me after my India trip to show he really had meant to take me there himself — and bandeau and patent T-strap Alice shoes. Marcel, who is elegantly tall, piles on all the hats from the hall stand. Fabian, archivist and scholar of Indian history, who is a slight, sparkling figure, takes up a white pillow and straps it on to his head thrusting up two high rabbit ears. Ruark, potter and artist, always capable of making a sensational entrance because of his striking dark young handsomeness and his paraplegic's moon-walking lurch, rolls a sheet of cartridge paper into a trumpet.

We arrive just as people hush for the speech. Thrust open of door, herald with trumpet announces in high measured tones: 'Make way for Alice — the Rabbit — and — the Mad Hatter.' We enter arm in arm. The whole dear Blackman family are clustered, Daisy in mock-satin harem pants and mock leopardskin battle jacket, hair vintage grape, Pop in R.S.L. retirement gear, grey long cardigan over low-slung belt, sister Doreen in nylon-frilled floral with serving apron and elbow-length black gloves. We stand to attention. Joan delivers her speech. Applause. 'Give us a song, Joanie,' sings out Daisy. She doesn't. Daisy trills her laughter at seeing us, Doreen goes on handing out drinks. Pop will wait for a beer at the local. Charles and his young wife step forward in courtly grace to receive us. Embraces on all sides. Two marriages meet.

For years I have had a repeating dream. It is about a child I have lost, lost by neglect, left unattended amid traffic, forgot to keep hold of, an infant child too small to care for itself. How could I have done such a thing? How can I find it? Now I dream that child's finding. A middle-aged woman finds me. She is a good, scrubbed and darned, wholesome and bespectacled, aunty woman. She has had the child all the time, a good child. But the child has just died. She pulls out the bottom drawer of her chest. There is the little person, sweet, smelling of embalming as in a coffin. I have another dream soon after. I give birth in ecstasy to a baby. It walks and talks almost at once. Its head is huge. It runs over to the chest of drawers and knocks. I lift it up and stand it on top of the chest. These are dreams of the archetype of the Holy Infant, the poem within.

These are all images, exterior and interior, snapshots, colour transparencies, shuffled out to patchwork a story.

Transparency is perviousness to light . . . disphaneity . . . pellucidity . . . opposite of opacity . . . A transparency is a picture, print, inscription or device on glass or some other translucent substance made visible by means of a light behind.

(*Oxford English Dictionary*)

It is an experience, its metaphor to be seen, like meaning in a dream understood. Life seen from the interior is all metaphor. This is the seeing with the other eye which is 'akin to eternity'.

Marcel and I are passing through Bali, lives now in full embrace. We rise just before dawn, that time when birds begin to flutter, rooster to crow, broken-tailed cats leap out, bare feet on the paths, brooms sweep, bells somewhere. We go by bumping taxi through millet fields to an ancient temple. We drive up a dusty rocky hillside, mountain on one side, lake on the other, as the sun rises. The driver stops. Before us is a tall double wooden door elaborately carved with lotus flowers. We open the door, lift feet over the threshold and pass within. There is only the door: no walls, no roof: same ground beneath us, same sky above us, same mountain, same lake. But it is all perfectly changed. Tradition, numinosity, has made this sacred ground. We proceed far forward to long low steps, then tiers of tombs, of the ancient dead, something between catacombs and letter boxes: an antithesis to the European basilica.

I recognise this passing over the threshold of the Balinese temple as metaphor of my threshold of seven years earlier. Mine had a triple door. A few months after the Karnak sortie with Jung, I went to a university seminar on Jungian sand play therapy, a form of self-portraiture using miniatures on a landscape tray of sand: quite wordless, altogether symbolic. Announcement was made of a conference soon in Bombay, 'Modern Science and Ancient Wisdom'. At once my friend and I said, 'We'll go.' I had no money for the trip but knew now that, on the Wanting Willing Waiting system, the need becomes the means: or, being on the side of the angels, best to leave it to them. So it transpired, as my religious grandmother would say, that I was robbed. All my fine jewellery, the crafted silver necklaces and bracelets, the Paris fur coat (which had had several trips to Europe without me anyway) and some shipwreck Dutch coins, all went into thin air – and were never really needed again. So insurance gave me India. Angels move in most mysterious ways.

Not I only, but the world around me, was changing. At Bombay the trumpet sounded, as indeed it had done in 1891 when the World Congress of Religions opened East to West. Here now the leaders of India's five great religions – and the spokesmen of the new physics and psychology – Sheldrake, Grofe, Kapra among them – and Bede Griffith from his Christian/Hindu ashram, Muktananda from his ashram at Ganeshpuri and Mother Teresa, in the new religious forms – many others – all spoke. A thousand of us gathered in a hotel more sumptuous than anything I had known, for ten days were served utterly exquisite food, given evening performances of music, dance and ceremony in the National Theatre – guests in a palace.

The past and the present seen in the light of each other, the change and the continuity took shape in our minds. Each one of us seemed to be changing, insiding out, encountering those 'hints half guessed, gifts half understood'. Later, visiting temples, we had this knowledge grounded. At a press conference an American voiced our embarrassment, shame, to the guru Muktananda. 'Here we are, such rich people in your country of such poverty.' The answer came gently. 'Ah, I have the same embarrassment in your country. You people are always running out of time, trying to make up time, losing time, chasing time. You in your country have plenty of money. We in our country have plenty of time.' In India I felt I had come in from the outside to some interior place where one drank from the well of eternity. The glass that I drank was a knowledge of life as paradox. Fogs cleared. What India taught me was Both; not Either Or, but Both.

I went again to Karnak: another year, a longer stay, this time with Marcel, this time myself a student. Ibn' Arabi, the medieval Sufi scholar known as son of Plato, Doctor Maximus, was intensively studied, his *fusus*, the revealed wisdoms of the twenty-seven prophets of the Abrahamic religions from Adam to Mohammed, only now put into English. The next year I took Olive, now ninety-four. The Sufi way was already embodied in her.

> Great poets disappear into their own great works. In this they resemble great sages who awake one day to the awareness that they have become transparent. 'I am nobody. Who are you?'
>
> (Stephen Mitchell, Introduction to Rilke's
> *Sonnets to Orpheus*)

Marcel and I skip a class, sit out on the grass under the bunya nut tree beside the 'palace', that building of bamboo and river stones. What moves us both about Karnak is its traditional monastic simplicity, the harmony of buildings made out of and into the surrounding landscape, and the way of life, the dedication to service, the order in utility, respect accorded to cleanliness, generosity and beauty, that gives the serenity of still life to the interior, of grandeur to the exterior: *as without, so within*.

Marcel had been nomading about – Uvea in New Caledonia, east coast Tasmania, back home to Le Touquet in northern France, now Cairns – and I had been gypsying about the big cities collecting oral histories of distinguished Australians for National Library archive – shelves of transcripts, the histories and biographies. The six months of study, the grounding in Sufi understanding, the way the sweet mysteries of life are all seen to be interwoven, had brought us together, resonating his quest for 'a university in the bush' and mine for the maturity of the adolescent's blueprint 'Friends, Nature, Books'.

As lovers we needed to inhabit this common ground. Wisdom being inherent in the language, the simplest procedure was to take it literally and find some land, and take the most direct route of 'wanting, willing and waiting' to bring us to it. My mother, never having believed in Catholics or white bread all her life, was now living her dwindling years in a hospice, well-being with both. Practical in her generosity, she ordered me to sell my parental home at Indooroopilly and buy land for this new marriage. Wisdom validates. The under-market price for which I sold the one to a young friend was the exact comedown price of the other.

Our 'Indooroopilly', in the crook of a mountain not far from the sea, was common ground indeed, 'tiger country', not arable, surveyable only by default, a landscape to have challenged my surveyor father. We consulted a diviner in Wales, giving him latitude and longitude, topography of escarpment with some rainforest. He tuned us in, telling us the historical times of Aboriginal communities here or nearby and the consequent 'dark' and fortunate places, and the underground water flows beneath a house site. We had it in our hearts to build here, out of sight and sound of the trafficked road, a place to feel like home, able to family-in twenty people for weekend or longer periods, our own House of Hospitality, Contemplation and Study.

II

FIRE

Easter 1986: Flame outdoors in the bush, a campfire, a hangi, a gathering on an uninhabited dark hillside far down from the road, under cloud. The night that Halley's Comet does not appear to us. A celebration of genesis. It rains lightly. Cars are parked or bogged. A tent is erected hastily, too close to the cow paddock fence, bales of hay strewn within. People in raincoats, dry-as-a-bone coats, and no coats at all, move about with greetings, with billy cans, with clink of drinks. By torchlight and hurricane lamp we move up to the knoll to raise a toast where a house will be built: the consecrated house site is all space and sky.

Marcel lives in that tent for a year weathering his vision while the house takes shape, stone, mud, tall straight tree trunks, limb of cedar for stair rail, gathered. His fire cooking gets better. The pots get blacker. His hair and beard turn grey. Within the tent he, who carries his world around on his back, mostly books and journals, has set up his desk; outside his bushman's spick and span of pots and pans nailed to tree trunk, tap on gravity feed, tongs and grate over ring of stone. Beside the camp fire he reads late by primus lamp. I come at weekends, dabble in mud bricks, gather the everlasting daisies that smell so ridiculously like fresh cake inside the tent. In that vastness of bush, infusion of wood smoke, that happiness we have glimpsed together suffuses all.

Chris the builder, fresh from his mudbricking of the Clare monastery, at Stroud, lives in the loft over the first built barn, enters by clodhop ladder. The three of us draw mudmaps. I write my famous words of warning in the smoke: 'Takes longer; costs more; is smaller.' A year later, the house built, we recognise our three roles. Chris had sculptured the shape of it, the triple saddle slung roof like a Balinese temple; I the interior configurations of space, the pathways of use; Marcel the structure core of stairway, drying room below, mezzanine out over kitchen. Together we had made the skin, flesh and bones of it. The attic, planned as low and cosy, turned out to be lofty and luminous.

Easter 1987: A party in a shell of a house, but a shell with a hot shower, a kitchen with a gas-bottle cooker. A menagerie of old friends, familiar as household pets – long marble table on trestles, the pews, tall Welsh dresser, Norfolk carver with harem of dining chairs, and a spin-sterly silky oak chest of drawers bereft of other bedroom pieces – have seemingly stumbled down from the Sydney tribal ground of 159 and found us out here, herded them-selves indoors just in time to summon up a party comme d'habitude: just like the dog that followed his master from one end of France to another, or the old cattle dog that arrived at 'Four Oaks' several months after his owner from out west.

The mudbrick walls are dry, the rafters high, the slate floor slanting – having been last-minute slave-laid on Maundy Thursday – strong enough now to take footsteps in the dance. A violinist, someone with a didgeridoo, and the dancers round and round the marble table singing. This is the consecration of the house. My daughter, a Spaniard now, is here with her honeymoon husband. We toast her loss to us, their lifelong happiness and marriage fruitfulness.

My mother sees the photographs of their Spanish wedding and of the house upright before she dies. With her last breath she gives the nun who holds her her last worldly possession, the blue knitted shawl I had brought her home from the Marseilles backstreet little old ladies' handcrafts shop. 'But her great gift to us all,' says the nun, 'was her blue blue eyes.' Those deep sea Swedish eyes that loved me. She bade me leave her bedside a week before. 'If you haven't got your fare home, go and ask the bursar.' Good accountant to the end, she cleared her sheet by the last day of June, dying as she had lived, in the wisdom of humility. Strangely, now and hereonafter I am here on earth without her.

For Marcel, exile from his mother tongue, and for me, exile from the written word, dance was our language. It pulsated through the house, endless and effortless, and in our blood. It gave the mysterious conjunction of our love a form, a style of life. Improvisation, the creating mystery of the artist, captured Marcel's errant vision and gave it architectural form. Configuration of house party study weekends shaped our purpose. Friends came to this little paradise in Nature and opened Books for the joy of study together. The old Socratic magnet of 'seeking wisdom' drew us together, a peer group of diverse preoccupations, generally twelve, around a table, text of poet or philosopher, ancient or present, as teacher: I the chairman, Marcel the chef. 'It is all beautiful' – first Visitors Book entry.

Another, 'As H. L. Mencken said, It seems an original idea, or if it is not, then it is enough that it is a good one'.

Easter 1988. Our life is theatre. Marcel, a cook with flair, makes front-stage of his kitchen. The house is whole, weathervane and guttering, wide country verandah and bricked western yard. It is time to hang the wreath. With a rehearsed cast of friends we put on Ibsen's *Master Builder*. Scenes in the house are watched by audience in doorways or crammed into the mezzanine; then scenes on the verandah, then down on to the flattened grass for the final scene, the upward look, the downward fall. Norwegian supper is served between the acts. 'Miss Wangel was up long ago' floats in sugar and almond above the birthday cake.

Olive, in her hundredth year, is dying. Her dying is translucence, transparency articulate: for us an illumination. Olive, in old age, had this dream: 'I am standing alone in the attic of the house. Someone comes to me, a tall fair man. It is the Christ. He tells me to go downstairs to the president who is waiting for me. The first flight of stairs is narrow. I look into the bedroom on the first floor. It is empty. I look at myself in the mirror. It is all right. I go down a wider staircase. At the bend in the stairs there is a larger darker mirror. At the bottom of the stairs the door to the president is closed. I wait in the hallway. The door opens a little and a dark man indicates to me to wait in the further room. This room is small and dark. Eventually I make out that there is a man-hole in the middle of the room. This grows bigger, as big as the room. A figure is coming up from the depths. I press back against the wall. The figure that climbs out is large. It is a lion. The lion just touches me in passing and goes into the president's room. I go upstairs. I look for a long time into the dark mirror on the way. I find now that the bedroom is not empty. There is a figure in the bed, a dark man. It is the Christ. He is dying. I go over to him. I kneel down at the side of the bed. I look across and see that the president and the lion are kneeling down on the opposite side. The lion looks up at me and winks.'

At the end she hardly eats, has abandoned her body — a crucible of thin bones with some living water still — but not her insight, her dignity. Her spirit, like some great plumed bird, hovers over the whole topography of her long life, seeing it whole. This is the transparency of unification. She says, in commonplace: 'They will keep asking me if I am afraid of dying. But I am not going to die. My body is, and about time too. I was long ago in a little child's body as I am now in an old woman's body, but I came before and go on after. Do not ask me where I go any more than you can ask the babe in the womb where it thinks it's going.' In elevation — and one may wait days for the words to come, or for her to come back to words — she says: 'Encouragement is one of the greatest forms that love can take.' And later: 'All lovers are one Lover. All love is one Love.' This is Eliot's 'the condition of complete simplicity costing not less than everything'. She has always imaged herself as the hermit with his lantern going into the dark bush, because it was there. Now she sets down her lantern. She goes to her death inner lit like a bride to the altar.

In every wink a caprice,
and in every caprice a scent,

> *and in every scent a beauty,*
> *and in every beauty a love,*
> *and in every love a wink,*
> *and in every wink a caprice,*
> *and in every caprice a scent,*
> *and in every scent a kind of recommencement.*
>
> (Ibn' Arabi)

Marcel and I go on pilgrimage leaving the house with friends. Us whitefellers, we 'walk all around'. We take up backpacks and go to a Temenos conference in Dartington Hall in Devon on 'Art in the Service of the Sacred', Kathleen Raine the president, its papers supply topics for next year's 'weekends'; to holy Lindisfarne and Iona, to plays in Edinburgh and Dublin, to painter and sculptor friends in Ireland, to families in France and Spain, to Lourdes and Montserrat, to the beginning places in Murcia and Andalucia of the Sufi scholar studied at Karnak. The gateway of the Alhambra welcomes us strangely: 'To be blind is great sorrow. But to be blind at the Alhambra is the greatest sorrow in the world'. We are given free entry, life-long passes. In three days I get to know its stories and arabesques, its courts and contours, its whispering hall, and loaded pomegranate tree; shed my coat in midwinter sun in the ladies' court while running my hand down the frozen rivulet beside me.

We return to a rain world, an Easter all wetness and frogs and blessed isolation. The house is Barbara-homed with reassembled childhood things – kitchen safes and a table, bits of a Swedish grandfather's bush carpentry, parental cane chair and table, rocking horse, bears and dolls around the verandah. The beautiful blue Alice, Blackman triptych painting, goes to the Gallery of Western Australia, in Perth that seeded me, and in her honour Marcel thereby fulfils his dream, builds his wing with a submerged long library and theatre octagonally wide and sonorously high, domed with stained glass, echoes of his seminary boyhood – a splendid place for many a convivium: and our wedding.

MARCELEBARBARATION, The Secret Wedding.
A Solemnisation in Three Acts. One Performance Only.
Tomorrow Sunday at 10 a.m. at the Octagon Chapel.

A Don Juan with broad hat, black cape flapping, pulls out the scroll from his shining scabbard, strides the dumbfound hall and towncries the announcement. It is just before midnight. Over a hundred friends in fancy dress or country clobber stand about the theatre in mid-dance. They have gathered for Marcel's fiftieth birthday. The party has been grand, bleu-blanc-rouge ribbons on pillars and posts and in the colours of the huge heartshape cake in loaves and fishes motif (love and kisses) for the chef extraordinaire. Children have had high tea, cakes as far as the eye could see, then given their concert offering. Our play this year has been *Don Juan*, Marcel as Commandatore Don Carlos, then a Christmas of a feast; then the dancing, skits and speeches, until we two clear the floor for our song and dance duet – 'We're getting married in the morning!' – and we did.

The dramatis personae is read. Most hear their names for the first time, including best man, the son (in Pijinjarra

print T-shirt) to give his mother away and two godsons, one
boy and one babe, for bell ringers. And so it goes:

Act I: Outside the Octagon. Such early morning choreography
of ablution and carpet laying, tying of white and gold ribbons, draping of tables in embroideries. A couple in evening
dress crawl out from a tent, others crumple out from backs
of cars and spread wings into Sunday shirts, girls shaken
into sportswear or sarongs, spruce newcomers. I, signing
documents on the warm ironing board, am attended by my
maidens putting wreath in plaited hair, and seek among
them a shot silk lipstick to match my dress. Adrian, a music
master, is honing the rabble into a four-part choir.

Act II: Within the Octagon, Sc. I: The Wedding Ceremony. To
Bach's organ Fantasia, mountain-loud, we proceed down the
long verandah. The children are lined up — this is a hetero-
sexual marriage — boys on one side with lighted candles,
held upright, girls on the other with posies of flowers, petals
open. They fold in procession behind us. Little granddaughter, still in Easter Parade petticoat green, is bouqueted
before us as flower girl. *Tallis's Canon* greets our arrival at the
sacred centre, sun shafting exactly through high stained
glass. I am nervous, aware of a high dome of peopled silence,
sibilance of children cross-legged on the carpet around us,
extravagant scents of flowers, Marcel's large hard trusty
hands; the celebrant's endearing mispronouncements of his
complex French family names, our adding 'Before God and
our friends here gathered', our exchange of necklets. Words
are fired. Andrea, my theatre mate, reads the Shakespeare
sonnet, James one of his Rumi translations 'Two Oceans

Meet', Ross a raft of Wordsworthian intimations and Diane the entry on marriage from the *Macquarie Dictionary*. Pronouncement 'man and wife' and I am swept up and swirled in the air by bridal kiss. A bullocky's whistle from Andy. Stamping and cheering. Outbreak of choir in the Laudate Dominum, Taize chant.

Sc. II: The Signing. Downstairs in the library. Cat comes too, paws the exact place on page.

Act III, Sc. I: Outside the Octagon. Exodus to a Peruvian Gloria Deos, with bongo drums and babe now awake shaking hand bell. Confetti and cameras. 'Birth of Botticelli', someone says.

Sc. II: On the Terrace. Two Birthdays and Three Cakes. Croissants and a jeroboam of champagne. Jesse, who is five, kneels up on the table stabbing his ice-cream cake, a clown. My son, mid-thirties, cannot get his carving knife through his cake garishly decorated with windmills and butterflies; finally lifts high a first slice, a whole ambrosia cheese under its hard thatch of wax.

Act IV, Sc. I: The Cutting of the Cake. A great two-tier fantasy, brought out from hiding under the bed, made by my matron of honour, my India-going mate, is swathed in veils adorned with silver cashews and baby Easter eggs, doves on branches and, atop the tower of it, a bridal couple doll, formerly on my daughter's Spanish wedding cake. Granddaughter's hand is with us on the knife. Little persons, chin-high to the table, capture birds and eggs. After the speeches a final African Amen with bongos, two didgeridoos, clapping, teaspoons percussing coffee cups, all of us a choir. A transparency of ecstasy by spontaneous combustion. 'The happiest, most beautiful wedding I ever saw,' the celebrant phoned next day to say so. That luminant moment was the marriage of spirit and place, our Marcelebarbaration its metaphor.

A week later, on Easter Sunday, our neighbours', good friends', house is burnt to the ground while they go down to the beach for an hour. We, a kilometre away, see, hear, smell nothing. Suddenly Shirley stands in the doorway. 'All gone,' she says. 'Burnt right to the ground' – years of building – all that love, that dream, that work, that hope. Nothing remains. Sudden conflagration, a vertical inferno, source unknown. Nothing: piles of melted glass like spilt honey. Twisted tin a foot off the ground that was their roof, some upright poles still smouldering, the new combustion stove alone standing inviolate, its dial almost at zero – 'I didn't do it'.

The devastation images the inner shock. *House you have gone/ And widowed your owners*. The house has gone under the hill. No one was hurt. Next morning we walk with them over the ruin, lovers seeking tokens – a heap of small green tiles, enigmatic sculptures of molten glass, fragments of red cedar, ashy scraps of charred books still readable – among them a torn corner about Vulcan the god of the forge, another about Hercules. *Hercules in his delirium threw his offspring into the fire and then, we are told, slew his wife*. At first there seems no meaning to it, no cause and no meaning. As time flows over a little, it moves into myth. It is as though, as in a Lorca play, the Fates were at work, the Avenging Angel summoned by so many shades, perhaps out of something blood-rooted in the land itself. The Merciful Angel says, 'It must happen quickly. Let us take these people away to a beautiful place while it happens. Let no one be hurt. Let us bring them back to disaster of house and the love of friends existing together.'

A few weeks later we mount an Indooroopilly Weekend 'Fire – A Blessing'. Some thirty people come, heave two long days into the demolition. The performance is dramatic. Men tie ropes and pull down sections of wall. The tank is toppled and rolled sloshing up the hill. The star, the big bob-cat, moves in, with great dexterity like an alien monster into 'kitchen' and 'bathroom'. 'Save the bath!' So the demon pauses and rescuers rush in. Then the monster noses into corners and they crumble, softly the mudbrick crumbling down, noisy the scratchy roof iron falling. The monster, devious as an ant with a large crumb, nuzzles, rolls, positions, opens jaws upon a huge charred beam, takes it forward, teeters on a slope, almost topples over as its back legs leave the ground, drops the tasty morsel of the beam, opens jaws again and this time delivers it down the slope. Close on the heels of the bob-cat the shovellers swarm in, woman with babe on back at one of the wheelbarrows. The tractor scoops, and all retreat as the monster re-approaches.

Light fading, billy is boiled, a neighbour with scones. A cloud has hovered. Rain falls. People are patient. Tired people back at Indooroopilly, slaking thirsts, seeking hot showers, feeding children first. Another great meal. Then the theatre of the spirit. We gather in the Octagon. Readings from Indian mythology about the gods of fire and their worship, about the exodus of Moses between pillar of fire and pillar of cloud, about man's distinction as a fire user, about the states of fire destroyer, comforter, servant. Readings of poems about bush fire, fire on the snow, fire in the belly. Shirley makes confession, her testament of losses, close to tears, but always at the brink spreads her arms and rises above it, drinks in deeply the love surrounding her, the hope for the new house. Dennis, deephearted, speaks his thanks to us all for our support in work and love, finishes with his best pun ever. 'This is a celebration of Awake! not a wake.' A transparency of transformation through loss.

Transparencies are not stacked in the chronology of experience, rather in the metaphysic of meaning, an anthology of archetypes subject to tense. Here now the event, hereafter the metaphor, thereafter the event. The origin of that fire was diagnosed, a faulty chimney in the first built-over house. A risky assumption in the beginning inevitably took effect. Between the house of wedding and the vacant space of separation, *House you will burn and widow your owner*.

Easter 1993. *Dream Play*: fragments of memory, brief scenes, dissolves, toss-up of transparencies: Marcel running about dragging lengths of hessian, panels of wood, mattress, chairs, leads, to the building of his castle; Matthew making a rag and pole boat and a teepee fire stack; Gillian painting cardboard organ pipes and a huge blow-up beach ball globe, the world which Indra's daughter comes down to dwell upon; Marina sewing sacks into shifts and the clover-hole stage door slung in mid-air. Children come bursting in while parents lug out boxes and bedding from cars, straining forward to find the other children, the places where they will again sleep; new people coming aboard this mudbrick ship wondering at its decks and gangways.

Some eighty souls bigger and smaller on the night – makers and participants of the play, largely outdoors, makers and participants in my indoors theatre of the kitchen, become pasta palace. *Dream Play* scenes flaring up in dining room and theatre portico, lamps carried. I swap stirring spoon for lacy cloak to play the mother for a moment. People confused by scripts in differing translations. Talcum powder called upon to flour-bag the hair. Leaping moments of Strindberg's words, lives overheard, compassion and mercy for human follies. Gentle rain from Heaven falling on the final scene of fire. I see the motifs of this play for ever adhering to the walls and spaces of Indooroopilly, moving through and beyond us. Indooroopilly is truly a dream, a play, a growing castle, a place of 'feeling for the poor people', us all.

Poles of solitude and conviviality, producing and reviewing, my nodes of Sagittarius and Gemini. 'The purpose of parties' I wrote in a youthful diary. 'Heaven will be like a great happy party where all the people one knows and loves will meet and get to know and love one another, a place where one would meet and begin the knowing and loving of many new people, a place where people of all ages would be the same age, a co-existence of little children, growing-up people, sad and merry people all together – and one's being at one and the same time part of each person and each mood.' So every party of which I am part of the making is for me a little part of Heaven. I love to move about in it all, angling my way among people, catching the corners of activities, answering some questions and escaping others, hearing the stories that extend my picture of the person.

Sometimes, being blind, I expect to be invisible. Sometimes, being blind, I see what is invisible. Without my doing anything, what I wish happens – I the glass that lets the light pass through, projecting the image into form, the idea into action. A transparency of muse, of catalyst.

The writer too is a nobody, transmitting shades, shaping other people.

> Eyes of flesh perceive the world and mankind as densely material. In such eyes life is a losing struggle for permanence, although sometimes full of beauty. Eyes of flesh acutely perceive details of time, place, person, action and ideas, but in relation to one another rather than to anything beyond them. Eyes of fire perceive each thing as the outer sign of an inner fact, or the local sign of a distant power. For such eyes nothing is only matter. All things are caught up in the mysterious ultimately Divine Whole that challenges understanding over a lifetime. Eyes of flesh focus on the thing itself, eyes of fire on facts, but still more intently on their participation in the larger meaning by which they are raised.
>
> (Roger Lipsey, *An Art of Our Own*)

Easter 1994. A dream: Marcel and I are walking along a road together companionably, carrying bags. We are walking along the middle of a quiet road. There is something across our path. I look down and see it is a cord, or fissure.

As I gaze it grows into a crack, a gap, a railway track. Marcel, having been a pace ahead, is now on the platform on the other side. He is wearing army uniform, pack on back. He looks so handsome, so happy. He smiles, waves, blows a kiss. His train comes in fast and when it goes off the platform is empty. I stand alone on my side. People come up and offer to carry my bags. We start to walk away, slowly, up a green slope.

Twelve years after the Mad Hatter, the tall handsome man with foreign accent, made his happy entrance, his head was turned towards India. He bought a one-way ticket to Tibetan Buddhism, gave up all worldly goods and disappeared into thin air. His mysterious creative force grounded in Indooroopilly, in the sure hands of the angels, gets completed. The dance goes on. *And there is only the dance*. I move into a higher octave of solitude, the domain of the writer; as in my beginning, the solo rider on a bicycle built for two.

We see what we are doing as the beginning of something. Amazed, and only after painful severance, we can see in hindsight that it was the focusing and bringing into first being, short-lived but necessary something that completed itself, broke new ground. 'Love the people and the soil. When you fall down, get up and keep going without halting to admire the place or stopping to lament. Hold fast to your work and never let it go.'*

A framed portrait of Marcel hangs high on the wall, watches down over the gatherings and feastings, the radiant solitudes, the books turned, discussions taking flight at

* From a radio interview with a contemporary Chinese novelist.

the table, the readings, the music sounding in the theatre. Indooroopilly has its own momentum. Our traditions grow. At New Year party a bonfire is made, a Joan of Arc pyre, on which is hoisted our Guy Spoons. Into his fire, as in the final scene of *Dream Play*, we throw all last year's unfinished business, lost hopes, missed moments, our simple forgivable human failures, and, out of the flames watch and salute the new year's promises and prospects castle our hope into the air.

Upstairs in my window sky attic I lie in my bed, or sit out on the wide balcony with a tea tray, or lie in the rock room below in a warm scented bath. Immediately outside is the bush – cool, tall, dense, deeply green rainforest, my roped walk leading off down rough steps and pelt of rotted undergrowth to a splashing waterfall. Malaysian pentatomic chimes, tethered to a post, translate weather and landscape into sound for me. Perhaps it is the musical instrument, even more than the wheel, that is mankind's greatest invention. Intimately I am given news of tranquillity of landscape in the occasional, barely perceptible, sustained presence of a single chime; or of turbulence in crescendo gamelan, wild theme and variations of that tempestuous wind that shakes nests, combs out brittle twigs, flexes branches and strengthens roots. Every ambience is translated into a joy of sound, distilling for me the diverse abiding happiness of my earthbound world. Susan, a friend, has this dream: Barbara is in the kitchen, downstairs, cooking. The floor is wet. Water is coming in under the doors. It deepens. Barbara goes upstairs and lies on her bed. The water rises, up the stairs, is lapping the bed. 'I'm alright,' she says. 'When it comes up to me, I'll just float on out.'

'So pure the wine

So clear the glass

Sometimes I see the glass and no wine

Sometimes I see wine and no glass'

– Rumi

CREDITS

Some of the chapters, or parts of them, have appeared in different forms elsewhere. 'My Life with Joey', as a broadcast on ABC Radio National; 'Grandmothers', *Quadrant*, 1975; '15 Edmondstone Street', *Imago*, 1995; 'Four Oaks in the Forties', *Sydney Morning Herald*, 1974; 'Barjai Days', *Meanjin*, 1995; 'Daise of Our Lives', *Imago*, 1995; 'The Fish Bowl', *Voices*, 1995; 'The Good Ship Mora', *Meanjin*, 1996; 'Portrait of a Friendship', *Island*, 1994; 'Our Life with the Bears', *Sydney Morning Herald*, 1974; 'Days of Wine and Roses', *Quadrant*, 1989; 'A Year in Paris', *Sydney Morning Herald*, 1970; 'Pleasures of Solitude', *Quadrant*, 1975; 'The Cat That Got Away', *Sydney Morning Herald*, 1976; 'Tell Your Mother Lovely', *Sydney Morning Herald*, 1974; 'On First Looking into Blackmans' Home Life', as a broadcast on ABC Radio National and in *Overland*, 1995; 'Nature's Poems', *West Australian, Sydney Morning Herald*, 1979, and *Vogue*, 1980; 'Into My Looking-glass Land', *Sydney Morning Herald*; 'Unlikely Gifts', *Vogue*, 1982; 'Whitefellers Walk All Around', *Australian*, 1983.

The author and the publisher would like to thank the following for permission to include material:

'God bless this tiny little boat . . .' is taken from *The Prayer Tree*, © Michael Leunig 1991. Used with permission of the publishers, HarperCollins*Religious,* Melbourne.

The extract on pages 395–6 is taken from *An Art of Our Own: the spiritual in twentieth century art* by Roger Lipsey, © 1988. Reprinted by arrangement with Shambhala Publications, Inc., 300 Massachusetts Avenue, Boston, MA 02115 USA.

The extracts on pages 32 and 33 are taken from *The Man Who Mistook His Wife for a Hat* by Oliver Sacks, by permission of the author c/o Rogers, Coleridge & White Ltd, 20 Powis Mews, London W11 1JN, in association with International Creative Management, 40 West 57th Street, New York, NY 10019 USA.

Every effort has been made to trace owners of copyright material. However, due to the fact that many quotes are transcribed by the author from tapes, it has not always been possible to source copyright owners. The publishers welcome any further information regarding copyright ownership.

Lovesong Elizabeth Jolley

Miss Vales: I never ever clap eyes on him.

Mrs Porter: Well, he's around all right, EV, coming and going all day he is – up and down the stairs, in and out the whole day long and half the night . . .

To Mrs Porter's establishment – a Home away from Home for Homeless Gentlemen – comes Dalton Foster, recently and reluctantly returning to the community. Dalton is intent on a fresh start. So is Miss Emily Vales, fellow lodger, and recipient of Mrs Porter's tea-leaves predictions . . .

Across the park from Dalton's cold, bleak room is the large, overdraped house of his childhood, where now another Consul's family lives. Intrigued and well-meaning, they welcome him into the house, unaware of Dalton's past links – and his yearnings.

'Love at its most desperate, lit by flashes of Jolley's wild humour, and sweetened by her patient tenderness.'

Helen Garner

The Multiple Effects of Rainshadow   Thea Astley

'Don't ask me why. No "why" will ever explain hatred, will it? It's true you never forgive the people you have treated badly.'

In the little hours of a January morning in 1930, on an island off the Queensland coast, a man goes berserk with a rifle and a box of gelignite. Is he evil? Or crazy? His violence is in fact a mirror for the brutality of Australian life – and is a dim reflection at that, in a country where atrocities by whites against blacks are so ingrained few question them.

The effects of the rampage ripple out to link the lives of those who witnessed it, across the north and down through the decades. It is a time when silence in the face of tyranny is at its loudest. When allegiance to English niceties is confounded by the landscape and by the weather. And change is a slow wind that brings little real difference.

The Multiple Effects of Rainshadow finds Thea Astley back in the territory she is a master of, writing with the iconoclastic wit and insight that are her trademark, in a voice that marks her as a diva among contemporary novelists.

Before I Wake   John Scott

With evening, cloud begins to close across the sky. Blanket upon blanket. As if it wished to hatch some unnatural thing from this town.

I will tell you what these clouds, what this incessant humidity, have hatched. In me. They have hatched the past.

Jonathan Ford, childless at 43, moves restlessly through other people's lives. From Australia to Europe he pursues a series of ill-fated relationships with the vulnerable and the insecure. In turn he is pursued by his past, whose echoes he finds all around him: in Danielle, a young French poet condemned to perpetual childhood. In his mother Violet, wickedly irreverent even as she struggles through her days alone in a council flat. In the flawed genius of the painter Malcolm Richardson. In many lives, ordinary and extraordinary, that he changes in the profoundest ways. It is through two sisters, themselves once hostage to the past, that Ford finally awakens to the present.

This is a story to treasure, a journey through what it means to be human, told with exquisite feeling by the award-winning author of *What I Have Written*.

'The most appealing and engrossing novel I have read in a very long time. John Scott is, quite simply, one of the best writers of fiction at work anywhere in the world today.'

Deirdre Bair